Essays Brazilian

Fabio Akcelrud Durão
and Friends

1st Edition

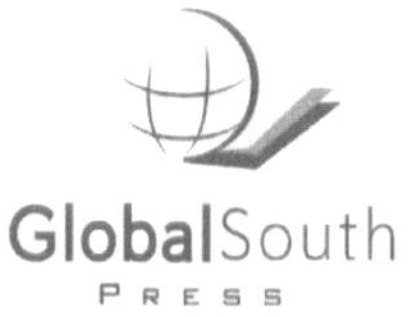

Published in the United States by Globalsouth Press Inc TM.

For more information, please contact info@globalsouthpress.com or go to http://www.globalsouthpress.com/

Book design by
Karla Pastore

ESSAYS BRAZILIAN
By AKCELRUD DURÃO, Fabio—1st ed. — 2016
Includes bibliographical references and index.
ISBN: 978-1-943350-36-0

1. International Studies — Brazil
2. Cultural Studies — Brazilian Culture
3. Literary Collections — Latin America

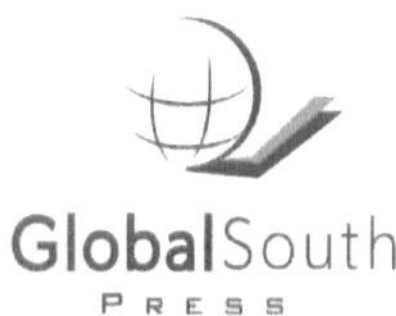
GlobalSouth
PRESS

para Leni

CONTENTS

INTRODUCTORY **NOTE**

This book was not originally conceived as one. Its chapters were written under different circumstances and with particular aims in mind; their collection, however, generated a whole that goes beyond the sum of its parts. Herein the reader will find essays devoted to Brazilian literature, art, music, film and theory, which, plunging into specific objects, eventually project a coherent image of the country's culture in the late twentieth and early twenty-first century. Several of the most dramatic dilemmas facing cultural production in general take here a distinctly Brazilian shape and development: the question of engaged literature; the desacralization of language; the relationship between the public and avant-garde art; the role of labor in the constitution of artworks; the absorption of techniques developed abroad; the interaction between high and popular culture; the commodification of the latter; the drama of adaptation from one medium to another; the process of subjectivation in a regime of semiotic overproduction; the theoretical characterization of pain; the baleful function of multiplicity. The list is only apparently random, for these topics interact and create a number of cross-references,

thus crystalizing ideas and insights with a broader scope of validity than the particular artifacts from which they emerged.

The fact that a certain consistency appears behind the critic's back suggests an image of objectivity, as if the ideas were thinking the researcher rather than the other way round. In this case, however, a further factor must be taken into account, for more than half of the texts here collected were written by four or even six hands. Collaboration with scholars from different fields allowed for a broader scope of inquiry, but it also showed, as I can now see with pleasure, that just as ideas are more than what is put subjectively into them, relationships are more than a sheer encounter of isolated individualities: they give birth to worlds of their own, some of which materialize in this book.

The same applies to the practice of translation; that is why I am very grateful to Lara Bourdin for her rendering into English of "Ferreira Gullar: Poesia e Intensidade" and "Monologismo do Múltiplo".

POETRY

Ferreira Gullar: Poetry and Intensity. (with Mario Frungillo)

Activism and aestheticism, social content and formal immanence, commitment to ethics and search for the new, Brecht and Beckett: beyond these oppositions one could cite many more; one could expand upon their assumptions, their consequences and their histories; one could illuminate the theoretical postures, the editorial and cultural policies, the appointments in universities that they entail. This is, in fact, a problem as urgent as the risk of losing control and landing back on the entrenchment of exclusionary positions, which ultimately impoverish themselves – a potent dilemma in developing countries in general, and in Brazil in particular, which is poor enough to be incapable of hiding its misery, and rich enough to host a rich culture of contestation. But if these two critical positionings lead to disagreements when they involve the elaboration of panoramic visions, the delimitation of canons, or the design of the physiognomy of literary historiography, imagine the complexity of the case of Ferreira Gullar, whose work incorporates *both* the impulse toward literary-political activism and that toward vanguard experimentalism. Indeed, the central question for readings of Gullar's work resides in how to articulate the political and the aesthetic; or how to articulate *littérature engagée*, literature committed to a transformation of the concrete world, and linguistic innovation, whose aim is to amplify the horizons of the representable. There is unquestionably a possibility of reconciliation, when approaching negativity in reality opens the door to what is novel, when the inclusion of social oppression in verse corresponds to a conquest at once representational and technical from the perspective of poetic writing's internal evolution. This possibility of reconciliation is short and fugitive, however; it exhausts itself in the instant after its enunciation. Depending on one's perspective, this instant may have occurred long ago: at best, as early as Baudelaire, but no later than with the avant-gardes of the early 20th century. As such, in Gullar, the two vectors are not easily reconcilable. Political mobilization can hardly dispend with communicability, while the true search for the new refuses to be subordinated to any imposed finality (even if the latter is ethically or morally laudable). For this reason, one just has to call to mind the *cordel* and the neo-concretist poems placed side in Gullar's complete works, to dissipate any illusion of reconciliation between these two opposites.

Of course, these examples represent what is most distant in the poet's production (despite having been written only a few years apart), and there are other cases, most notably in his *magnum opus*, the *Poema Sujo* ("Dirty Poem"), about which it would be possible to argue (as Damaso [2006] has done) that a successful synthesis has been accomplished. Nevertheless, the persistency of an unresolved conflict can be sensed in the fact that critics have so far emphasized one or the other of these polarities, attempting to mark the poet with the stamp of their own theoretical preferences. In an important article, Alfredo Bosi (2003) begins by recognizing the difficulty of inserting Gullar in a homogeneous narrative that harmonizes materiality and spirituality. However, he concludes his text with words that clearly give stronger emphasis to the latter: "As the contradictions are deepened and internalized, skirting the frontier between life and death, there emerges that universalizing sentiment that makes the poetry of matter take on accents of metaphysical drama. What was a solitary and fleeting instant of perception, what was a drive of the body and soul of a single individual, enters a process of communication, crosses the barriers of time and takes on the (still vulnerable) consistency of a meaning" (2003: 185). Conversely, João Luiz Lafetá, in what is perhaps the most decisive essay on the author, describes Gullar's poetry as of collective content, albeit one that is subject to lyrical form. In his words, in Gullar, "*personal identity* reveals itself as a *cultural identity*, inserted within a more ample *national identity*" (2004a: 210), where "national" ultimately becomes indistinguishable from society as a whole and ends up absorbing individuality (and poetry) entirely. It is interesting to note that the harmonization of opposites, whether it be for one side or the other, goes very well with the rhetorical structure of the route, the trajectory (Camenietzki, 2006) or even the itinerary (Bosi, 2003; Villaça, 1998: 94ff). Already in the meaning inherent to these nouns, there is the invitation to an idea of coherent and organic development, in which even missteps can be seen as necessary detours on the road to a certain plenitude. Needless to say, such a model presupposes a linear and cumulative temporality, which equates the life of the poet with forward movement and progress.[1] Conciliation and teleology go hand in hand, whether it be at the service of Christian idealism or that of a limited materialism.

---

1 For a critique of the apologetic character of "trajectory," see Pécora (2006).

Rather than opt for one of these vectors – that is, try to reconcile the desire for the social and the impulse toward the new, or even insert them in a pacifying diachrony – it would be more interesting (and productive) to search for a perspective from which both movements can be seen as something derivative, as manifestations of a more ample and comprehensive poetic principle. The concept of *intensity* can fill this role, for it is capable of giving intelligibility and providing a name for constitutive poetic features in Ferreira Gullar which would otherwise remain disparate. What is more, the concept of intensity offers a privileged means of taking on the historicization of Gullar's poetry as a whole, as well as its social symptomatology.[2] It is worth emphasizing, however, that rather than being first defined in order then to be applied to the poetic material, intensity here should emerge as concept-in-process, as it were, inseparable from the interpretative process.

II

The search for intensity is perhaps most clearly identifiable on a lexical level, namely in the use of words that could be brought together under the label of "rawness." Firstly, there is in Gullar's work a constant impulse toward the description of the body in its ultimate materiality, the body as a pulsating and naked concreteness. On this conception, the

2 This apparent depoliticization should not come as a surprise, for it has been common currency in Marxist literature for a long time. As a renowned author has said: "Literature can be called revolutionary in a meaningful sense only with reference to itself, as content having become form. The political potential of art lies only in its own aesthetic dimension. Its relation to praxis is inexorably indirect, mediated, and frustrating. The more immediately political the work of art, the more it reduces the power of estrangement and the radical, transcendent goals of change. In this sense, there may be more subversive potential in the poetry of Baudelaire and Rimbaud than in the didactic plays of Brecht." (Marcuse, 1978: xii-xiii) Cf. as well Adorno's classic essay (1992).

body has primacy over any sort of spirituality or even over the very consciousness of the self: "Who am I inside my mouth? / Who am I in my teeth / behind my teeth / in my tongue that moves / trapped at the back of my throat? What name do I have / in the darkness of my esophagus?" ("Who am I?" *Barulhos*: 354[3]). In its most extreme degree, this primacy of the somatic over the spiritual takes the form of decay; a motif that also runs through Gullar's œuvre. In the prose poem "Carta de um Morto Pobre" ("Letter of a Poor Dead Man") from *Luta Corporal* (1953), one already reads:

> Fui sempre o que mastigou a sua língua e a engoliu. O que apagou as manhãs e, à noite, os anúncios luminosos e, no verso, a música, para que apenas a sua carne, sangrenta pisada suja – a sua pobre carne o impusesse ao orgulho dos homens. [...] Porque estou morto é que digo: o apodrecer é sublime e terrível. (22)

> I was always the one who chewed his tongue and swallowed it. The one who, in the mornings and at night, turned off the bright signs and, conversely, the music, so that only its meat, dirty bloody bite – its poor meat impose it upon the pride of men. [...] Because I am dead I say: decay is sublime and terrible.

Decay, here, goes very well with "night" and "meat" – both rendered swift by the lack of commas in the adjectives

3 References to Gullar's poems include the title, the name of the original volume, and the page numbering of the last edition of Toda Poesia (2006).

–, with the bright signs and the poetic craft itself; they are the perfect opposites to clarity and the gradual flowering of spring. Some forty years later, we find a recurrence of the term (one among many others). This recurrence is representative of a poetic constant:

> Escuta: nada se ouve
> no poroso talco
> no fundo poroso pó
> debaixo das tábuas
> sob os pés da família
>
> Escuta só: é pulvo
> é pudre é podre é púlvura é
> pólvora
> quase azul ("Sob os pés da família", *Muitas Vozes*: 492)

> Listen: nothing is audible
> in the porous talc
> in the porous dusty depth
> under the floorboards
> under the family's feet
> Just listen: it is pulvo
> it is pudre it's rotten it is rottenness it is
> powder
> almost blue ("Under the family's feet," *Many Voices*: 492)

Of course, in this case, the cohesion is more acoustic than imagistic, and the idea of decay dissolves itself in the insistence of the /p/ sounds. Nevertheless, in their dissimilarity, these two examples show that the lexicon of rot, even when it names poems,[4] does not lead to the thematization of decay, does not make it an object of reflection or meditation: if the analogy can be allowed, it never shifts from adjective to noun. Moreover, however tempting it may be to insert rot into a temporality of decline, it is clear that the effort does not go far, for rot is never exposed as a process; when it is introduced, it already is as it is, a vehicle of impact more than an element of any metaphysics.

But in order to complete the lexicon of intensity, one must add the concrete vocabulary of sex and eschatology. Sex, also running insistently through Gullar's œuvre, is distinctive: un-sublime and available, apparently universal (despite being inherently heterosexual and objectifying toward the feminine[5]), it dislocates what would traditionally be the central place of love in the West's poetic tradition; that is, an unattainable, ethereal, spiritual or unrequited love. Paradigmatic, in this sense, is the last stanza of the first page of *Poema Sujo*:

azul
era o gato
azul

---

4 Cf. "Bananas podres" and "Bananas podres 2" (Na Vertigem do Dia, 315, 331).

5 Gullar's sexism, like that of a great part of his generation, would merit further study. An extreme case is "Definição da Moça" ("Definition of the girl") (Muitas Vozes, 470), which asks four questions, beginning with "Como defini-la/quando está vestida/se ela me desbunda/como se despida?" ("How to define her/ when she is dressed/if she drives me crazy me/when she strips?" only to end with "Como possuí-la/ quando está desnuda/ se ela toda chuva?/ se ela toda é vulva?" ("How to possess her/ when she is naked / if she is all rain?/ if she is all vulva?") The feminine does not exist for itself alone, here; it is nothing but a source of satisfaction for the poet.

era o galo
azul
o cavalo
azul
teu cu
(233)

blue
was the cat
blue
was the rooster
blue
the horse
blue
your ass

"Blue," as we shall see below, is the adjective that comes closest to expressing the transcendental in Gullar's oeuvre. Color of the sky and the ocean, (in)vocative of the imagination, it is here inserted between the names of the author's favorite animals, prime objects of domestication,[6] in a clear phonetic sequence: /g/, /a/ e /u/, then /l/, and finally /k/: "cu" is the pinnacle of the poiesis of the opening page of Gullar's greatest poem.[7]

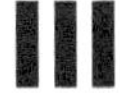

As far as the effect of isolated terms is concerned, Gullar's word combinations also merit our attention. Here too a poetics of intensity makes sense. Whether it be in the

6 E.g. "Galo galo", or the book *O Cavalo sem sede*.

7 One can observe that the editions of *Toda Poesia* published after 1980 do not respect the careful spatial organization of the *Poema Sujo*, whose first page originally ended with that stanza.

concrete descriptions of fruits, in the childhood impressions, or in the unusual combinations, which sometimes push the limits of intelligibility, Gullar's images, as recurrent as they may be, never articulate a subjacent theory. Unlike in Wallace Stevens' work, for example, where poetic images are submitted to the theoretical-systematizing effort of supreme fiction – such that the recurrence of an obscurity can suggest significance, even as it negates the signified – in Gullar, the hermeticism is sporadic, even in its moments of greatest difficulty. As such, more interesting than attempting to undo and organize the images in what would be a grammar of the unfamiliar, or than trying to confer the naturalness of a system upon hermeticism, is to highlight Gullar's unusual encounters in terms of the shock that they provoke. In doing so, the meaning stays in the second rank, in front of the "simple" effect, as in fireworks. In other words, the perplexity in the face of the concatenation of images does not endure as an enigma, but vanishes in a discharge of intensity, often in rapid succession, as in "Pele Que Só se Curte a Blasfêmias" ("Skin that Only Likes Blasphemy"):

> Na escritura das flores
> não há uma só palavra decifrável
> nome de amigo, nome de anjo algum
> ali se pronuncia
>   O metal é escuro,
> a ave solar
> deixa seu rastro no relógio de pedra de Intihuatana,
> mas a carne do homem foi o seu pouso diário
> e mesmo seu pasto
> O penacho que orna a cabeça de Osíris,
> De flores feitas,

Avança, quando ele vem,

Sobre uma população sem rosto.
(*O vil metal*: 87)

In the writing of flowers
there is not a single decipherable word
name of a friend, name of an angel
there it pronounces
                              Metal is dark
the solar bird
leaves its footprint in the stone clock of Intihuatana,
but the meat of the man was his daily landing
and even his pasture

The feather that crowns the head of Osiris,
Of flowers made,
Advances, when he comes,
Over a populace without a face.
("The vile metal")

However bold it may be, the first image is clear: flowers write, but their message is illegible. Still, the theoretical-poetic potential that lies in this observation is not explored; the inscrutable in nature, or the inaccessibility of natural beauty, for example, could have been developed further, but they are not. Obscure metal (gold/money, as in the book's title?), and (its opposite?) the solar bird (mythical? the sun as bird or the bird that belongs to the sun?) in an act of flight over the mystical pyramid of Macchu Picchu (*Intihuatana*, in Quechua, means "the place where the sun stays"), while the meat of man probably refers to the practice of sacrifice. From Peru to Egypt in the space of a stanza: Osiris enters to integrate in the semantic fields of birds and flowers. "He" could have "Osiris" as its referent, but with a bit more of a stretch, it could even refer to "man"; "populace without a face" could refer back to the spectators of the ritual, even though "populace" evokes something of a modern urban atmosphere, an idea that the anonymity of "without a face" ultimately corroborates. An approximation of the primitive to the contemporary? The perpetuation of barbarity in civilization? Maybe, but without imagistic solidity. The dissonance between the writing of flowers, between the value of metal and gods does not lend itself to theoretical departures, but remains simply as it is, a procession of figures that don't even point to a meta-poetics – which by no means way should be seen as negative.

IV

Gullar's articulations of sounds are also notable for their intensity. There is in practically all of his best poems an excess in the phonic layer that cannot always be integrated with the meaning to create a harmonic unity. The most obvious example of acoustic prominence in the Gullarian corpus is, without a doubt, the "Roçzeiral" (*Luta Corporal*: 55-57), an experimental poem that has already been described as being made of "groans, of sounds without meaning, [...] a rage-full dismantling of language," in which "his words – and they are not words – don't mean [anything]" (Lafetá, 2004a: 153). This is hyperbolic. Compared to John Cage's last writings, for example, or even to some Dadaist experiments from the early 20th century, the poem certainly channels some meaning:

Au sôflu i luz ta pom-
pa inova'
orbita
FUROR
tô bicho
'scuro fo-
go
Rra

The lexical items are not all identifiable, of course, but they are far from being indecipherable. With but a little effort, one can overcome the strangeness and see "no roseiral o sopro e luz, o bicho escuro de fogo" ("in the rose garden the breath and light, the dark creature of fire"). In any event, the phonemic play in Gullar certainly has something of an overflowing effect, even in cases less extremes than "Roçzeiral," such as "Personal Question" (*Barulhos*: 376):

essa palavra avesso esse
verso
espesso mais que pêlo
essa pele-
palavra
que envolve a voz
e voa ao revés

tão rente a meu corpo
feito um sopro –

o poema
que em si mesmo se solve
(em seu mel).

this word inside out this
verse
thicker than fleece
this skin-
word
that involves the voice
and flies to the reverse
so close to my body
made a breath –
the poem
that dissolves in itself
(in its honey).

The metapoetic theme is characteristic of *Barulhos* and *Muitas Vozes*, the author's last two books, both published after a silence of almost twenty years. Here, the sound's relief is evident, perhaps because of the insistence on the /a/ and the /ɛ/, or because of the alliterations of /s/, /v/ and /p/ in the first five verses, or of /v/, /j/ and /R/ (to follow Gullar's Rio-style pronunciation), among other repetitions. What is interesting, in this case, is the revalidation of the theory of mimicry between sound and image, which is otherwise inapplicable to a large portion of his work. In the *Poema Sujo*, for example, arguing for a harmony between the acoustic features and the content described would mean going against the text's impetus, an intensity that resulted from the *tension* between eschatology and sex, on the one hand, and remembering, on the other. But because in "Questão Pessoal" the object is the poem itself, all the vowel and consonant games call back to themselves in an explicit self-referencing, i.e., with "its honey." Even though the latter could offer a semantic anchoring, an image that would fix the poem, the acoustic work would make the concept unfamiliar in a final, phonetically appropriate, /seumɛu/. There is certainly a discussed "point," namely, the relationship between the individuality of the author who creates the poem, on the one hand, and the universality of poetry, on the other: the old 'topos' of the singular vs. the universal. Nevertheless, this question dissolves in the text's movement of self-making; it almost functions as the process' motivation, to use the Russian formalists' terminology. As an element of the poem's self-making, the phonic layer is much more apparent than in "Roçzeiral," which should be its best example.

V

Even what is generally understood as political engagement can be usefully explained in terms of intensity. This intensity, however, is not linked to the more or less immanent play of words on the page; instead, it obtains its force through what one could name a collectivizing effect, a change of course for the reader that aims to strengthen their belonging to an interpretive community, to use Fish's famous concept (1980). This is important to emphasize: strictly speaking, Gullar's political poetry is not truly persuasive; more than any kind of conviction, what it puts into play is the intensification of preexisting ideas, beliefs or postures. At the time when the content of the discourse propounded by self-described leftists had a strongly universalizing slant, it was easy to ignore the importance of the circulation of affects *within* the group. It was *this* circulation that Gullar's poetry backed up; accordingly, the latter carried out its activism in the field of a consolidating leftist culture, and not in an ostensible direct communicability with the working mass. This does not mean that the one could not serve as a mediator for the other. All the same, the perspective of intensity sheds new light on the debate over Gullar's populism (cf. Lafetá, 2004a: 169-198; 2004b; Camienetzki, 2006: 71-83), which ironically furnishes an excuse for his worst poems. To put it bluntly, when the poems related to the *Centros Populares de Cultura* (CPC) are conceived as a means to intensify the communication within leftist groups their questionable literary quality is at least partially justified.

"Cantada" (*Dentro da Noite Veloz*: 173) is not one of the worst, but it aptly illustrates the dynamics of the collectivizing effect in Gullar. The text has a reasonably regular comparative structure: "You are prettier than" is repeated seven times in a crescendo that makes competent use of formal variations to avoid the monotony of parallelism. In the first instance, there is the alternation of the items being compared: "the silver-lined ball of the cigarette paper," the "puddle of water," "zebra," "nail," "Boeing 707," "flowery garden," "the sea in Ipanema," "Petrobrás refinery," "Ursula Andress," "Alvora Palace," "dawn," "sapphire-blue sea of the Dominican Republic" – these skillfully bring together personal items and objects from mass culture, industrialized artifacts and natural landscapes, in a set that keeps the reader or listener's attention. Moreover, the Petrobrás refinery and the Alvorada Palace could be seen to reconcile the political and the aesthetic; the fruit of the mobilization of "petrol is ours" and the greatest work of the communist Niemeyer are highly relevant in that they represent an expansion of the lyrical gaze, the inclusion of national objects until then unpoeticizable.

The variety expands all the more with the rhythmical irregularity and the variation of the expressions, locatives or adjectival sentences, including the semantic and phonic confusion between "Pálacio da Alvorada" and "alvorada." We thus arrive at the second stanza, where the colloquial vocative "olha" [look] creates a greater intimacy with the receiver and sows the ground for the breaking of regularity that occurs with a "tão bela quanto o Rio de Janeiro," an indirect declaration of love to the city. All of this concludes with the conclusion "você é [...]/ quase tão bonita/ quanto a Revolução Cubana" (you are [...]/ almost as pretty /as the Cuban Revolution."

If one is a partisan of the Cuban Revolution, the poem reaches a climax of intensity, the apotheosis above all the text's semantic richness; if one is not, the text crumbles as an embarrassment. There is no space for persuasion of any kind here; we are dealing as much/only with strategies for constructing intensity in accordance with sides already taken, a dynamic that permeates Gullar's openly political poems.

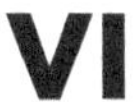

With the hypothesis of a poetics of intensity Gullar's adoption of free verse, both in its more common version, as well as in its spatialized form, becomes more interestingly intelligible. Indeed, one could posit a continuity between these two kinds of word arrangement, as if the demise of rhyme opened the verse to the immensity of the page. It is not merely a matter of rhyme and metric regularity losing their a priori necessity, their justification based on what is given by tradition; the very white of the page turns into a space of potentialities in which meaning can be distributed. The spatial organization of the words becomes relevant in itself and the emptiness comes to interfere with the meaning's dissemination. The paper begins to resemble a plane of immanence, such that there emerges a difference of meaning between two words when placed side by side or with space intervening. For example:

mar azul marco azul
blue sea blue mark

mar azul marco azul barco azul
blue sea blue mark blue boat

mar azul marco azul barco azul arco azul
blue sea blue mark blue boat blue bow

mar azul marco azul barco azul arco azul ar azul
blue sea blue mark blue boat blue bow blue air
(*PoemasConcretos/Neoconcretos*: 97[8])

The method used here is not complicated. It unites the repetition of the phonemes (with slight variation) and the insistence of the blue, which ends up becoming a suffix as acoustic as semantic. As such, we once again have a structure of increasing intensity, but that comes through a process of spreading rather than condensation. From this accumulation another type of intensity is delineated; the visual, which also lends itself to allegorizations: is the poem the sail of a ship? Or

8 It is important to note that the pages in this book do not have numbers.

an inverted staircase that leads from the sea to the air, now to the ground, or that, conversely, goes from the sky to the water? In any event, the status of the first "mar azul" is different from the last, whether it be considered weaker, because it is followed by emptiness, or stronger, for the same reason. For now, it is interesting to observe the curious logic of spatializing intensity in Gullar's poetry. Contrary to what one may think, the most purely spatial poems, those grouped in *Poemas Concretos/ Neoconcretos* (161-174) are not the ones in which the spacing is most intriguing. Precisely because the arrangement of words on the page is the primordial factor, there is an obviousness that is weak in comparison with the cases in which the distribution of verbal matter is combined with other elements, as in the *Poema Sujo*, where blocks of prose are interspersed with spatially regular verses, left-aligned, and passages typical of the concretist conquests:[9]

bolacha não
cookie is not

vale quem term
worth who has

vale quem term
worth who has

vale quem term
worth who has

vale quem term
worth who has

nada vale
nothing worth

nada não vale

9 One also notes, in the "cordel poems," that the space of the page does not play any significant role. There is no justification for this. Even if one wanted to maintain the acoustic regularity, with well behaved rhymes and meter, it would be possible to deal with the distribution of the words as a means of reinforcing the meaning being communicated.

who doesn´t have

nada não vale
nothing in not worth

nada não vale
nothing in not worth

quem nada
who nothing

tem
has

neste vale
in this vale

(Poema Sujo, p. 249)

Because of the words' spatial distribution, the two meanings of "vale", "to be worth" and "vale" appear much harder-hitting, and the criticism vis-à-vis the "vale/valor" becomes more severe.

VII

The prism of intensity also illuminates new aspects of Gullar's worldview that have so far gone unnoticed. Indeed, intensity confers upon the poems an expressivity that at times translates into excess, even aggression. This development comes from the fragmented and atomized poetic universe, which is marked by the incommunicability that permeates Gullar's entire production. This universe goes on transforming itself, finding its resolution in a specific moment only to ultimately reveal itself in a manner similar to that of the first poems. It is necessary to note that fragmentation is linked to intensity simultaneously as its condition and its result. The continuity of the intense, as energetic as it may be, leads to the establishment of homogeneity, as it is absorbed without contrast with its contrary.

This atomization and incommunicability can already be found in many of the poems of *A luta corporal*: in the anguished cry of the rooster, otherwise "useless" and "a mere complement to the dawns" ("Galo galo," *A luta corporal*: 12), or in the balcony "on the margin of the afternoon" ("O trabalho das nuvens," *A luta corporal*: 16). In "As pêras" ("The pears"):

> As pêras, no prato,
> apodrecem.
> O relógio, sobre elas,
> mede a sua morte?
>
> Paremos a pêndula. De-
> Teríamos, assim, a morte das frutas?
> [...]
> O relógio
> não mede. Trabalha
> no vazio: sua voz desliza
> fora dos corpos.
> ("A luta corporal": 18)
>
> The pears, on the plate,
> rot.
> The clock, overtop them,
> measures its death?
>
> Stop the clock. Would we de-
> Lay, thus, the death of the fruits?
> [...]
> The clock
> does not measure. Work
> in nothingness: its voice slides
> off bodies.
> ("A luta corporal": 18)

The pears rot alone on the plate, and this doesn't change anything, for "O dia / comum, dia de todos, é a / distância entre as coisas" ("The day / the common day, day for all, is the / distance between things"). The day is passing "Não entre os móveis. Pas- / sar como eu / passo: entre nada" ("Not between the moving objects. Pas- / sing like I / pass: between nothing"). In a world thus compartmentalized, incommunicability doesn't just affect people, it affects even objects, inanimate things. Even time, the flux of time (a constant theme in Gullar) is watertight. The clock marks a time that is not that of pears, for if it were to stop they would continue rotting – which leads one to think that the opposite would also be true: if they stopped rotting, the clock would continue marking its own time, indifferent to them. This indifference also expresses itself constantly in the poems that deal with someone's death, in the recurrent idea that things follow their course indifferently, ignorant of everything. Seen from this angle, the intensity present in Gullar's poems could be interpreted as an attempt to break – out of discomfort, out of aggression – the incommunicability of things.

The expression of such a world naturally gives to each fact and each occurrence a character of individuality is so profound that, from the perspective of political engagement, Gullar would inevitably have to be accused of alienation. These poems would thus necessarily have to be considered as opposites to the political poems that Gullar wrote later on. In fact, after the cordel poems, one notes a change of tone in his poetry. The harshness of poems like "Roçzeiral" has disappeared. And *Dentro da noite veloz* is full of a poetry that has collectivity as its theme, beginning with the opening poem, "Meu povo, meu poema" ("My people, my poem"), in which "Meu povo e meu poema crescem juntos" ("My people and my poem grow together") (p. 155). Even the aggressiveness of poems like "A bomba suja" ("Introduzo na poesia / a palavra diarréia" ["I introduce into poetry / the word diarrhea"]), which recalls a process that was already present in his earlier books, has a character of urgency and immediacy, for it communicates a concrete fact to the reader: diarrhea is responsible for high mortality rates in the poor regions of the country. But it suffices to recall the problematic ending of a poem like "Cantada," analyzed earlier on, to doubt the efficacy of this procedure. And, lastly, in poems like "O açucar" ("Sugar"), incommunicability endures:

> O branco açúcar que adoçará meu café
> nesta manhã de Ipanema
> não foi produzido por mim
> nem surgiu dentro do açucareiro por milagre.
> [...]
>
> Em lugares distantes, onde não há hospital
> nem escola,
> homens que não sabem ler e morrem
> aos vinte e sete anos
> plantaram e colheram a cana
> que viraria açúcar.
> Em usinas escuras,
> homens de vida amarga
> e dura
> produziram este açúcar
> branco e puro
> com que adoço meu café esta manhã em Ipanema.
> ("O açúcar", *Dentro da noite veloz*, p. 165-166).
> The sugar white which will sweeten my coffee
> in this Ipanema morning

was not produced by me
neither emerged in the sugar bowl by miracle.
[...]
In distant places, where there's no hospital
nor school,
men who can't read and die
twenty-seven years old
planted and harvested the cane
that would become sugar.

In dark mills,
men of life sour
and hard
produced this sugar
white and pure
with which I sweeten my coffee this morning in
Ipanema.

The tone has certainly changed. There is a perceptible impulse toward solidarity that extracts from the poem the harshness that is so omnipresent in Gullar's earlier works. Moreover, the search for immediate communication repels all possibility of hermeticism. It is nevertheless impossible to deny that that incommunicability between beings persists, perhaps unconsciously (i.e., repressed?), for in spite of the solidarity between poor men who produced his sugar (and who know nothing of him), the poet does not stop sweetening his coffee. One is almost tempted to introduce a verse from Brecht as a key: "nevertheless I eat and drink." And when Che Guevara is imprisoned, the stars that shine on the helicopter that brings him to the place where he will be assassinated "nada sabem do sonho, /da esperança, da alegria, / da luta surda do homem pela flor de cada dia" ("don't know anything of dream, /of hope, of happiness, / of man's deaf fight for the flower of every day"), and the men that live in the shacks he flies over "não sabem o que se passa / naquela noite de outubro // quem passa sobre seu teto / dentro daquele barulho / quem é levado pra morte / naquela noite noturna" ("don't know what is happening / on that October night / who flies over their roofs / in that noise / who is carried toward death / in that nocturnal night") ("Dentro da noite veloz", *Dentro da noite veloz*: 198).

The impasse thus remains, even in Gullar's political poetry. But his experience as a political poet, his attempt at a collective poetry, one that would break with that uncomfortable, anguished feeling of fragmentation, opened new perspectives for the poet's later production. The impasse would only be broken through memoir-style evocation.

This evocation manifests itself as early as "Uma fotografia aérea" ("An aerial photograph"), from *Dentro da noite veloz*. Looking at a photograph of the city of São Luís do Maranhão taken from an airplane at some point in his childhood, the poet brings this moment back to the forefront of his consciousness and believes in the possibility of having heard the motor's rumble on that afternoon. It is in this image of the city contemplated from above that he imagines himself, as a boy, becoming a part of that landscape, that precarious fragment of memory that he can deny (he can rip up the photograph if he wants). It isn't the first time that the poet contemplates the city from above. In "A vida bate" ("Life beats"), from the same book, but located many pages before, one reads:

A cidade. Vista do alto
ela é fabril e imaginária, se entrega inteira
como se estivesse pronta.
Vista do alto,
com seus bairros e ruas e avenidas, a cidade
é o refúgio do homem, pertence a todos e a ninguém.
Mas vista
de perto,
revela seu túrbido presente, sua
carnadura de pânico: as
pessoas que vão e vêm
que entram e saem, que passam
sem rir, sem falar, entre apitos e gases. Ah, o escuro
sangue urbano
movido a juros.

The city. Seen from above
is industrial and imaginary, it gives itself in whole
as if it were ready.
Seen from above,
with its neighborhoods and streets and avenues, the
city is the refuge of man, it belongs to all and none.
But seen
from close,
it reveals its turbid present, its
musculature of panic: the
people who come and go
who enter and leave, who pass by
without laughing, without speaking, between whistles
and gases. Ah, the dark
urban blood
moved by interests.

There is no communication between the people who go by without speaking, "loaded with suffocated flowers." Only from above is it possible to know that "inside, in the heart [...] life beats. Subterraneously, / life beats" ("A vida bate," *Dentro da noite veloz*: 181). It is only with distance, be it that of the view from his apartment window, or that of the picture taken from the airplane, that the whole, apparently fragmented, makes sense. It is only seen through the temporal distance of the years that have passed, and the spatial distance of the exile's eyes, as in *Poema Sujo*, that it will at last be possible to bring those fragments together into a whole that makes sense. The incommunicability between things comes undone in a simultaneity that accommodates all the formerly isolated beings. What unites them is the poet's conscience:

[...] debruçado no parapeito do alpendre
via a terra preta do quintal
e a galinha ciscando e bicando
uma barata entre plantas
e neste caso um dia-dois
o de dentro e o de fora
da sala
um às minhas costas o outro
diante dos olhos
vazando um no outro
através de meu corpo
dias que vazem agora ambos em pleno coração
de Buenos Aires
às quatro horas desta tarde
de 22 de maio de 1975
trinta anos depois.
(*Poema sujo:* 251)

[...] peering over the veranda's parapet
I saw the garden's black earth
and the hen foraging and pecking
a potato among the plants
and in this case a day-two
one from inside and one from outside
the room
one on my back the other
before my eyes
leaking from one into the other
through my body
days that leak now both right in the heart
of Buenos Aires
at four o'clock, this afternoon
of May 22, 1975
thirty years later.
(*Poema sujo,* p. 251)

In the simultaneity constructed by the poet's memory, opposites don't cancel themselves out, but don't repel one another either. They are part of a dissonant concert, a reality that can't be accepted as a whole (for we are still dealing with a world that needs to be transformed) but whose joints are becoming recognizable, at last.

VIII

Lastly, intensity allows for a new social reading of Gullar's œuvre at a time of his abandonment of political activism and turn to the right.[10] If, following Adorno's famous claim, literature can be considered as an unconscious historiography of its time, Gullar's writings testify to mass culture's consolidation and to the definitive implantation of Brazil's cultural industry, not as a technical infrastructure, but as a way of being, a structure of feeling. His poetry, would thus register, both by incorporating and resisting, the period in which mass production of symbolic artifacts no longer seeks to refer to preexisting compositional models – either from popular or erudite culture – but rather builds its own self-enclosed world of sensation, already preceding and conditioning perception (Adorno, 2004). It would be worth evaluating the relevance of the dynamics that Jameson (1992) posited with regard to the 1960s, of the cohabitation and proximity between the contestation of the capitalist system and its deepening. The dialectics of marginality make a lot of sense for readings of Gullar, the persecuted poet, the poet of overflowing intensity, the author of verses that could be seen as having an intrinsic exteriority but that are today situated in the center of the national literary establishment.[11] Indeed, the

---

10 Declarations from a 1998 interview: "Acho que é hora de profissionais. Eu discuto, acompanho a política, leio os jornais. Mas militar nessa situação é para profissional. [...] O que eu considero de fato encerrado é a concepção de revolução marxista. [...] não existe mais comunismo. Quer dizer, existem algumas pessoas nisso, mas não tem cabimento." ("I believe it is the time of professionals. I discuss and follow politics, I read the papers. But activism in this situation is for professionals. [...] What I in fact consider closed is the conception of the Marxist revolution. [...] communism no longer exists. That is to say, there are a few people involved, but they have no place.") (*Cadernos de Literatura Brasileira*, no.6 p.48)

11 Two undeniable gauges of success: to be the luxurious object of the previously cited *Cadernos de Literatura Brasileira* (1998), edited by the cultural foundation of a powerful bank, and to have a Sunday column in the *Folha de São Paulo*, Brazil's most widely distributed newspaper.

search for intensity, as well as the atomism and the isolation that it incites, go hand in hand with the commercialization of culture and language that has been deepening in Brazil since the mid-1960s. Certainly, at stake is a broader process, which in the end points to Baudelaire, and, in Brazil, to the modernist movement; nevertheless, the specificity of the constellation proposed here should suffice for Gullar's moment to be considered as a special chapter in this history in which change and continuity are so intimately articulated. If Gullar's poems cannot be reduced to this process, if their intensity is not simply absorbed by the logic of semiotic overproduction (Durão, 2008b), the commercialization, the outdoors or businesses in general, which have the same social origin, it is because there is something in the poet's work that, in some way, goes beyond them. Be it due to its lack of immediate finality, structurally impossible for commodities, or be it through the conjunction of different types of intensity, as we have seen, the lyrical in Gullar will always reside in this: in the potential of simultaneously registering a specific historical tendency and evading the mere register, in letting the economic come through while making it subject to the formal economy dictated by the text.

FICTION

Not Exactly Sex and Drugs: Reinaldo Moraes Pornopopéia between monadology and the partition of the sensible

The field of literary studies is founded on the underlying premise that works of literature may be treated as vehicles of knowledge. Trends in literary theory can – and should – be judged not only by their own philosophical stance, their conceptual content and internal propositional coherence, but also by the kind of knowledge they derive from literature. This article proposes a reading of *Pornopopéia*, a recent Brazilian novel that received much attention in the media (e.g. Pécora, 2009), but not in academia (exceptions are Paz [2012] and Marques Filho [2015]), according to two different models, the monadological one, as exemplified by T.W. Adorno, and that of the partition of the sensible, developed by Jacques Rancière (e.g. 2005). The underlying motivation is that such double interpretation may prove fruitful both as a means for confronting these hermeneutical perspectives through the mediation of the same object, and as a way of illuminating an otherwise elusive literary piece.

The knowledge yielded by a monadological interpretation has as its foundation a strict separation between the artifact and its surroundings, such as the author's intention, the reader's reception or its immediate social context. Considering a text a monad helps the constitution of the aesthetic as an autonomous sphere, but in the same gesture functions as an obstacle for its social relevance. From a philosophical perspective, such severing of the work from its environment should be viewed both as symptom of, and an attempt to deal with a deep crisis of thought, precisely insofar as conceptual, systematic knowledge became suspicious in a reified totality ever harder to be totalized. It was not without a sense of *faut de mieux* that Adorno's aesthetics (1997) identified in art's tense articulation of the imagination with strict aesthetic rationality a promising modus operandi for the absorption of social truth. From the point of view of the sociology of literature, the opposition between what is inside and what lies in the exterior proves to be a precondition for their articulation. For our purposes the following famous passage by Fredric Jameson may be a good starting point:

> The sociology of culture is therefore first and foremost, I would like to suggest, a form: no matter what the philosophical postulates called upon to justify it, as practice and as a conceptual operation it always involves the jumping of a spark between two poles, the coming into contact of two unequal terms, of two apparently unrelated modes of being. Thus in the realm of literary criticism the sociological approach necessarily juxtaposes the individual work of art with some vaster form of social reality which is seen in one way or another as its source or ontological ground, its Gestalt field, and of which the work itself comes to be thought of as reflection or a symptom, a characteristic manifestation or a simple byproduct, a coming to consciousness or an imaginary or symbolic resolution, to mention only a few of the ways in which this problematic central relationship has been conceived. (1971: 4-5, italics in the original)

One may certainly criticize this as being too much of a formalization (true, in accordance with the book's title, *Marxism and Form*), something that fosters the *application* of theories, which may eventually lose literary works from the field of vision (Durão, 2011a), but still it is useful as a characterization of an interpretative stance that aims at acquiring knowledge from the clash between the interiority of texts and their social import. In its strongest version, the monadological reading draws its insights from literary form considered as crystalized social content. The result is a paradoxical one, for the more a text separates itself from the world surrounding it through an investment in its internal articulations, the more it may bring within itself its own exteriority. In Jameson's enterprise, the aim of interpretation is a reconstitution of the social totality through the visibility yielded by the literary artifact; this is not an irrelevant ambition for access to society as whole may be not only considered a necessary step for political action, but also attests, as it were performatively, the superiority of Marxism as an interpretative master code over other theories, which now are seen as commanding, even if truthfully, only restricted parts a totality.

To be sure, there are other uses a monadological reading may serve. In its weakest form, when the knowledge brought by the work already exists as a sociological idea, the text makes it more concrete, gives it sensuous contours, thus be contributing to a fuller understanding of it. Further, by being present in different rational-discursive spheres, the contents presented may aspire to a greater scope of validity, as a *Weltgeist*, as it were. But when the knowledge extracted from the work is new, the very division of the world into separated conceptual realms ruled by their own internal logic is challenged and literature seems to appear at the same time *alongside* and *above* other discursive practices and forms of rationality (Menke, 1991: vii- xiii).

It is exactly this that is achieved by Brazilian critic Roberto Schwarz (2001) in his reading of Machado de Assis. Dealing with *The Posthumous Memoirs of Brás Cubas* (1997) he begins by isolating one recurrent narrative trait as an underlying formal element (note then that form is not something given beforehand or pre-conceived, but is itself already imbued with critical imagination), namely the narrator's flippancy, his propensity to negate and deny what he has just asserted. This volubility is then interpreted as a particular ruling class position in post-independence Brazil.[12] The coexistence of slave-based production and political coming of age allowed the ruling elites do adopt a colonial or modern worldview depending on the circumstances. This literal opportunism was masterfully captured by Machado de Assis in a comic, entertaining mode that effectively glues what otherwise would be a bizarre amalgam.[13] From Schwarz's reading results not only a concrete picture of 19th century Brazil, which still reverberates in the present, but a substantial contribution to sociological knowledge itself, hardly obtainable otherwise.

12 Independence was proclaimed on September 7th, 1822, by D. Pedro, son of the King D. João VI. Abolition came only in May 13th, 1888, but it took decades for the black population to be incorporated into the wage labor market. To this day blacks have not been fully included socially if one thinks of the satisfaction of basic human needs.

13 For a good contextualization of Schwarz's reading of Machado de Assis, see Arantes (1992) and Ohata & Cevasco (2007).

The crisis of the monadological approach parallels that of the category of literary work itself. If for an aesthetic monad to exist it has to seal itself off from the outside world through its form, then it has to be new: monadic artifacts must be uncompromisingly unique. This has become increasingly difficult[14] in a world so utterly pervaded by so much language, characterized by uninterrupted, ever louder and brighter semiosis. It is not that masterworks are no longer being written, as conservative critics often claim, but rather that they have to vie with a multitude of other artifacts, whose abundance eventually promote a change in the very character of language. When semiotic productivity reaches its maximum, silence is converted into interval and works have to make an immense formal effort to become individualized vis-à-vis past art and present linguistic production (Durão, 2008b). In fact, it is tempting to turn much of the most recent developments in theory (say, the emergence of Barthesian text, or the notion of the canon as a stifling, oppressive entity) upside down and consider them as symptoms, results of and not causes for, the precariousness of strong works. For the monadic approach one either has a powerful object capable of yielding knowledge (that is why it is powerful), or one has nothing. In this case what should be done with the avalanche of objects or messages, *both* from high culture *and* the culture industry, which do not really evince an absolutely new formal organization?

14 It is curious to observe that the impact of Roberto Schwarz's work (as well as Antonio Candido's, his mentor) was such that in certain academic circles in Brazil the crystallization of social content into form became an abstract, a priori aim of interpretation. This led to a reification of the procedure, for deprived it of the spontaneity that should inform the critical imagination.

It is in view of this that Jacques Rancière's theory of the partition of the sensible becomes particularly relevant, for it provides another angle to deal with aesthetic objects. The question now no longer relates to the process of individuation of artifacts, their separation from everything else (including other works, which they normally abhor), but how art participates in a division of the world of perception that dictates who is entitled to exist, and therefore to act politically. As is well known, Rancière articulates an overall view of art divided into three stages or degrees; although historical, they do not strictly correspond to periods or moments in a supposedly self-unfolding of art.[15] The first is what he calls its ethical regime, in which works do not exist as autonomous entities, but are constituted instead according to their supposed truth and effects on subjects and the community. In the representative regime artifacts acquire a new level of existence for now they cease to be subordinated to external criteria and appear as objects governed by their own rules, such as genres, adequacy of tone to subject, distinctions of what is high and low etc. What characterizes the aesthetic regime is the establishment of the sphere of art as a realm no longer subjected to any a priori normativity; as such leads to a radical form of equality, both on the treatment of materials and the projected position of its recipients. The potential to say anything does not interest Rancière as a sheer wealth of meaning, which is always so suspiciously close to a rhetoric of accumulation; rather, the aesthetic regime is relevant through the myriad of ways it allows art to challenge, rearticulate or question society's organization of what can be sensed and thought as existing.

15 For good commentaries, see Corcoran (2010: 14-24); Tanke (2011: 73-108).

This has been superbly illustrated by Rancière's recent *Aisthesis* (2013), which provides a real poetics of how the most diverse artifacts from different aesthetic realms, from the *Belvedere Torso* to James Agee's 1941, *Let Us Now Praise Famous Men*, challenge an ideal of order in representation. The book presents its materials in chronological series, always beginning with a quote from its object (in this it reminds one of Erich Auerbach's *Mimesis*). The progression of increasing equality in the world of art is developed through close readings without any overarching hypothesis proposed beforehand. The aesthetic regime of art thus emerges as an irresistible phenomenon from the artworks themselves, not as a result of any theoretical imposition. As such, art is in itself political and a form of practice. One of the most frequent criticism of the monadological model, that it leaves no room for action is here totally avoided, because art itself is viewed as a way of being, one which invites readers to transpose it to society at large. The interaction between the two spheres, however, a complex one: "For literature deals with democracy not as some 'reign of the masses' but as excess in the relationship of bodies to words. Democracy is first and foremost the invention of words by means of which those who don't count make themselves count and so blur the ordered distribution of speech and mutism that made the political community a 'beautiful animal', an organic totality" (Rancière, 2011, 40). In other words, political democracy reorganizes the sensible through language in order to allow for the oppressed to appear; literary democracy creates a surplus of signs for persons and things that challenge their ordered, well-established placement.

Rancière himself repeatedly criticizes the monadological conception of art, which, he argues, eventually leads to an ontologization of the work conceived as a total other. This version of aesthetic autonomy is then attacked as part of a larger tendency, which includes Deleuze, Badiou and Negri. But there are other ways to deal with aesthetic autonomy that do not lead to immobility in a supposed absolute otherness. For the constitution of the monad may be dynamic; it can be not the starting point, but the *result* of the interpretative process (Durão, 2008c). In fact, it is possible to criticize Rancière's aesthetics from the point of view of the monadological model by suggesting that its multitude of perspicacious insights, its interpretative ingenuity and intimacy with art all converge to one single idea, namely that art *is*, that it exists as a sphere of democratic potentialities. Like other prestigious approaches to literature, Rancière's would not be exactly hermeneutical, for it does not purport to uncover a hidden meaning, something the text would not know about itself. By not recognizing nonidentity inside the artifact, Rancière's theory would ignore the dialectic character of art, as part of society, and also participating in social domination. If aesthetic monadology is centrifugal, since it proceeds from the work to society, the partition of the sensible is centripetal, because ends in the space of aesthetic practice. Both models are then able to criticize each other without there being mutual correction or reciprocal annulment. This incapacity to invalidate or improve one another justifies underlying presupposition of this paper that the monadological and the partition of the sensible models illuminate different aspects of literature as an aesthetic phenomenon. It may very well be that their efficaciousness is best measured a posteriori, according to the results they yield.

Perhaps as interpretative models both perspectives could be dealt with pragmatically, more according to the situation one is in and to what one is after. Be it as it may, the fact that both approaches have something unsatisfactory about them be itself be viewed as yet one more sign of the crisis in the relationship between art and knowledge – a link which itself became relevant, as said before, under a deep social crisis. Thus the objective of this essay: as a methodological exercise, it aims at experimenting with both interpretative procedures in one of the most intriguing recent Brazilian novels. If successful, the analysis will not only point to the theoretical strengths of each, but will also help characterize an otherwise baffling work.

Reinaldo Moraes' *Pornopopéia* was published in 2009. The book is exactly what its titles says: a pornographic epic. Noun and adjective are in tension and modify each other. Pornography withdraws any claim to seriousness of this long paratactic narrative; the epic size of the story transforms the pornographic by making it continuous, not allowing for the existence of breaks, of moments of rest, that normally characterize the pornographic. It is true that there are strong elements of the picaresque in the plot, but the tragic end and the considerable degree of self-reflection on the part of the first person narrator point to another direction. It is not easy to summarize this 660-page-long story, filled as it is with so many events. The main character is José Carlos Ribeiro a sexually insatiable, drug obsessed, failed film maker, who narrates the series of occurrences that randomly but inexorably lead from his late night, frustrated attempts to write the script for an institutional advertisement video for the Itaquerambu sausage factory to his imminent murder by what seems to be undercover policemen. The storyline is full of coincidences, properly noted by the narrator, and is centered on a statistically improbable event, the killing of the drug dealer Miro in his own car by a stray bullet as he was sitting next to Ribeiro, who then runs away with Miro's leftover cocaine supply. Afraid of the police, Zeca, as his friends call him, leaves São Paulo city for Porangatuba, a fictitious paradisiacal seaside resort on the border of the States of Rio and São Paulo where his friend's Nissim's wife's brother-in-law owns a house. There he starts an affair, not without much libidinal diligence and self-persuasion, with the sixty-three-year-old Rejane, owner of a luxurious inn. The relationship is fully motivated by self-interest, for José Carlos manipulates Rejane to provide for him and hide him, telling her that his problems were family-related. The key point for the outcome of the story is Zeca's postponement of a trip to a private island, where he would have sex with Josilene a naïve, poor local girl, who works at a tourists' restaurant and dates a policeman. After the choice was made to depart the next day, all events in the narrative conspire to Ribeiro's downfall: Josilene's boyfriend finds out about her and beats her up, probably with her parents' consent, to the point of disfiguring her, and Rejane discovers the real reason of Zeca's need to hide. The book ends with the protagonist's imminent capture by undercover police, who will most likely kill him.

The plot thus combines the lightness of the picaresque, which derives from the apparent lack of necessity in the concatenation of events, with the inevitably dramatic fact of the extinction of the narrative voice, the annihilation of the "I".

But the process of narration is also important. The story is told in blocks of real time writing, which in the beginning give the impression that the words of the text were being composed as they were typed on Ribeiro's laptop, apparently with no revision of afterthought possible. This ultra-realism of the act of composition also emphasizes the addressee, a "you" at first unnamed towards which all sentences are ultimately directed. It is only on page 562 that reader learns that the computer file of *Pornopopéia* was going to be sent to the translator of Charles Bukowski's *Women* (*Mulheres* [1984]), none other than Reinaldo Moraes himself. José Carlos instructs him to edit the material in any way he wants, provided that all names, including the author's, are changed[16], and the linguistic low level is maintained:

> Respeite o meu baixo nível, é o alto favor que lhe peço. Faça da minha vulgaridade um parque pras suas diversões. Vai fundo nas *cenash obscenash*, como ouvi de um crítico de cinema carioca sobre as mais floridas sequências sexuais do *Holisticofrenia* [José Carlos' underground, only film]. Evite lirismos lambisgoias, insights psicossociológicos modorrentos, e, sobretudo, morais-da-história digestivas ao gosto do distinto público de classe média de shopping. Mesmo os neologismos vagabas e as palavras-valise-sem-alça, sem falar nas

---

16 "Invente um pseudônimo. Ou tasque seu próprio nome, se quiser. Por mim, tudo bem. Só não quero ver o meu nome associado a livro nenhum. Seria admitir o fracasso de toda uma vida dedicada ao cinema. (Dedicada ao alcoolismo e à putaria também, mas deixa para lá.)" (p.434) // Invent a pseudonym. Or just throw in your own name, if you want. It's alright, as far as I'm concerned. I just don't want to see my name associated with any book. That would be to admit the failure of a lifetime devoted to the cinema. (Devoted to alcoholism and fucking around, too, but never mind that.)" All translations of *Pornopopéia* are mine.

> badalhocas trocadilhescas, pode limar numa boa, se te parecerem muito bestoides. Só deixa o que você achar mais engraçado e esdrúxulo, digamos. (436)

> Do me the great favor of respecting the low level of my language. Turn my vulgarity into a park for your amusement. Really go for it in the obscene scenes, as a carioca film critic once said about the more colorful sexual sequences of the film "Holisticofrenia." Avoid cheap lyricism, stupefying psycho-sociological insights, and, above all, the comforting moral endings better suited to the middle-class tastes of distinguished mall-going readers. The trampy neologisms and the unbearable portmanteau words, not to mention the punning pubic hairs, you're free to delete if they seem too stupid. Just keep what you think is funny and twisted, let's say.

This of course generates indeterminacy as to what was originally written by Ribeiro and what was modified by Moraes. In any case, it is important to note at this point that it is as impossible to identify with the first person narrator, as it is inadequate to criticize him. His falsehood, his lack of concern with, and instrumentalization of people, his addictive obsession with his own pleasure all make him someone not to be trusted, let alone liked or admired. On the other hand, all his vices, including his outrageous chauvinism are so openly exposed by him, and in such hilarious ways, that carrying out ideological analysis of Ribeiro's sexism would be ludicrous. Accepting to read *Pornopopéia* at all already means complying with the grossness that is structural to the work. The mixture of odious character and charming exposition is in reality a constitutive principle and as such has to be accepted as internal to the text. This is something Moraes's narrator shares with the Machado de Assis of *Brás Cubas* and *Dom Casmurro*. But unlike Bentinho or Brás, Zeca is not easily identified socially. It would not be accurate to think of him as a *malandro* or trickster, someone who cleverly lives zigzagging the borders separating of legality from criminality (Candido, 1993); his hedonism and urbanism are too strong for that, as are José Carlos' familiarity with literature and culture, which mark him too much as an educated character.

Indeed, mixed with several references to mass culture – as when José Carlos masturbates on a 1995 issue of the chief celebrities-oriented magazine in Brazil (414-416), or the five or six "paulocoelhos" (551) at his disposal at a seaside inn – *Pornopopéia* evinces a disguised but firm set of literary and artistic sources, including Mallarmé, Proust, Freud, Picasso, Matisse, Goddard, Heidegger (who is associated to Steinhäger[17]) and others. The text is clearly self-conscious as a literary work and its affiliations are directly mentioned. Besides Bukowski, one finds allusions to Philip Roth's memorable scene in *Portnoy's Complaint* of Alexander's masturbation with a piece of liver (272; 273[18]), which is now adapted to a squid ("uma

17 "Cato o notebook, disposto a registrar os últimos quinze minutos da história da humanidade, visto do meu ângulo pessoal. Sete horas. É cedo ainda. Para o homem, digo. Para o ser continua sendo irremediavelmente tarde, como diz o garotinho na 'Chinesa', do Godard, citando um filósofo alemão, o Heidegger, acho. Se não for o Heidegger deve ser o Steinhager." (p. 381) // "I grab my laptop, all set to record the last fifteen minutes of the history of humankind as seen from my personal perspective. Seven o'clock. It's still early. For man, I mean. For being it's still irremediably late, as the little boy in Godard's *La Chinoise* says, quoting a German philosopher, Heidegger, I think. If not Heidegger, Steinhaeger."

18 "Gozado é que o esquema narrativo dele lembra esse papo que eu venho levando com você." (273) // "Funny how his narrative structure resembles this chat I've been having with you."

atividade lulonanista", 499), also to be eaten unbeknownst by an innocent family. What one should observe here in passing is that this posture of light-hearted mockery and lack of respect for high-brow culture is more internal to culture than serious approaches full of respect and awe, which fail to see how culture is not that what it purports to be. And yet, it would be a mistake to associate *Pornopopéia* to the genre of Beatnik literature. Bukowski's *Women* is a good term of comparison. Even though sex and drugs are also present in Bukowski's novel – although not as extremely as in *Pornopopéia* – the glamour of the outsider, the charm of being literary by fiercely negating mainstream literature is unavoidable. There is something inescapably cool this kind of character. In Moraes's novel the lure of the alternative, which so easily pervades countercultural literary production, is totally absent. Not only is Zeca despicable as a person, but also ideologically the novel is not strictly leftist, for although anti-petty bourgeois sentiment is pervasive in Moraes' work, it never coalesces into a proper political stance, and very often what seems to be social revolt derived from petty subjective frustration. This sharply differentiates *Pornopopéia* from the Brazilian *geração do mimeógrafo* or *poesia marginal* of the 70s, the first undeniable, because self-conscious, marginal[19] literary movement in the country, even if (or precisely because) reference to years of the dictatorship can be found in the character Alê, a decadent musician, who sings Torquato Neto, quotes Waly Salomão and is well schooled in the ways of Tropicália.

19 Note that in Portuguese "marginal" means both "at the margin" and "criminal".

Pornopopéia's main formal trait is that of synonymy. The whole narrative may be conceived as a sustained attempt to build a story with elements that would systematically deviate from the usual, established sense while at the same time retaining a kernel of meaning. Moraes deploys the whole gamut of linguistic possibilities offered by Portuguese to generate this effect. Apart from neologisms and pervasive colloquialisms, the novel extracts the maximum potential of augmentatives, diminutives, nicknames and mixture of registers. Now, this linguistic tortuousness has a social equivalent that is ironically incorporated within the novel itself: the idea of proximity, familiarity or informality that was so successfully conceptualized by Sérgio Buarque de Holanda as the cordial man (1997: 139-52). This is perhaps the best well-known notion in Brazilian cultural criticism. It refers to the weakness, originating in colonial Brazil, of the division between public and private, which renders the process of Weberian rationalization partial and incomplete. The social drive towards increasing impersonality, as in the constitution of state bureaucracy, would penetrate Brazil only imperfectly, being resisted by an extended version of the family and a "familiarization" of public relations. The structural avoidance of a neutral language and the absolute primacy of synonyms create a sense of gratuitous conviviality, something emerging solely from the presence of the other, just emphatically as it were. This Brazilian utopia of cordiality, a nidus for all kinds of nationalist ideologies, is dealt with in a complex way in *Pornopopéia*. The tension between language and character has already been mentioned; now it should be remarked that the literary circuit – José Carlos (his real name?) writing to Reinaldo Moraes, who rewrites (how much?) the manuscript – joins the opposites of textual proximity, painstakingly produced, with the distance inherent not only in the disconnection between writer and recipient of the computer file *Pornopopéia* (though never mentioned as such in the novel), but also in the mediation of fictionality. To be sure, the contrivance of creating a supposedly real frame for a found manuscript, as in Hawthorne's *The Scarlet Letter*, is an old one, but in *Pornopopéia* the editor of the manuscript is never felt as such. Furthermore, the concern here is the social content of this formal device, as it mixes distance and proximity. Would the work be staging a hilarious requiem to the death of an ideal of Brazilian conviviality, however unreal and ideologically misused it has been? Interestingly enough, there seems to be a relation of inverse proportionality here, for the more this kind of a gregarious, easy-going, hedonistic mode of being becomes denied socially, the more *Pornopopéia*'s self-referentiality, the fact that it is constructed as a work comes to the fore. In other words, the more disinterestedness of being together becomes socially problematic, the more the novel firmly establishes itself as successful literary artifact, which thus distances itself from society showing its failure.

III

If for the monadological model the circuit of cordiality/ intimacy is central, for the partition of the sensible what is important is a specific kind of presentation of the body and its drives. Here, the focus does not lie on the process of synonymy derived of linguistic productivity, but on the contrary on the exhibition of the body and its fluids as demystified objects, sheer sources of pleasure. They are not dealt with disgust or scientific neutrality, nor with pride or a desire to *épater le bourgeois*. Rather, body parts and its products become the means of sensuous satisfaction for the narrator, and for the reader something funny. Here is a passage from the pseudo-religious orgy (in Portuguese, *suruba*, not *orgia*), part of the cult of the Zebuh- Bhagadhagadhoga: Zeca, high on acid, is contemplating Melquíades, the 6+ feet tall black dancer, who was supposed to be gay, but has sex twice in the novel with Sossô, a desirable soon-to-be seventeen-year old – or, better, he is observing his penis. The other participants of the "rite" are a fat woman, an extremely fat woman, a very thin man, Ingo, the cithara player, and Samayana, the mistress:

> Cara, me desculpe insistir nesse assunto, mas a pemba do homem era uma borduna bororô, uma autêntica encarnação antropomórfica do divino Zebuh da piroca master, nada menos. O resto é pinto, bilau, neca, piupiu, pilinha, pirulito. E, pelo visto, a cobra preta ia fumar. Não fumando no meu derrière nem nos tenros orifícios da Sossô, beleza, pensei. Por mim, ele podia ficar à vontade pra desbastar as badalhocas merdosas do magrão, as adiposidades grementes das gordas, o carnão fardado em seda que passava por nossa divina mestra e até aquele furo no cavalo da calça do Ingo, se a gônada saísse para frente. (195)

> Man, sorry to insist on this, but the man's bratwurst was a Bororó baton, an authentic anthropomorphic incarnation of the divine Zebuh of the master dick, nothing less. Everything else is a mini cock, willie, winkie, twinkie, wee. And from what I could see pigs

> were going to fly. As long as they didn't fly up my ass or Sossô's, it's all good, I thought. As far as I was concerned, he could be my guest to prune the shitty ass hairs of the thin guy, the sticky adiposities of the fat chicks, the succulent flesh clothed in silk under the guise of our master and eve that hole in Ingo's paints on his crotch, if the gonad poked through."

And here is the anus of José Carlos' wife, a professor of sociology at the University of São Paulo (USP), being compared to the one of a prostitute he just had sex with:

> A Lia, por exemplo, muitíssimo cá entre nós, nunca apresentou um cu tão chupável quanto o daquela puta da Augusta. O cu da patroa sai pra trabalhar de manhã cedo, passa o dia sentado ou sendo massageado pelas nádegas na cadência do andar e caga sem apelacão nos banheiros da faculdade, onde é limpo a seco com o papel higiênico de segunda que o governo oferece nos toaletes da suas instituições ensino, desenvolvendo, por conseguinte, toda sorte de grumelos e badalhocas aderentes à pilosidade local, de resto jamais desbastada na depilação pelas mulheres ditas honestas, pois está na Bíblia, no Alcorão, nos Upanishades: "Se quereis pastar no rebanho das eleitas, não depileis vosso rabicó". (141)

> Lia, for instance, absolutely between us, never presented an ass as suckable as that of that whore from Augusta Street. The missus' ass goes to work early, spends the day sitting or being massaged by

> the buttocks in the cadence of walking and shits mercilessly at the university's WC, where it is dry-cleaned with the second rate tissue the government provides for the toilets of its educational institutions, therefore developing all sorts of little pimples and minute leftover shitballs adhering to the local pilosity, incidentally never depilated by "honest" women, for it is in the Bible, in the Koran, in the Upanishads: "If thou wilt graze on the herd of the chosen ones, do not depilate thy butt."

It would be inaccurate to argue that sexual organs are estranged or de-familiarized here. They remain what they are, but the way they are handled make them fit to be visualized and experienced without any sense of abjection or heroism. This is also true for the more sensitive case of sexual relations, which are depicted, as in this passage, without innuendos:

> Esguichar porra na cara da mulher é o que há. Na boca, no nariz, nos olhos, na bochechas, na testa, no cabelo – é lindo. E fica mais lindo ainda quando elas lambem e sorvem a porra, que é pra você se sentir o governador-geral da putaria. As boas fêmeas gostam disso. Algumas das más também. E não é só em filme pornô, não. Bom, você deve saber disso tanto quanto eu.
>
> A minha puta sabia tomar uma pica por via oral. Começou com um bem-realizado tour de língua em torno da chapeleta, pra depois alojar o negócio sobre o leito da língua dentro da boca. Meu pau ficou descansando um pouco naquele berço esplêndido como um pequeno deus na manjedoura, antes

> que ela iniciasse o trabalho de sucção. Quer dizer, a mulher se esmerava em prolegômenos refinados até no boquete. De tirar o chapéu – ou a chapeleta. (137)

> Gushing cum on a woman's face is the best. On her mouth, nose, eyes, cheeks, forehead, hair – it's beautiful. And it's even more beautiful when they lick and savor the cum, so that you feel like the governor-general of sex. Good females like it. Some of the bad ones too. And it's not only in porn films. Well, you must know this as much as I do. My whore knew how to take a dick orally. She started with a well- done tongue tour around the head, moved on to lodging the thing over the tongue's bed. My cock found a short repose in that splendid cradle as a little god at the manger, before she initiated the work of suction. That is, the woman strove in refined prolegomena even in the blowjob. Giving head, both of them.

My claim here is that descriptions like these should not be regarded as objectively offensive (however much one may feel personally outraged)[20], first because of their already mentioned comic nature (they do not take themselves seriously), second because sex and drugs are a source of pleasure for all involved in the story. A quote like this may be repelled as sexist, which it is, but in a different, more literal meaning: not as the prevalence or superiority of the male over the female, but as a sexualization of existence.[21]

---

20 Interestingly enough the depiction of sexual organs and of intercourse hardly tends to arouse sexual desire in the reader.

21 Indeed, that the novel may create precisely this kind of semantic noise may itself be seen as an achievement.

For all of Zeca's partners with enjoy intercourse with him (again unlike Bukowski's *Women*), and one would very well be entitled to imagine the same scene being described by the prostitute in very similar terms.

Moreover, Moraes' handling of the body has demystifying effect. Not only is here no symbolism attached to it, not hint of transcendence, no residue of spirituality, but also its presence is very often a means to destroy illusions. This is how Zeca listens to the precepts of the fake-Hindu creed at the preamble of an orgy:

> A bhagadhaghamaithuna, de acordo com a Samayana [the attractive female master], requeria a nossa mais completa e irrestrita nudez – "de corpo e alma". Sempre a eterna dupla sertaneja de todas as religiões Body & Soul. (179)

> The "'bhagadhaghamaithuna' according to Samayana, required our most complete and unrestricted nudity – "of body and soul". Always the eternal country music duo of all religions, Body & Soul.

Accordingly, desire is not transcendent and the desire to desire seems to be unproblematic:

Minha impressão é de que a gente nasce com um estoque fixo de gozadas pra gastar ao longo da vida, do mesmo jeito que as mulheres trazem de berço um número contado de óvulos nos ovários. A maior parte dos homens morre sem ter gasto nem metade da munição gozosa a que tem direito. Bem ou mal, esse não vai ser o meu caso, posso te garantir. Vou gozar até o último item em estoque. Meu organismo demanda o gozo 24 horas por dia, e até falando, lendo, trabalhando ou mesmo dormindo eu quero gozar de algum jeito. (223)

My impression is that we are born with a fixed stock of cumshots to spend in our lifetime, in the same way that women bring from birth a limited number of ova in their ovaries. The greatest number of men die without laying out even half of the ejaculatory ammunition they are entitled to. I'm going to come until the last item on stock. My organism demands orgasms 24 hours a day, even talking, reading, working, or even sleeping I want to come somehow.

All of this leads to the conclusion that in Pornopopéia one witnesses a particular form of language circulation, in which words and discharges of desire coexist. The Brazilian word for "horniness" is tesão, a term with a peculiar performative function; it is an excess of desire that can be applied to extra-sexual contexts but which always brings a superabundance of libido to them. "Tesão" cannot be used objectively; it always implicates the speaker; it is itself "tesudo", "tesão-ful" as it were. In Pornopopéia, it is inextricably intertwined with linguistic creativity. The result is the emergence of a configuration of language in which sex-and-drugs and writing as production of sentences become almost the same thing. To put it differently, it is not only the case that tesão becomes completely visible and accessible, thus reconfiguring what could be called a partition of desire; it shows itself at the bottom of narrative production, as its very motor.

There are several interesting implications deriving from this. Once *tesão* partakes of the horizon of the sensible, language's impact is altered. The manner in which swear words are used in *Pornopopéia* drains them of their illocutionary force. Any intention to use them is frustrated because they are literalized: according to the internal logic of the novel a "screw you!" could only be replied with "thank you". From the point of view of the reader, since words are used so freely (also socially: *Pornopopéia* is now available as pocket book for only 25 reals (approximately 7 dollars) they tend to generate an intriguing subjective dynamics. It is likely that the reader will have a sense of satisfaction seeing himself or herself reading this multitude of asses and cocks and cum, and not being prude or square or uptight; however, it is probable that at one time or another disgust will eventually creep in and a sense of abjection will turn her away from the book. As a book *of* desire, *Pornopopéia* is a challenge as well as a promise.

The interpretative insights offered by the monadological and partition model are not reconcilable. A joining together of the circuit of proximity and the liberation of desire would lead to a kind of positivity that would be detrimental to both. For the former it would suggest the existence of a happy conviviality as immediately present in society, and male to boot: it would be conformist. For the latter, it would inscribe an anthropomorphic aspect in the production of desire: it would be sedate. Presiding both, of course, is a work that is only the more interesting (and exciting) for being so different from itself. To be sure, such irreconcilability is uncomfortable; as critics, we always tend to look for unity, a final single generalization. It is tempting to articulate this opposition on a higher level as a sign, perhaps a tragic one, of the predicament of aesthetics today. This is a possibility. Another would be a more pragmatist one, which would deal with monadology or the partition of the sensible according to the particular situations. The monadological model is one that unveils social problems, in *Pornopopéia*'s case the fate of a Brazilian kind of conviviality; the partition of the sensible unveils horizons of social action; here is a light-hearted liberation of the body associated with linguistic productivity, which in the Brazilian context could be historicized as a struggle against its catholic past. In both cases, however, we have *Pornopopéia* to thank: it's not exactly sex and drugs.

ART

Objectifying Failures in the last São Paulo Biennale: the cases of Nuno Ramos and Gil Vicente. (with Flavia Trocoli)

I

Strange is the relationship between truth and scandal. If the latter's unavoidable basis in self-righteousness, marketing and opportunism embeds it in falsehood, its galvanizing potential, the sheer fact that it manages to mobilize the attention of all, suggests that truth, albeit obliquely and surreptitiously, is necessarily present in scandal. To be sure, a fuller phenomenology of scandal would have to take into account the current tendency for the managerially planned self-scandalization of things as integral part of their promotional campaigns – scandal here may even preexist the emergence of that which it is a scandal of. But the crisis of scandal is but a fraction of a generalized failure of the event, what is quite often too easily and glibly called *événement*.[22] What happened at the recent 29th São Paulo Biennale Arts Exhibition was a rare case of real scandal in its old sense, and in not only one, but in two independent instances. The protagonists were Nuno Ramos and Gil Vicente, artists with quite different styles and artistic perspectives, who presented highly dissimilar works, but who ultimately evinced the same logic of a failed achievement in their compositions. It is this logic that we will try to explain below in connection with the scandal it is the both the result of and challenge to.

22 Indeed it is remarkable how theories of the event managed to acquire currency precisely at a time that seems to be absolutely impervious to events in their emphatic sense, as that which breaks through and annuls existing structures. A clear of proof of this is the fact that the ecological crisis, perhaps the greatest in the history of civilization, has not been yet socially recognized as such.

But before dwelling on the works, it is important to note that the 29th Biennale was haunted by the ghost of failure and crisis, which had been hovering since the end of the 2008 exposition. In this previous occasion, curators left a whole floor empty as protest against the scarcity of funding, which prevented the occupation of all spaces available. Due to the 2008 disastrous attendance, the 2010 Biennale was running the risk of simply not happening. But even the best expectations were surpassed. Without vacant spaces, the exhibition showed 850 works by 159 artists and was visited by almost one million people (which contrasted sharply with the 161 thousand of 2008). Perhaps it was not by chance that the organizers chose as main motto for the event the line "There is always a cup of sea to sail in "from Jorge de Lima's major work Invenção de Orfeu (1952), which aptly epitomized what the São Paulo Biennale wished to achieve, namely, to assert that the utopian dimension of art is contained within itself, not without it or beyond it. It is in the "cup of sea" – or in this near infinite where artists insist on producing their works in – that lies the power to move forward, despite everything else. As Jorge de Lima's poem goes to say "the power to sail on even without ships/even without waves and sand".

Ramos' work bore the ironic name of *White Flag*. It was composed of three gigantic dark-brownish sculptures in geometric forms, which for many resembled enormous tombs, placed at the central span of the 30,000 square-meter modernist pavilion, projected by Brazil's most famous and cherished architect, Oscar Niemeyer, and located at the Ibirapuera Park in São Paulo city. They extended themselves over the three floors of the building and were made of highly com- pressed burned sand; it was only the manually-generated pressure which kept them standing and the contrast between their size and the appearance of fragility and instability was sharp. Each sculpture had a pole attached to it, as well as loudspeakers which incessantly played three paradigmatic songs: the folklore-sprung lullaby "Boi da Cara Preta" [Black-Faced Ox], sung by Dona Inah; Max Nunes and Láercio Alves's "Bandeira Branca" [White Flag], sung by Arnaldo Antunes; and João do Vale and José Candido's "Carcará" [Caracara], sung by Mariana Aydar. Each cycle ended with a chorus saying "nada é" [nothing is], before starting again. These are all pieces loaded with meaning and it would be difficult to convey the affective appeal they have for Brazilians. "Boi da Cara Preta" is a melody one would listen to as a child in bed, whose lyrics say that the black- faced ox will catch children who are afraid of ugly faces; "Bandeira Branca" is a carnival song one opens ones arms to sing, almost as an automatic reflex, upon hearing it; "Carcará" is a leftist song in mixolydian mode, immediately associated with the Brazilian Northeast, the poorest part of country and which has been providing cheap labor to the south for almost a century. But the most important element – at least as far as scandal goes – has not been mentioned yet, for a net enclosed the whole of this enormous work so that the three vultures that inhabited the installation would not escape. This eventually happened, as they were finally evicted, but not before much public controversy.

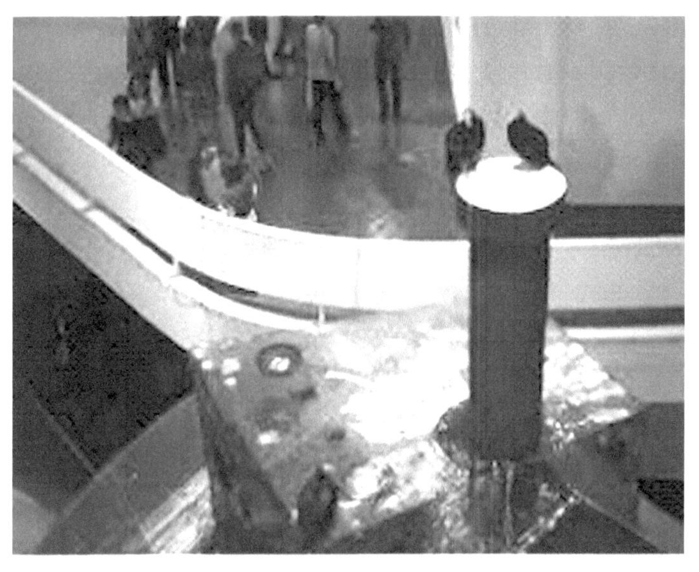

White Flag 2008-2010, installation view at Centro Cultural Banco do Brasil, Brasília, 2008. Courtesy: Galeria Fortes Vilaça, São Paulo. Photo: Mila Petrillo

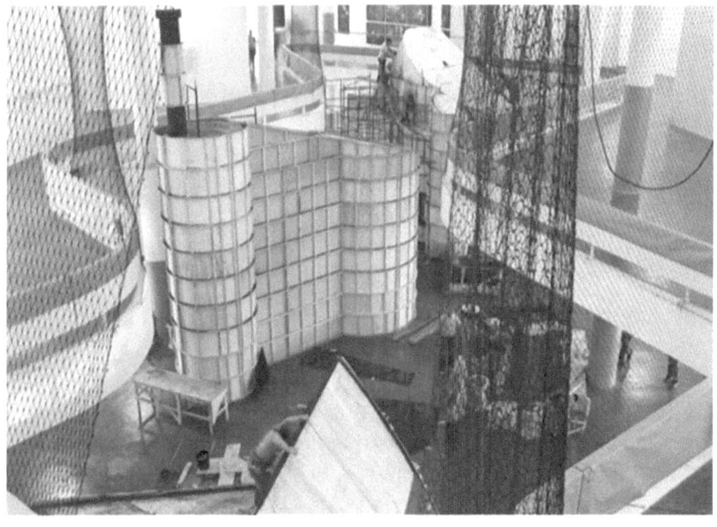

The vultures resting on one of the poles after being fed.

Even before it was shown at the Biennale, *White Flag* generated protest from ecologists, who gathered thousands of signatures on the internet demanding that the birds be returned to their original habitat. This was followed by graffiti (in bad Portuguese) on one of the sculptures saying "free the vultures" [*liberte os urubu*], and finally a formal case brought to court, which ultimately withdrew the vultures from the site. Our main argument will be that this outrage does not deserve to be taken at face value; rather that it was a misplaced reaction for effects of meaning that were taking place in Ramos' installation.[23]

But before dwelling on this, it is important to point out, to avoid any possible misunderstanding, that the vultures were being handled adequately and that the proper government venue, the Brazilian Institute for Environment and Natural Renewable Resources (IBAMA) had fully authorized the use of the birds in the artwork, before the decision was overruled by the Brasília headquarters of IBAMA, which left the installation vulture-less for a considerable time until the end of the Biennale. *White Flag* had already been exhibited in Brasília in 2008 and in 2006 Ramos had used three donkeys carrying sizeable loudspeakers on their backs – in none of these occasions there was anything resembling the uproar of the Biennale.

---

23 In view of the nosy unilateralism of the ecologists' attacks (as well as the support from the greatest part of mainstream media) and, probably most importantly, due to the mortifying silence of critical discourse, Ramos published a letter in *Folha de São Paulo*, the biggest Brazilian newspapers, called "Bandeira Branca, amor – in defense of the haughtiness and the will of art". In it, he proposes a first reading of his own work in order to provoke other interpretations and displace that which he considers grounds his attackers' position, namely that his work "should be taken in an absolutely opaque and literal fashion, as a kind of corpse without meaning". See http://www1.folha.uol. com.br/fsp/ilustrissima/il1710201005.htm.

The public's rage, so we claim, does not spring from the use of the birds themselves, but must be connected to the *compound of sense* of the artwork. Two main features of the installation deserve to be commented on here. In the first place, even though *White Flag* is an enormous three dimensional artifact full of empty spaces, it cannot be penetrated; it must rather be viewed and listened to, but still only imperfectly so. The installation can only partially be seen, because of the way it was fused with or melted into the architecture of the Ibirapuera building. There is no vantage point from which it may be apprehended as a whole. If it cannot be walked into, it does not let itself be contemplated from the outside either. At the same time, *White Flag* resists listening as well. The repetition of the songs spatializes sound and the endlessness of the cycle prevents the spectator from either really starting or putting a closure to the sound material.

The second important characteristic of the work is its negativity, which can here be envisioned on at least two different levels. As far as the material is concerned, as has already been mentioned, the work is precarious and constantly seems to be on the verge of crumbling, in spite (or perhaps because) of its colossal size. The conflict here is one of matter versus volume. But this instability in the realm of the signifier is paralleled in that of the signified, for it is simply impossible to extract an overall meaning from the accumulation of negative parts.

The relationship with space, the geometric forms and their massive character, the songs, the colors, the title, the vultures: all of them point to something black and dreary, but they do not let themselves be articulated into a message;

worse still, they seriously threaten to ruin the work as such, which then would be not much more than an accumulation of disjoined parts. Ramos himself is aware of this formal trait, this instability of his art, which is always on the brink of becoming something else; he even theorizes about it commenting that it is typical of Brazilian culture, which mixes both exhilaration, because everything remains to be done, and mourning, because everything seems always about to disappear, because it is so difficult for things acquire the state of being, to become existent (See Ramos, 2007: 12-13). If this unsteadiness is a central feature of Ramos' work as whole, the biennale was the occasion for a curious logic to take place. To put it succinctly and somewhat provocatively, it was the ecologists' reaction that, by denying the work its status as object, endowed it with meaning.

Those who faced *White Flag* from a moral perspective, and not through the ethics of the artwork, which is to follow to the limit its own compositional freedom, actually ended up mobilizing an internal sense of the installation they could not enter. In "Carcará", we listen: Carcará: pega, mata e come/ Carcará: nunca vai morrer de fome [Caracara catches, kills and eats/Caracara will never starve to death].[24]

That which prevents barbaric killing, the sheer extermination of the other, the persistence of its nature as just food, is the mediation of a third element, representation itself, which is what all artworks (however unwittingly), including *White Flag*, accomplish. To put it in other words, once the work is rejected as such and treated as a non-thing, it can answer its destruction (so infinitely different

24 The song is easily available online.

from its dematerialization) with its own immanent content, which otherwise would be hard to discern. It then shows itself as some- thing at the same time that it lays bare the barbarous fury that uses a spurious claim of animal mistreatment and demands expiation from the artwork's sin for desiring to be an object.

Gil Vicente's Enemies series of drawings was the other source of out- rage. These were naturalistic portrayals of world leaders about to be killed by the artist himself: George W. Bush, Lula, the Pope, Eduardo Campos, Fernando Henrique Cardoso, Queen Elizabeth II, Jarbas Vasconcelos, Kofi Annan, Mahmoud Ahmadinejad and Ariel Sharon. The drawings were charcoal on paper in natural size (1.50 × 2.00 m), adopting several perspectives, using knives and guns, and showing the victims in different positions and with differing degrees of expression.25 All titles of the pictures began with "Auto-retrato matando" [Self-portrait killing] followed by the name of the victim.

Many saw in these representations not only a gratuitous act of violence, but also a lack of respect for world leaders. In fact, Vicente was careful enough to represent national and regional politicians as well, thus effectively mediating the global and the local; he also included secular and religious leadership as well as the whole political spectrum obtaining today, from center left (Lula) to the extreme right (Bush, Sharon). Noteworthy, too, was casualness of Vicente's clothing in these executions, which included shorts, loose t-shirts and flip-flops.

---

25 All drawings can be downloaded in high resolution at the artist's site http://www.gilvicente.com.br/.

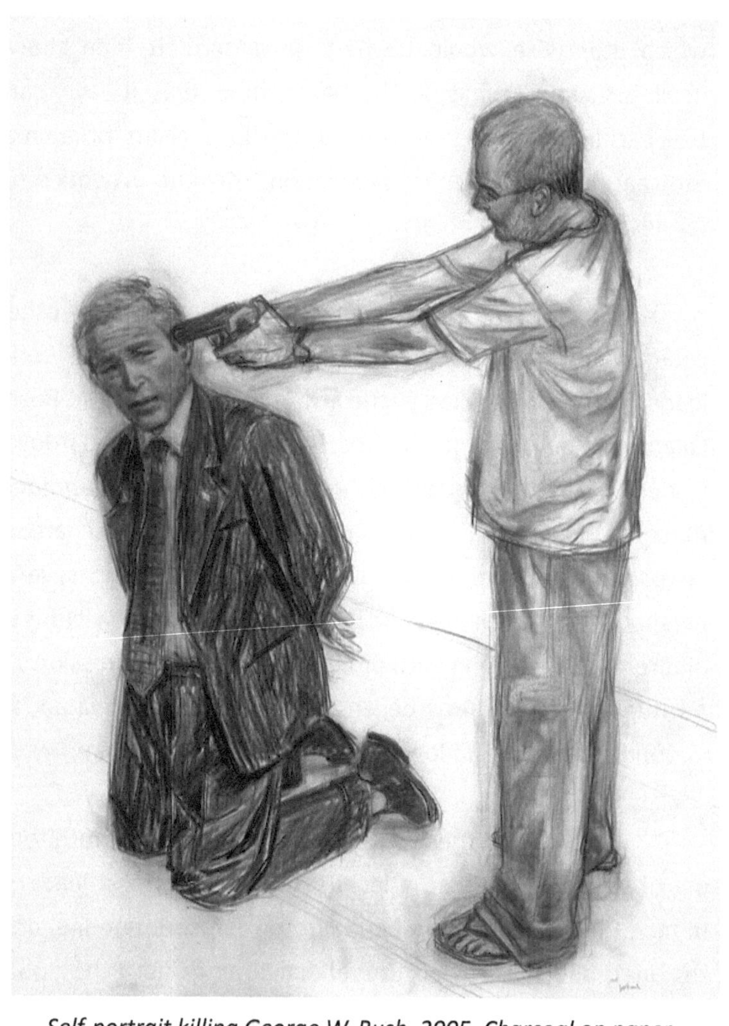

Self-portrait killing George W. Bush, 2005. Charcoal on paper, 200x150 cm. Credit: São Paulo Bienal.

The very opposite of *White Flag, Enemies* shuns any idea of dissolution or splintering. If in Ramos' work, as we pointed out, no sense of wholeness can be easily or naturally conceived, vultures, songs, sand and nets remaining disjointed until the failure of the aesthetic organized the installation,

Vicente's drawings are highly static, centered and symmetric. The viewer sees himself before figurative representations of remarkable similarity to their originals. There is no indetermination, no spectacle, and no difficulty in positioning oneself vis-à-vis these images. Indeed, the series of drawings is so easily approached that it may even invoke the universe of mass culture with its comic strips and graffiti on walls, something that Vicente repeatedly rejected.[26] However, this proximity to popular representation was in fact encouraged by the artist himself, as he exposed his work and advertised his exposition in public spaces, as in ATM booths in the city of Campina Grande, in the extremely poor northeastern State of Paraiba.

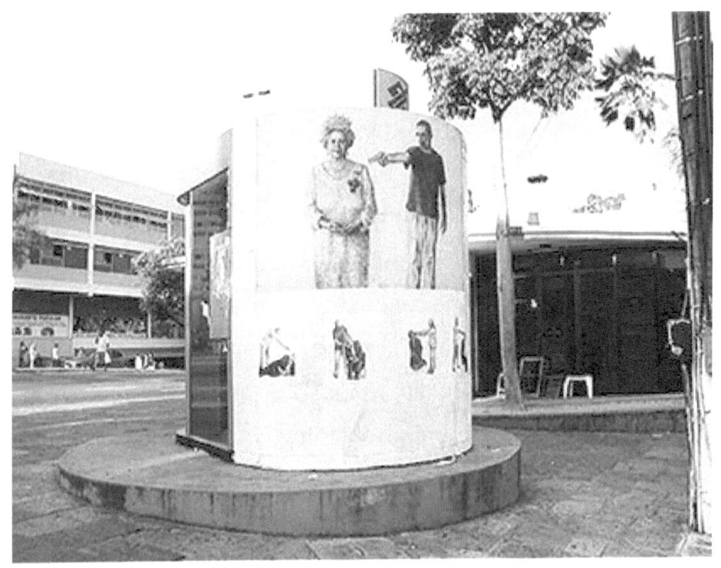

26 http://veja.abril.com.br/noticia/celebridades/gil-vicente-comemora-a- repercussao-gerada-com-a-oposicao-da-oab.

The only apparently complicating factor in these drawings, interestingly enough, are the titles themselves, which place the artist, and not the celebrities, on the foreground; this raises the question of who is the subject and who the object of the pictures, even if their structural fixity and opposition vis-à-vis one another remains beyond dispute.

On September 17, 2010, the Brazilian Association of Attorneys at Law [Ordem dos Advogados do Brasil, OAB] requested the removal of the drawings alleging that they incited violence in the public and claiming that "Although an artwork expresses its author's creativity freely and without any limitations, there must be limits for its public exposure".[27] In this case, the biennale's curators defended artistic autonomy and maintained the drawings at the exhibition. Since there was no time to follow all the legal proceedings, and perhaps because they considered they would lose, the OAB did not bring the case to court. But the controversy remained in newspapers and on the internet and, again, the result of scandal contributed to a re-articulation of the works' internal content. In *Enemies* one can find the same logic at work pointed above. Had it been "simply" received as an artwork, with all the detachment and impartiality required by aesthetic rules, it might be that one would not find anything much remarkable about these drawings. But after they had their status as works legally questioned, they suddenly became extremely revealing. The axis here is not indetermination, as in Ramos' case, but naturalism.

27 O Estado de São Paulo newspaper, 10/17/2010. http://www.estadao.com.br/noticias/arteelazer,bienal-diz-que-mantera-desenhos-de-gil-vicente-apesar-de-pedido- da-oab,611568,0.htm.

From this perspective, several formal characteristics, which would otherwise go unnoticed, suddenly acquire significance. First, one sees oneself forced to argue, against the lawyers, that the pictures do not represent death but a moment of suspense, a not-yet or on- the-verge-of, which in their stability uncannily draws them close to Ramos' *White Flag*. The Vicente on paper cannot be found guilty of murder, because murder, on paper, has not taken place. These are highly dramatic instants of suspension, and it is only the viewers' anticipation or projection that can see death happening here. This actually points to an important social truth covertly revealed by scandal: once the protection from the aesthetic sphere was withdrawn, or, perhaps better, since the aesthetic sphere was not strong enough to offer protection, the drawings fell into a social void that actually goes deep in a Brazilian structure of feeling. When the lawyers denied the aesthetic rule, this minor act of barbarism allowed one to contemplate the really big one, namely that viewers will feel pleasure in this representation – or even worse: envy, the desire to be in the artist's (cheap) shoes. More than the actual figures, the drawings would then represent the anger against established politics and its exclusive and excluding nature; it is the wrathful frustration for that which may not be politically represented that the attorneys feared. Perhaps one has to visit Brazil to witness how pervasive this feeling is, how relentlessly it is repeated by so many people in all social strata that politicians are all the same, that corruption is everywhere in Brasília, that their only concern is to get rich.[28] These two factors – namely, 1. That

28 This feeling is exactly what the recent movie *Tropa de Elite 2* – the single most profitable and the one with the largest audience in the history of Brazilian film – relies on and fosters. The claim that all political institutions are rotten was typical of fascism.

after the denial of their artistic character, the drawings' formal features become more pronounced and 2. That after they leave the world of art they start to express Brazilian barbarism – can now be combined and it is tempting to interpret the blurred contours of the drawings as an element of fantasy, the minimal exclusion from the scene of a realism that would complete the act of aggression, perhaps even a residual presence of the law as a mediating term that would prevent the carcará logic mentioned. A curious reversal then takes place, for it is only as the representations are subjected to the extra-artistic, the real law of society – from which, as artworks, they are exempt – that it becomes visible that it was this law that they were dramatizing[29] as on the verge of withdrawing themselves, while in the popular imagination it has been long gone.

To conclude, and to summarize what has been already shown, both in *White Flag* and *Enemies* a paradoxical logic occurs, for it was only because of the failure of their being received as art that enhanced (or maybe even established) their status as strong artworks. Their stepping away from the sphere of art was incorporated to the material of the works as such. It was not only the case that their failures were necessary steps in their achievements: the failures ultimately contributed to their strong objectivity as such. Had they succeeded as instances of unquestioned art, had they been detachedly commented upon according to the rules of aesthetic appreciation, even (or especially) with their messages (whatever they might be) fully apprehended, they would have failed as events. Perhaps

29 It is irresistible at this point to observe that Gil Vicente (1465?–1536?) was the father of Iberian theater and the greatest representative of Portuguese letters before Camões.

there is something that can be theoretically extrapolated from this. In the first place, there may be something to be said here concerning the otherwise barren debate between formalism and reception theory about where the meaning of art would be.

Form in this case, and as a result objectivity as such, is a function of a reception that denies it. With one more step, one could argue that this dialectics of achievement through failure would correspond to the (frail) state of art in Brazil, or maybe even Latin America as a whole. But one could interrogate it from still another, broader, the point of view concerning the problematic status of objectification today. In a world so aggressively permeated by language (the everywhere of the imperative of advertisement), where all of us are bombarded on a daily basis by signs and fluxes of messages, one may very well claim that objects disappear, that without silence, ruptures or interruptions form cannot emerge as such and objects melt away in semiotic flows (Durão, 2010). In this context, the hardly-won, precarious objectivity achieved by *White Flag* and *Enemies* becomes exemplary. Herein lies the truth of these two incisive scandals.

Arthur Bispo do Rosário and The Ruse of Brazilian Art.

São Paulo's Biennial is by far the most important art event in Brazil. Its thirtieth edition, titled *The Imminence of Poetics* [*A Iminência das Poéticas*], took place from 7 September to 9 December 2012, at the Exhibition Centre in the Ibirapuera Park as usual, and was attended by more than 520,000 people. With generous state support, abundant advertising and free admission, the *Bienal* naturally belongs to the fabric of large-scale events in the city. Every other year it shares the listings with the carnival, São Paulo Fashion Week, Book Fair and many other activities. As always, one simply had to enter the Ibirapuera main building before seeing seas of people – although not the habitual gallery highbrows or inescapable poseurs but school children, teenagers kissing in between installations and unassuming families in jeans and soccer jerseys; in short, the common people. One just had to behold all this to have the impression that art and community are not mutually exclusive terms, that here, at the margin of the world market of art, the crisis of the aesthetic – the uncertainty concerning the status of art – wouldn't be so unavoidable after all.

And yet, doubt emerges: the noisy school children running all over, the hormonal adolescents obviously thinking about something else, the families taking advantage of free admission could all be enjoying themselves in quite a different way, even the very opposite way of how one would assume art should really be appreciated. The question is a serious one and by no means rhetorical: whether the *Bienal* is a true artistic event, whether it allows for what one would deem a genuine aesthetic experience or whether it is but a simulacrum of itself, shallow and inane entertainment like any other in the city of São Paulo, its only particularity deriving from the cultural capital associated with the word 'art'. To put it somewhat extremely, if one takes into consideration the weight of the *Bienal*, its failure as a sonorous void, nothingness amid so many works and things, could be indicative of the fate of art as a whole in Brazil. The claim that no true art has ever taken shape in the country will surely sound exaggerated, if not absurd, for readers in the developed world; and yet this overall nagging sense of inauthenticity has been a lingering, strong *topos* in Brazilian cultural criticism. It was famously articulated by film critic Paulo Emílio Salles Gomes when he observed that "we are not Europeans, or North-Americans either, but wanting an original culture, nothing is foreign to us because everything is. The painful construction of ourselves unfolds in the rarefied dialectic between not being and being "others". (Salles Gomes, 1973: 58; see also Schwarz, 1987: 29-48)

This longing for the genuine may, to a certain extent, be explained by the conditions of colonization that shaped the country. Unlike other undeveloped nations such as Egypt and India, which are so easily haunted by non-Western, ancient civilizations, or Mexico, Peru and Bolivia, which were formed with the extinction of great empires, Brazil has never had a technically well-developed pre-modern society in its past. The indigenous populations were decimated by the arrival of the Portuguese and eventually absorbed by the stronger and conflicting cultures brought by whites and Africans.

To be sure, this feeling of inauthenticity may project as its opposite: a sense of normativity in Europe; as though their art had its proper, unproblematic place; nevertheless, it does not logically follow that, because art may so easily appear to be artificial in Brazil, its organic character in Europe is positive or non-ideological. Be that as it may, the possibility of envisioning the *whole* of art as untrue is epistemologically rich and in other contexts not so readily explored.

In this light, only works that somehow address such a complicated state of affairs – as Machado de Assis's, for instance – would merit the label of 'art' in an emphatic sense, not work which celebrate things Brazilian, say, the country's exuberant nature, its amicable, spontaneous people and so on. The present moment, however, would be peculiarly dramatic because, as a latecomer that never managed to create an emancipated tradition of its own in the past, the nation would have finally mustered the necessary resources for artistic production (free entrance and all), precisely at a time when the concept of art would be too evanescent to stand solidly on its own two feet.[30] If the *Bienal* suddenly seems to acquire such decisive character, there must certainly be ways to determine whether anything at all has happened aesthetically in it. Even though one could try to empirically establish, through questionnaires and the like, whether there was art in the *Bienal*, it is more interesting to investigate how the hesitancy concerning the existence of art in Brazil may inhabit the works

30 Interestingly enough, this narrative of belatedness would parallel that of developmentarism in the history of the country. For when Brazil reached a point where modernization finally appeared to be at hand, it was too late for national projects in view of the dominance of global capital and the unbearable costs of national modernization. See Schwarz (1999).

themselves, how artifacts can embody, in their own form of existence, the impossibility as well as promise of the art. That artworks are self-contradictory; that they contain force fields in themselves keeping strong opposites together is not a new idea, but rather a touchstone in the materialist aesthetics of TW Adorno. However, the ways in which non-identity is expressed in Adorno's thinking are blind to the question of underdevelopment and all the problems related to it, such as the peculiar shape taken by progress (not as sheer advance, but always as catching up with developed countries); the unequal but combined nature of backwardness (never a simple lagging behind, but itself a product of advancement elsewhere); and the establishment of specific types of relations of dependence, among others. The attempt here is to develop a reading that does justice to the dialectic of art in Brazil, not from abstract or general presuppositions, but through the immersion in objects and what is made with them, something rooted in their concrete conditions of production and reception.

It would be hard to dispute that the work of Arthur Bispo do Rosário held a position, if not of rigorous centrality, at least of prominence at the 2012 São Paulo Biennial. Not only were his works the object of ample news coverage and general public attention,[31] but his compositional techniques and aesthetic procedures could be detected, coincidentally or not, in pieces by several other artists, Brazilian and foreign alike. Rosário's minimalism, his penchant for assemblages and bricolage, reliance on junk, re-functionalization of everyday things, mixture of words with shapes and colors, the utmost

31 A Google search with the words "Bispo do Rosário", "Bienal de São Paulo" and "2012" yielded around 37,000 hits on 28 June 2013.

submersion in the objects he was creating – which imbued them with signs of so much *work* – are only some of the defining traits of a kind of aesthetic practice that could be identified in one way or another in artists such as Alexandre Navarro Moreira, Anna Oppermann, August Sander, Benet Ressell, Cadu, f marquespenteado and many others in the *Bienal*.[32] In sum, the strength of Rosário's production would allow one to reorganize around it much of the non-electric/electronic art that was being presented at the *Bienal*. To be sure, Bispo (as Brazilians like to call him) was not unknown in the country's art milieu; his presence at the exhibition actually marked a second wave of interest in his work. In 1982, his work was presented at the collective exhibition *À Margem da Vida* [*At the Margin of Life*] and in 1995 he reached the apex of his fame when he was chosen to represent Brazil at the forty-sixth Venice Biennale (something to which we will return). Rosário died in 1989, before being able to see his work exhibited abroad. However, even if he had been alive he would have surely remained unmoved by the thrill of stardom, at least in the way we conceive of the term, centered as it is on an inflated image of the self. For Rosário was not what one would think an artist is.

Arthur Bispo do Rosário was born on 16 March 1911, only twenty-nine years after the abolition of slavery, in the poor town of Japaratuba in the impoverished province of Sergipe. He began an apprenticeship as a sailor in the Navy in February 1925 in Aracaju, the state capital, before being transferred to Rio de Janeiro, the then capital of the country. Expelled from the Navy

32 See the São Paulo Biennale 2012 Catalogue (Pérez-Oramas et al., 2012).

in July 1933, according to him because the officers didn't like his semi-professional boxing (Hidalgo, 1996: 79)33, he worked until 1937 at Rio de Janeiro's power company, finally settling down as a servant and jack-of-all-trades for the wealthy carioca family of lawyer Humberto Magalhães Leoni. Work relations were servile: Rosário lived at the property and his labor was paid with food, lodging and the bare necessities. To the Leoni family he swore loyalty. His obsequiousness was extreme and it is said that once he offered his hands as an ashtray for his master's cigar (Hidalgo, 1996: 49; Dantas, 2009: 30).

On the eve of December 22nd, 1938, however, all that would change. Rosário woke up in a trance; followed by his angels he went to several churches of the city, finally reaching the Saint Benedict monastery, where he made his annunciation to the surprised monks as God's envoy, the new Messiah commanded by the Almighty to redeem humanity. Two days later, he was arrested for disturbance of the public order; in his file, a few words describe his legal profile: black, no documents, indigent. He was then hastily interned at the Hospício Dom Pedro II, Brazil's first insane asylum, which had already housed the black writer Lima Barreto (1881-1922). After a month, Rosário was transferred to the Colônia Juliano Moreira, where he was diagnosed with paranoid schizophrenia, and received Patient Card 01662. He would live there for over fifty years until his death, a sojourn interrupted by several periods in the

33 His career lasted from 1928 to 1936. Although he seems to have won just one fight, there are several newspaper articles from the time attesting his aggressiveness and endurance. 'As he had particularly salient cranial and facial bones, he often provoked his opponents into punching him where he knew they would injure their hands' (Corpas and Morais, 2013: 34/244). (Page references refer to the original Portuguese text and the English version at the end of the book.) Might that have contributed to his mental health illness?

outside world with the Leoni family. Long after life in the Colônia Juliano Moreira became routine, Rosário started to work on miniatures and assemblages – his belief was that God had instructed him to gather, replicate and catalogue all the objects of the world so that they could be redeemed at an approaching Doomsday. This also applied to people, which accounts for the large number of proper names on many of his artifacts.

In 1980, Rosário was featured in a news story on Rede Globo's popular Sunday program *Fantástico*. The initial idea was to portray the lives of inmates at the asylum, but Rosário stole the scene. Two years later, art critic, Frederico Morais included some of his works in the exhibition *À Margem da Vida* at Rio de Janeiro's Museum of Modern Art, alongside pieces by patients from several psychiatric institutions. In 1989, the Juliano Moreira Colony Artists Association was founded with the purpose of preserving Rosário's work, which was officially declared of public interest by Rio de Janeiro's State Institute for Artistic and Cultural Patrimony [Instituto Estadual do Patrimônio Artístico e Cultural, Inepac]. In 2003, the exhibition *Ordering and Vertigo* was organized by curators Jane de Almeida and Jorge Anthonio e Silva at the Cultural Center of the Bank of Brazil with the explicit aim of "encouraging contemporary artists to discuss and reinterpret the work of Arthur Bispo do Rosário",[34] thus placing him at the center of Brazilian art and encouraging artists to relate to and even be influenced by Rosário's work. With this, the process of incorporation and legitimization was complete; the 2012 *Bienal* only served to finally corroborate this at the most important art event of the country, while the

34 Exhibition booklet, 2, available at http://www.janedealmeida.com/vertigo.pdf.

use of his art to represent Brazil in the 2013, Venice Biennale attested to his growing international recognition. His artworks have been fully catalogued for a total 804 pieces, which are regularly displayed at the Bispo do Rosário Museum located at his former asylum. It is in view of all this, of such wide success and almost unanimous and unquestioned acclaim,[35] that one feels the need to interrogate what might be at stake in Rosário's case and in the constitution of the concept of art in Brazil.

Perhaps the best place to start is with the writing, mainly academic, devoted to him. Such an enthusiastic reception in museums and exhibitions could hardly have happened without positive critical assessment. Indeed, in the steadfastly growing bibliography on Rosário[36] one finds general and undisputed praise – interestingly from a variety of different perspectives which seek to justify the aesthetic value of the artworks. At the lowest level of the spectrum there are those who use Rosário to support an irrationalist, quasi-mystical stance (see Figueiredo, 2012; Bêta, 2012), lauding the free imagination which rises above inescapably oppressive and suffocating rationality. More serious academic studies construct Rosário, in one way or another, as hero or victim and most often a combination of both. This is evident in biographical approaches to Rosário's art (Hidalgo, 1996) and in more theoretical writings. From a Jungian perspective, Dantas (2009) sees in him the archetype of the adventurer who sacralizes the world; Soares (2000) lauds his lunacy as a (positive) sign of the postmodern; Burrowes

35 Criticism of the assumption that Rosário was an artist has been restricted to newspaper articles as Gullar (2011); none of the longer bibliographic items consulted for this paper challenged this position.

36 Corpas and Morais list some nine books, twenty-eight book chapters, fifty-nine papers, six PhD dissertations and twenty MA theses and more than 200 newspaper and magazine articles (2013: 281-90).

(1999) describes a Deleuzian poetics of fluxes and flows in his art objects; Seligmann Silva, after observing that "Bispo is recognized as a kind "reincarnation" of acclaimed icons of modernity such as Duchamp, Arman, César, and as a brother of Oiticica and Peter Greenaway among others" (2007: 144), applies Benjamin's theory of collecting to him, as well as the musings of German early Romantics on madness; Maciel (2007) views Rosário's oeuvre as an encyclopedia and compares it to the original eighteenth-century Enlightened idea in order to show the impossibility of cataloguing the world. And so on...

At this point it is possible to observe that such a visible process of institutionalization should raise suspicion concerning the characterization of Rosário as a marginal, oppressed figure, which he of course was. His victimization owes a great deal to the ease with which Foucault's critique of power has been taken by Brazilian intellectuals as a disparagement of reason per se. This misreading has acquired a commonplace force, thus working as a kind of presupposition, one does not have to prove or really argue for. As a result, mental institutions of any kind appear as inherently evil, regardless of what is done in them. The irony here, however, is that the more the asylum as an institution is criticized, the less art's institutional character comes to the fore. The common denominator in these studies – the assumption underlying all this growing body of work – is *the widespread, unquestioned belief that Bispo was an artist*. This is far from obvious; indeed, it is precisely this operation of immediately bringing an immensely creative, mentally sick person to the concept of art that must be challenged.

It is not difficult to point to the myriad of problems arising from this presupposition. In the first place, simply situating Rosário within the realm of art is to ignore the context and the intentions within which all his objects were created. Although one can always argue that conditions preceding the creation of anything are irrelevant to the actual result, this claim is not often raised to defend the artistic character of formerly non-artistic material originating from morally questionable sources. You will never find an anesthetization of paraphernalia from concentration camps or Hitler's personal menagerie. Those schooled in literary theory will remind us that, since the 1940s at least, from the New Critics on the author's intentions have been considered irrelevant to the finished product, but this tenet ignores the degree, certainly limited, of the artist's control over their material. If not an absolutely determining forced – a clear origin from which all the rest derives – intention remains one of the components of artworks.[37] Or even worse, how should one react to a passage like this:

> Frederico Morais told me, five years after [the first exhibition devoted to Rosário, at the Art School of the Lage Park, in 1989], in an interview, that already in his first meeting with Arthur Bispo do Rosário he proposed to organize a great exhibition of his universe. He was willing to set the Museum of Modern Art at his disposal, where Bispo could even have his own room, if he didn't want to be away from his work. But Bispo refused 'absolutely' ['*terminantemente*'], saying that 'that had nothing to do [*nada a ver*] with art, that what he did were registers [*que eram registros que ele fazia*]'. (Burrowes, 199: 71)[38]

37 For insightful comments on the impossibility of eliminating intention from artworks, see Adorno (1997: 198-200).

38 All translations are mine, if not otherwise noted.

Or again, in the words of curator Frederico Morais:

> We spoke for about one hour and I offered him the whole second floor of the exhibition wing of [Rio's] Museum of Modern Art (its premium space). He turned me down, saying that his works were just records [*registros*] and that he couldn't do without them. So I offered him a hall-cum-dormitory in the same wing, so he could accompany the exhibition round the clock. Again, he refused. (Corpas and Morais, 2013: 24/241)

Bearing in mind Rosário's explicit refusal to be seen as an artist, the gesture that converts him into one cannot be dissociated from violence. It is irrelevant how liberating critics may find art to be; here they are agents for the repression of madness.[39]

This leads us to the problem of Rosário's biography. Most commentators argue that his work stands on its own without needing biographical elucidations. Some may even claim that information about his life could prove detrimental to the immediate experience of his pieces. In spite of all possible disclaimers, however, the fact remains that virtually everything that has been written on Rosário in one way or another mentions his history of mental illness. In fact, it is possible to suggest that the biographic impulse lies at the very core of most critical discourse on him. The presence of Rosário's life is so strong in the work of critics that it becomes difficult to

39 Thus the sense of unfairness and lack of respect for the deceased in Morais's slightly triumphant tone: "Finally, on January 19, 1993, three and a half years after his death, I was able to realize my longstanding dream of holding an exhibition of Bispo do Rosário – the one he had refused me on our first meeting – at the Rio de Janeiro Museum of Modern Art". (Corpas and Morais, 2013: 29/242)

even imagine the existence of his objects irrespective of it; it is because it is so pervasive that one can so easily forget Rosário's biography. Furthermore, the appeal of his life story is generally selective and all the regressive features of his personality are normally dealt with as curiosities, presented anecdotally. His adoration of hierarchy and submissiveness were already alluded to; as for his morals, they were Victorian and his gender definitions, extremely normative and inflexible. In 1962 Rosário was hired (again without salary) as a keeper at the AMIU clinic, owned by Humberto Leoni's brother-in-law. He had to leave and return to the Colony after signs of aggressiveness towards female nurses motivated by their behavior and way of dressing, which for Rosário were too liberal. Rosário found the opposite of this immorality in Rosângela Maria Grillo, a psychology student who was a trainee at the Colony. His muse, she was viewed by him as the perfection of purity and is present in several of his works.[40] That all this has a clear sexual origin is obvious and, while it is always possible to say that his objects cannot be reduced to sexual repression as a form of causality, simply ignoring this particular source represents an impoverishment of understanding and loss of sense. Finally, to counter the view that Rosário was just a helpless victim of a baleful system, it is worth mentioning that when not in a trance, he would aid nurses to control fellow interns; here he was a collaborator and an agent of repression himself. Another difficulty relates to the force exerted within art from art's own past, which in Rosário's is obviously absent.

40 The way Grillo dealt with Rosário was itself praiseworthy. All her efforts were directed at bringing him to reality and making him give up on his fantasies. This sharply contrasts with the romanticizing of madness and disparaging of reason put forth by many of Rosário's commentators.

Again, a skeptical critic might remind us that for the last 100 years art has been rebelling against tradition, that the internal desire for art to destroy its conventions has been an important driving force in its development. Rosário's lack of connection with art preceding him would thus only work to his advantage. Still, one does not even need to point out that the negation of the past brings in itself precisely that which it negates; it is only necessary to compare Rosário's "Roda da Fortuna" ["Wheel of Fortune"], which very much resembles Duchamp's 1951 "Bicycle Wheel", to face an embarrassment. The comparison in this case can only be relevant as long as one assumes that Rosário was unaware of Duchamp's piece and was *not* copying him. In order for the Brazilian 'madman' to become an artist, he must not belong to the world of art. Isn't there something condescending in this, in failing to contrast works and reach judgment through confrontation? The same would apply to Rosário's rawness and primitivism. His materials were not properly chosen; rather, they were what he could get from visitors or what he could trade with other inmates; otherwise he had to make do with whatever stuff was available. His famous ORFA (*Objetos Recobertos de Fio Azul* [Objects Covered with Blue Thread]) were created by enveloping diverse items with blue yarn taken from his uniform, which was thus totally and literally decomposed. The need and scarcity which constituted Rosário's representational world obscured his technical limitations. Take for instance this drapery: misspellings such as *bolça* (*bolsa* [purse]) or the restricted universe from which the objects mentioned are taken (pencil, paper, tomato etc.) are more symptoms of poverty and privation than compositional strategies originating in freedom.

The same criticism can be leveled against two other defining traits of Rosário's objects. In a world saturated with and ruled by machines, from motors to computers, their handicraft character is refreshing; it highlights the materiality of things, their concreteness – but not the world Bispo was inhabiting. The hand was not the other of the machine, but it was itself a tool of meaning. Secondly, the childish nature of a great deal of his production, from the embroidery to the toys themselves, may appear as "the other" against the seriousness, pomposity or pretentiousness that so often plagues contemporary art. Again, in Rosário they are not the obverse of an all-too cerebral aesthetics, but rather technical limitations deriving from lack of formal training and the precariousness of the tools he was working with.

A similar logic holds for compositional strategies. Jorge Anthonio e Silva (2003: 60-66) identifies four main procedures in Rosário's work, those of ordering, cataloguing, filling and wrapping up. This is accurate but misleading if it is supposed to bring to mind disinterested artistic production for, more than sheer techniques, for Rosário such processes are means for coming to grips with the world. The assemblages try to bring the environment within themselves; they set in order that which otherwise would seem to be too evanescent. The ORFAS, on the other hand, wanted to make the world what it is by enveloping it. Take, for instance, the watering can. Rather than bringing forth the non-existent or the new, it strives to fix the thing as such, to deprive it of a threatening sense of unreality. The toil embodied in it guarantees that it is what it is and that is why this ORFA, like so many others, has to bear its name, *regador*, to make sure that the object remains what it is. In sum, together with whatever kind of independent existence they may have, these artifacts must also be viewed as symptoms, as a real and painful struggle to make sense, strangely connecting both meanings of the expression.

Further, and to keep focusing on symptoms, it is interesting to wonder if much of the response to Rosário's objects may be traced back to a particularly Brazilian inferiority complex. Reading the bibliography on him, one is struck by the subtle but firm note of satisfaction that underlines much of the listed writing. The fact that an uneducated Brazilian could be present at the Venice Biennale is often quoted as a source of pride. And yet, at stake here is a subtle colonizing logic, for if on the one hand organizers let Brazilian critics determine their own national representatives, on the other the learned or educated art (mischievously termed "official") in Brazil is undermined, possibly in ways which confirm the credentials of Venice as a center of artistic recognition and renaissance. Here we encounter a common topos of Brazilian cultural criticism which, while noticing the precariousness and deficient nature of high culture and its institutions – including of course those of education – celebrates popular culture, extolling its spontaneity and creativeness.[41] Nothing suits more this structure of feeling than the mentally ill individual who, uneducated, disregarding all the world of art with all its prestigious participants, created an opulent universe of his own.

That final argument here is both the strongest and the weakest. It is at its weakest because it is the least related to the aesthetic; it is at its strongest because it is most intimately

41 For a recent, celebrated example, see Wisnik (2008).

connected to the motivation that inspired Rosário's creations, namely that his objects originated in pain. For all the temptation to romanticize mental illness, for all the desire to see in its bearer a victim of a domineering reason, it is impossible to deny that it is a malady and that it makes the subject suffer (even if we agree that what was meant as cure often worsens and deepens the disease). The urge to order, to organize things, the need to produce objects were part of a psychic struggle to deal with the world, to be able to still relate to it. If reason is control, it is because it originates in the need for self-preservation, for mastering that which is menacing in nature, but which seems to have become invisible today.[42]

This is why one feels uneasy when reading the superbly illustrated, luxuriously printed bilingual volume by Lazaro, with its 304 large, glossy pages, or the richly presented series of pictures by Walter Firmo. Isn't there an incompatibility between such wealth of material and the misery which Rosário suffered?[43] To conclude, then, the world of art was not his and bringing him inside it generated difficulties that eventually hindered the proper appreciation of his production. Incidentally, the concept of *art brut*, that kind of aesthetic production carried out by all those excluded from so-called traditional art, won't resolve the problem, for it does no more than giving a name and suggesting a theory. As a matter of fact, supporters of Rosário the artist tend not to like the term very much – in the same fashion as they reject the label of "naïve art" – for it subsumes Bispo under a broader category. Be that

42 For the connection between barbarism and lack of visibility see Hullot-Kenotr (2010).

43 Indeed, it would be liberating to imagine how Rosário himself would defunctionalize this book and utilize it for further work.

as it may, instead of a true aesthetic experience, the "all *too* perfect adaptation" by artistic institutions of this immense body of work by a maker who never envisioned himself as author and who could but feebly criticize the sphere he was being placed in – this gesture of inclusion ultimately corroborates the sense of inauthenticity mentioned above, the nagging question of actually being the real thing. That in the present case everything is richly digitalized and abundantly commented on doesn't change the character of the phenomenon; it just enhances the magnitude of the suspicion of fraud.

II

If there is something barbaric about failing to acknowledge the original context of Rosário's production, if it is misguided (to say the least) to simply insert his objects within the sphere of art, this does not mean that they can't have any connection to it. Everything changes when one, instead of starting with Rosário as artist, begins by accepting his mental disease. He then ceases to be the solitary genius of inexplicable creative powers and becomes instead part of a long history of productive insanity and fanaticism in Brazil. This is a history that would include figures such as Antonio Conselheiro, the religious leader of the famous late nineteenth-century slave revolt of Canudos (Cunha, 2010), as well as writers Lima Barreto and Qorpo Santo. At the Juliano Moreira Colony itself, the recordings of another inmate, Stela do Patrocínio, were transcribed into a book (Patrocínio, 2001). The most interesting case for our purposes, however, is José Datrino (Guelman, 2009; Guelman, Amaral and Kutassy, 2011), the Profeta Gentileza (Prophet Gentleness), who may be rewardingly compared to Rosário. Also a *carioca*, he filled fifty-six towers of Rio's viaducts with his philosophy, misspelled words advocating gentleness against the devil and capitalism. If Rosário was all concentration in the minute, Gentileza was expansion in the public realm; if the former shunned people, the latter longed to connect with city dwellers. In both cases, however, their production was not only the result of restless minds, but also of social exclusion.

Once we perceive that Rosário was not an isolated case (and thus become able to ponder the relationship of at least partial causality of social environment and psychological breakdown), it is possible to turn to his objects as what they are and not as *a priori* artistic pieces. Their origin in delirium thus comes to the fore and one can witness how they struggle against the scarcity with and from which they were made. Now it is not necessary to overlook all the regressive elements mentioned earlier, nor the precariousness of the materials and techniques, for they belong to the artifacts in their desperate fight to exist. As this takes place, a fundamental reversal happens. When Rosário is *not* brought to art, when his mental illness is granted its founding role in the creation of these artifacts, then all the problems identified earlier disappear. The question of intentionality becomes legitimate, the dialogue with other manifestations, as we just saw, is possible and, most importantly, their inherent features emerge as what they are. The amount of work embedded in them, their fierce unyielding desire to exist, mark them as extraordinary. They cannot be considered just as ordinary things but demand that a name be found for them. There is no other one than "art" to do justice to that which constitutes them. But this art cannot be that which comfortably inhabits museums. The desperate urge to "be" that characterizes Rosário's work now becomes a yardstick to measure – and criticize – what is normally judged as aesthetic. The concept of art is thus utterly changed; instead of the conformist – but at heart indulgent and patronizing notion presiding over biennales funded by the state and banks – a different perspective emerges that says "art should be *this*". A curious logic indeed: when without mediation it is associated to art, it refuses to be artistic, but when it is taken on its own terms it refuses to be common and requires that a revitalized but dislocated concept of art be brought to it. This is an exteriority that, once it is recognized as such, modifies art from within. This is what was at stake at the São Paulo *Bienal*; this is the ruse of Brazilian art.

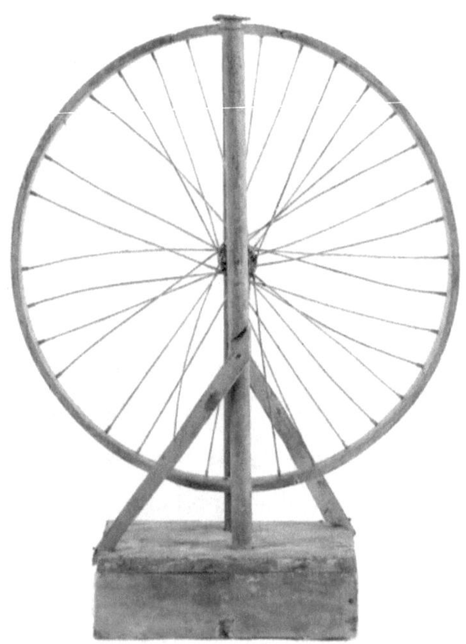

Arthur Bispo do Rosário. Wheel of Fortune, *no date. Metal, cloth, thread and plastic, 67x 29x51 cm. Photograph: Rodrigo Lopes. Credit: Coleção Museu Bispo do Rosário Arte Contemporânea Prefeitura da Cidade do Rio de Janeiro.*

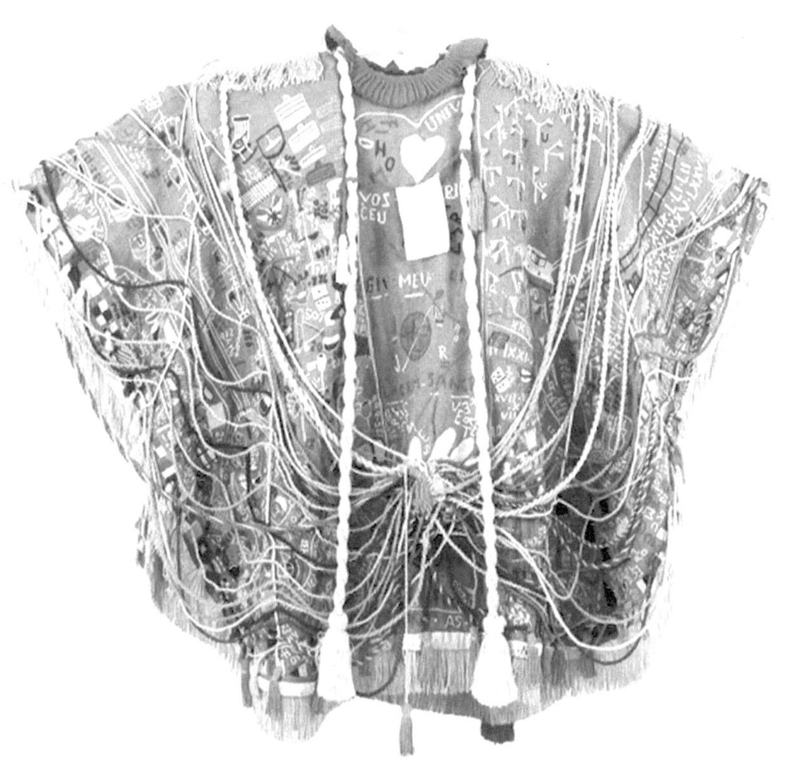
VOZ
CEU
MEU

Arthur Bispo do Rosário. Wheel of Fortune, *no date. Metal, cloth, thread and plastic, 67x 29x51 cm. Photograph: Rodrigo Lopes. Credit: Coleção Museu Bispo do Rosário Arte Contemporânea/Prefeitura da Cidade do Rio de Janeiro.*

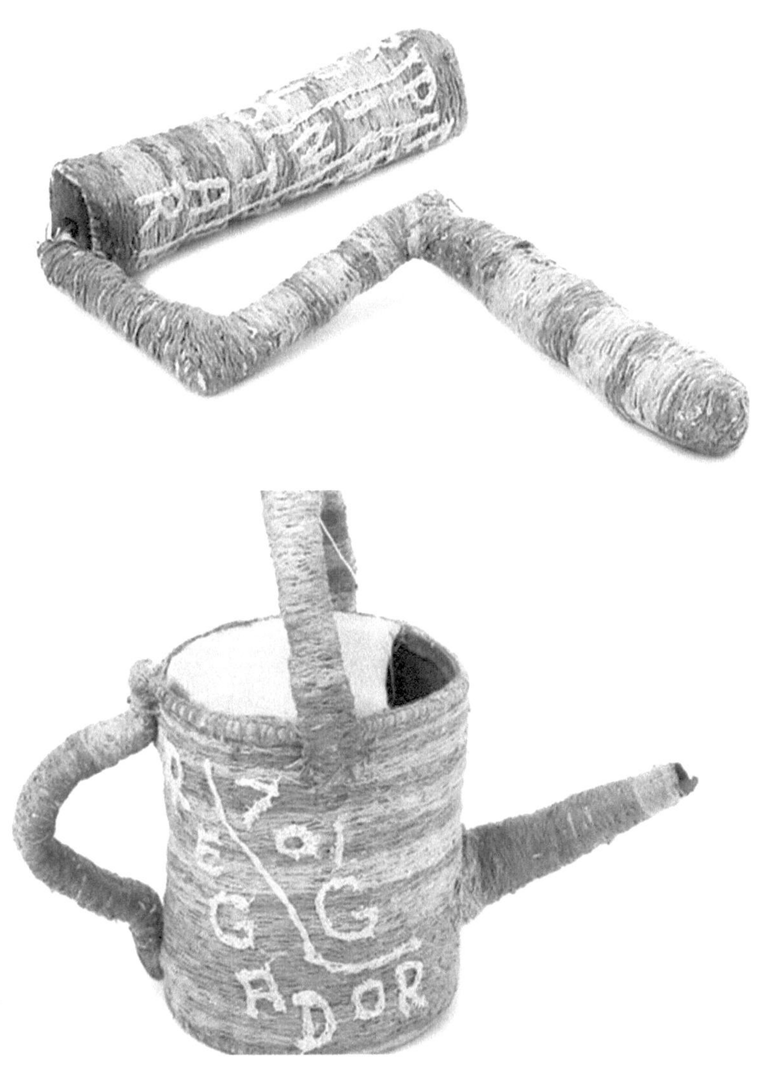

Arthur Bispo do Rosário. Attention Poison, *no date. Wood, cloth, thread and metal, 93x74 cm. Photograph: Rodrigo Lopes. Credit: Coleção Museu Bispo do Rosário Arte Contemporânea/Prefeitura da Cidade do Rio de Janeiro.*

MUSIC

The Adventures of a Technique: dodecaphonism travels to Brazil. (with José Adriano Fenerick)

Few revolutions in modern art were both as momentous and unambiguous as that of Schoenberg's twelve-tone method of composition. Occurring in parallel with the dissolution of a traditional perspective in painting and the omniscient narrator in literature, it surpassed both in innovation because of its systematic character: the very simple rule that in a twelve-note series no note should be repeated before all the others have appeared. From this innovation, a number of possible procedures emerged, together with a new set of prohibitions, which completely reorganized and re-conceptualized the very idea of what music was thought to be. History was waiting for the emergence of such serialism in music as it centralized this revolution: the tonal system itself, through its own internal development, furnished the means for its own overcoming.

This can be seen in the increasing lack of preparation of dissonances and the tendency to postpone their resolution, the accumulation of wandering chords, the use of chords with more than five notes, and the extension of modulation to ever more distant tonalities. The system of seven notes proved, however, so resistant to change that it survived, zombie-like, long after its demise was logically predicated. Schoenberg's "revolution" therefore deserves all the force that this term may connote.

Indeed, dodecaphonism's importance can be derived not only from the artistic horizons it opened, but also from the theoretical findings it stimulated. Adorno provided an influential, albeit not still fully explored, interpretation of what was at stake with the development of the twelve-tone composition in his *Philosophy of New Music*.[44] Embedded in the technique, he argued, were issues that influenced society as a whole; the musical form articulated vital social and psychological questions that were unconscious and in need of deciphering.

In a clear continuation of *The Dialectic of Enlightenment*, Adorno, in the *Philosophy of New Music*, interprets Schoenberg and Stravinsky as exemplars of the two related dialectics of progress and regression. Put in very broad terms, the latter epitomized the progress of regression: recourse to past musical forms, which are predicated on their availability and consequent lack of a binding character. Schoenberg's music, in contrast, exhibited the idea of moving forward or of developing, in the musical sphere, that process of rationalization (in the Weberian sense of disenchantment or *Entzauberung*) whereby nothing can be justified by merely being given. The possibility of submitting everything to such judgment corresponds to what the positive drive of rationalization; its bleaker side lies in dominating the material it is applied to. The twelve-tone technique represented an advance in relation to the tonal system because of the demythologization of the apparently natural hierarchies inherent in this system. Rather than an order ruled by the relationship between a tonic and its dominant, for instance, dodecaphonism presents a homogenized ideal of

44 Two reasons may account for this. First, only in 2006 did a completely reliable English translation of Adorno's central book on music appear; second, as Nho points out, historically the proper balance between philosophy and music has been difficult to maintain. The two extremes, as a result of an increasingly powerful social division of labor, have tended to prevail: either philosophical musings on music without connection to its inner logic, or musical descriptions devoid of a broader conceptual import.

musical notes. All of them had the same status, to the point that the repetition of notes became anathema. With this move, the nature of music was radically reconfigured and transformed into something more general and abstract because the note was considered in relation to twelve rather than seven basic possibilities and its so-called accidents, which made for more manageable material.

The systematic character of the twelve-tone technique made this musical innovation mobile. Yet, travelling across the oceans was not merely a set of rules and insights to organize the notes of a score, but an entire worldview, a particular employment of reason with its own attendant promises and dangers. In sum, the adventures of the twelve tone row in Brazil stage, micro-logically, the broader issues that are involved in projects of national modernization, import substitution, and, ultimately, reveal the patterns of the transnational circulation of organizing principles. In the implantation of this technique, three questions need to be considered: the nationalist reaction to the technique; the difficulties composers faced when trying to make use of dodecaphonism; and the attempt made to appropriate it into popular music which parallels the consolidation of the culture industry in Brazil.

Dodecaphonism's voyage to Brazil had one unmistakable bearer: Hans-Joachim Koellreutter. As in so many other cases, this important chapter in the country's cultural history of cultural happened as a result of (impending) war. Without the political turbulence of the period, it seems unlikely that Koellreutter, a socialist activist, would have left Germany for Brazil in 1937. It is difficult to overestimate Koellreutter's role as teacher and educator. Most of the important contemporary Brazilian composers, from so-called serious music to that which is also called "popular", had contact with him in one way or another. He not only introduced dodecaphonism to the country, but also developed a complete musical pedagogy of his own, which continues to be used today.

In fact, even though Koellreutter acquainted himself with the technique while under the tutelage of Hermann Scherchen in Geneva and Budapest, he never composed anything similar to the Second Vienna School before his arrival in Brazil. The musician who arrived in Rio de Janeiro in 1937 was a young composer, but primarily a flute virtuoso. His first compositions in the country remind one more of Paul Hindemith than Schoenberg, with whom he had never had strong musical affinities. It was precisely because of Koellreutter's role as a key representative of European music, and consequently as an educator and promoter of modern music, that he saw himself duty bound to adopt the twelve tone technique early in the 1950s. By this time, dodecaphonism had already been established abroad, but remained virtually unknown in Brazil, which justified Koellreutter's work of divulging the technique in an attempt to modernize musical composition. Indeed, from the start Koellreutter managed to gather around himself Brazilian composers who would later become formative names in Brazilian music such as Cláudio Santoro, Guerra-Peixe and Eunice Katunda; he was also in close contact with intellectuals, music critics, and established Brazilian composers such as Villa-Lobos and Camargo Guarnieri.

The result of the emphasis on group work was the creation of *Música Viva* in 1939, formed by students of Koellreutter, and which represented the first avant-garde collective music of Brazil. Several documents of the groups have survived, including musical programs, letters, statements of purpose and so on, as collected by Kater in *Música Viva e H.J. Koellreutter*.

These include among them a manifesto, perhaps previously unpublished, which is particularly useful in showing the philosophy of the members of *Música Viva*. Not only are musical innovation and freedom equated, but teaching and divulging musical techniques are also viewed as fundamental elements in the life of music. While ideas may be jumbled at points, the text still expresses the enthusiasm of bringing in the new:

> History registers now one more period of transformation. We are passing through a moment when one of the greatest movements of Humanity takes place. [...] Aware of this spiritual revolution which is spreading all over the Earth, and comprehending the imperatives of this new world, the *Música Viva* group demands an essentially altered behavior from the artist and especially the musician in view of the community; we condemn the individualistic mentality of the romantic musician and we appeal to "modern man" to establish the guidelines for the creation of a free music in a free and new world. (Kater, 2001: 246)[45]

45 Unless noted otherwise, translations are the work of the authors.

The realm of opening possibilities, however, is not restricted merely to formal questions; the manifesto states that this should be materialized through opening musical teaching and education. An otherwise unexpected mixture of socialism and musical experimentation becomes clear here:

> We place teaching above everything; we consider it the basis for any evolution in the artistic field and for achieving a high collective level. Educated in the mysticism of the "ego", in the concept of individuality, we have been conditioned to live in a decadent social organization. The result of this education is a low collective level, with only a handful of individuals of merit, who are ever farther from the majority's understanding, segregating themselves in elites that are noxious to the collectivity and the evolution of mankind. We therefore will combat the education that aims at instructing such elites and we demand an education that aims at a high collective level, an essential precondition for all evolution allowing the masses to understand the manifestations of the human spirit. (Kater, 2001: 248)

To be sure, the belief in an impending new era was misplaced; in addition, the emphasis on education is dangerously close to populism, especially if one bears in mind Villa-Lobos's orpheonic singing project.[46] But the manifesto is useful in showing the *possibility* of this otherwise strange equation of avant-garde composition and engaged art, to which Koellreutter's *Salmo Proletário* [*Proletarian Psalm*] from 1946 and the 1947 *Mensagem* [*Message*] attests. The intended result of this equation was political or existential

46 Villa-Lobos organized massive events, sometime in soccer stadiums, mobilizing thousands of singers, children, and adolescents from public schools.

liberation, and educational practices were viewed as driving social change. This context of absolute musical novelty engendered such unlikely conjunctions.

Parallel to this singular form of musical and political engagement, Koellreutter distanced himself from free atonalism and moved in the direction of more formalized composing techniques, i.e. towards dodecaphonism. The reason normally given for this shift relates to an episode where Cláudio Santoro, perhaps Koellreutter's most gifted student, spontaneously wrote dodecaphonic passages in his *Symphony for Two String Orchestras* (1940) without ever hearing of the technique. As a result of such natural inclination, Koellreutter started to teach him composition in twelve-tone rows, and "was encouraged to write his [Koellreutter's] own first piece based on the dodecaphonic series, his *Invention* (for oboe, clarinet and bassoon), which may be seen as his only composition rigorously following all the dictates of the technique" (Kater, 2001: 107). The story may indeed be entertaining, but one can still ask whether the introduction of dodecaphonism was not simply unavoidable and dependent on a natural progression over time. Furthermore, the rupture had to happen because the leader of *Música Viva* "was totally convinced of the latent identity between the principles of Marxism and atonalism"; the latter would work as "a substrate for a functional music, representing the new music of the time, which, grounded on a direct correspondence with dialectical materialism, should be in tune with the latest evolutionary stage of society and culture" (Kater, 2001: 90). Dodecaphonism, in Brazil, was therefore introduced at the intersection of new musical experiments, as well as through educational activities aiming at democratization, and a political engagement which aimed for some sort of revolution through an opening of knowledge systems as discussed above.

As could be expected, the introduction of the twelve tone technique was not smooth but faced strong opposition from native composers. When Debussy, for instance, was introduced in Brazil, musical culture was prepared for it because of a reasonably developed romanticism in relation to which impressionist harmony could be viewed as a continuation, albeit not a smooth one. Nothing of the kind happened with dodecaphonism, which appeared as hopelessly foreign. Music here allows for a clearer insight into what is at stake in the modernist desire to erect universes out of nothing, for "nothing" does not really exist. The resistance to the new in music makes visible what is obscured, for instance, in the construction of Brasília, perhaps the greatest example of the modernist demiurge complex. The nationalist claim to exceptionality – amounting to the claim that "we have something that the others lack, we don't need foreign imports" – has its own curious logic, which can be characterized as a reactive formation. It is not the case, in other words, that the "normativity of the soil" existed as such in the first place; rather, it emerged *after* the introduction of dodecaphonism. To be sure, immoderate praise of things Brazilian has been a common phenomenon in the cultural history of the country; the novelty here, however, stems from the distance between the imported compositional procedure and the supposed "Brazilianity" to be cherished. Indeed, just to think of a possible, tentative comparison, dodecaphonism did not prove to be as malleable as the novel form, as Roberto Schwarz's theorization of misplaced ideas in *Misplaced Ideas* and *A Master on the Periphery of Capitalism: Machado de Assis* illustrates. According to the latter work, Machado de Assis managed to transform the realist narrator into a dysfunctional figure, thereby laying bare its ideological matrixes. One may wonder if music, by virtue of its particular material qualities, would be more resistant to such acclimatization.

Be it as it may, the 1950s started with the "Open letter to musicians and music critics of Brazil", in which composer Camargo Guarnieri urged the nation against the "immense dangers that right now deeply threaten all of Brazilian music culture, that culture to which we are so closely attached" (qtd. in Kater, 2001: 119). Guarnieri's letter, aimed at warning young Brazilian composers against the "immense dangers" introduced by Koellreutter, is emblematic of the accusations that would be ceaselessly leveled against the twelve-tone technique: it is a cerebral music, a token of European cultural decay which could bring about the "destruction of our national character". Guarnieri says, further, that dodecaphonism managed to attract "some young composers of valor and great talent, like Cláudio Santoro and Guerra-Peixe, who, fortunately enough, after pursuing this erroneous direction, were able to free themselves and return to the right path of the artistic-scientific study and utilization of our folklore" (Kater, 2001: 120).

"*Our* folklore": for non-Brazilians (and for us writing in English) it is easier to see the irony here, which is typical of the problems involved in the construction of nationality.

In this case, it involves the defense of an autochthonous music being made by a composer with the most Italian of names. Nevertheless, this movement, which can be heard in Santoro's and Guerra-Peixe's work of the period, is not as whimsical as it may appear at first. The insertion of the twelve-tone row in Brazil did not happen in the course of the "natural development" (whatever the expression may mean) of a Brazilian musical language in the way it did in Europe as a result of the collapse of the tonal system. Adopting the technique in the country was, before anything, a gesture and not an imperative driven by a tradition of ruptures in the history of the development of a musical language.[47] In this sense, the rationalization effected by dodecaphonism was ambiguous, contradictory even. Composers could see themselves on the side of nationalism, as well as avant-gardism without apparently contradicting themselves. Even Koellreutter's most talented and promising pupils, Santoro and Guerra-Peixe, wrote both serial and nationalist pieces. The simultaneously composed their most daring scores – Santoro's *Three Sonatas* (1939-1940) and *Variations on a dodecaphonic series* (1946), and Guerra-Peixe's *Music n.1 for Piano* (1941) and *Piece for two minutes* (1941) – they also produced *Batucada, no Morro das duas Bicas* (1948) (Santoro), or *Suíte para Orquestra de Cordas (inspired in the folklore of Pernambuco)* (1949) (Guerra-Peixe), among

47 It is hard to think about musical "historical necessity" outside Europe. The way in which the tonal system developed out of its own original contradictions and specificities turned it into a highly organized, self-regulating musical language – a strictly European phenomenon. The internal advance of the system, as well as its underlying rationality cannot be abstracted from European modernity. Max Weber, for instance, identified in the unfolding of European music the specific trait of the modernity Europeans created as a model for Western civilization. Thus, the insertion of dodecaphonism into other continents transforms it into a graft, a more or less foreign element brought into a national or local tradition.

others. This duality would also have its own temporal pendulum, for in the 1950s, nationalism would dominate, while in the 1960s vanguard music would be the order of the day (Santoro, for instance, composed electro-acustic music at the time). In sum, they fluctuated between nationalism and avant-gardism. Thus, dodecaphonism was not employed as the result of convictions, or as a matter of principles, but rather as a momentary choice among others.

This is an aspect that is indicative of the modernity fostered by a certain vision of the country in the 1950s – a blended, "mestizo" modernity that daringly and ambitiously erects *Brasília*, a new capital, from scratch to stand as a symbol of national unity and integration, but whose constructed modernity placed it at the very center of the country. Although Santoro and Guerra-Peixe had been Koellreutter's first pupils to work with the twelve-tone series, they were only recognized as important composers of serious music based on their nationalist pieces, and even today only a relatively small part of their more avant-gardist work has been recorded or is performed regularly. This precarious articulation of a properly experimentalist space in Brazilian music, squeezed between the desire for revolutionizing expression and the compromises demanded by a national project, did not allow composers to pursue experiments beyond dodecaphonism, even if a few attempts were made in that direction in the following years.

In the late 1950s and early 1960s, a younger generation of composers started a new movement in São Paulo called *Música Nova*. Still guided by Koellreutter, though not following him as closely as the previous generation, the group hoped to reshape the scene of contemporary music in Brazil. Among the participants were Julio Medaglia, Rogério Duprat, Gilberto Mendes, Willy Correia de Oliveira, and Damiano Cozzella, all musicians who were closely attached to the growing cultural scene in São Paulo, which was quickly becoming the new cultural and economic center of the country. The infrastructure for contemporary art had been established with the founding of such institutions as the Modern Art Museum (MAM) in 1947, and the São Paulo Museum of Art (MASP), in 1948; the early 1950s witnessed the emergence of the concrete poetry movement, and the first São Paulo Biannual Exposition took place in 1951. The *Música Viva* shared much of the atmosphere of the city (Arruda). The group's purpose, as stated in their "Manifesto Música Nova", was "total engagement with the contemporary world" (qtd. in Gaúna, 2002: 88).

The intent was to go beyond canonical dodecaphonism and to explore all the possibilities of serialism as Pierre Boulez and Henri Posseur were doing in Europe. Moreover, through exchanges with Germany and the US, several members of *Música Nova* became acquainted with the work of John Cage and Stockhausen, with their techniques of indeterminacy, electronic and electro-acoustic music. Nevertheless, and in spite of its "total engagement with the contemporary world", *Música Nova* was at odds with mainstream Brazilian music of the time. In the words of historian Regiane Gaúna, "one may say that the *Música Nova* manifesto does not have an innovative character, but rather a founding one, because the ideas therein presented, common for artists in other countries, had not yet found a suitable space to develop in Brazil. Hence the urgency of such ideas for the transformation of the Brazilian music scene" (Gaúna, 2002: 88). For all its efforts and in spite of the favorable atmosphere of the time, *Música Nova* floundered due to the lack of an audience and the absence of reliable private or governmental sponsors.

If, given the frailty of the field, serious Brazilian music were not mature enough to nurture the radical vanguard of the period, Brazilian culture in the 1960s did possess another sphere that was sufficiently ripe to promote innovative practices: popular music. Because of his educational activities, Koellreutter had already been working with several popular composers, and had taught Tom Jobim (the father of Bossa Nova) and Tom Zé, for instance. The novelty came, however, when a number of "serious" composers (such as Julio Medaglia, Rogério Duprat, and Damiano Cozzella) from the *Música Nova* group started to interact regularly, and without an educational drive, with the field of popular music. This change of register made them collaborators more than teachers, and can be accounted for partially by the frailty of the field of erudite music in Brazil, but also because of "the possibility of carrying out a project of popular music which could prove to be different from the others" (Gaúna, 2002: 91).

This different project took the shape of *Tropicalism* in 1967-1968 which, by means of its all-inclusive aesthetics, made it possible to break away from the clear-cut distinction between: so-called serious music and mass culture, the archaic and the modern, and the national and the international. The result was a creative integration of erudite musical avant-gardes and the experiments of *Tropicalist* composers such as Gilberto Gil, Tom Zé, and Caetano Veloso. Thus, according to Favaretto, avant-garde musicians and the *Tropicalists* carried out a kind of group work in which the rules were collectively invented thereby precluding the former from imposing their musical material on the others (2000: 42-3)[48]. In this kind of collaboration, Favaretto suggests:

> Elements of avant-garde music were integrated into the popular song, such as: material originating in the two extremes of contemporary composition—those of Boulez-Stockhausen, on the one hand, which adopted the rigor and constructivism of the Vienna School (Schoenberg, Webern, Berg), and which included experiences of electronic and chance music (in which, however, the work of chance was controlled by the composer); and John Cage, on the other, who represented the lines of anti-music and of the happening, which brought about a sudden break with traditional concepts of art, by means of strategies of indeterminacy applied to the musical material as well as his interest in the reception of music. Through the creation of a non-discursive syntax, the two trends got mixed up in an iconoclastic use of tonality, similarly to what had been happening in literature, film and the visual arts. Ultimately, the discussion on popular and erudite music coalesced into one discourse. Ignoring the conflict between quality and quantity, and due to the interest in establishing new ties with an urban audience, working within the relationship production/consumption, erudite music had a lot to learn with the popular: for instance, in handling short bits of time and condensation of sound, as proposed by television. (2000: 44-45)

48 See also Dunn (2001), and Perrone and Dunn (2001) on the opening of horizons promoted by *Tropicalism* in Brazilian popular music.

Nevertheless, the dream of a happy conciliation between extremes did not last long. Popular music became a powerful branch of the culture industry, which, because of its structural drive for profit, very soon made the joining together of the erudite vanguard and popular music unviable; by the beginning of the 1970s this confluence was no longer effective. The consolidation of the culture industry in Brazil, fostered by a project of conservative modernization carried out by the military regime of the time, gradually occupied all available spaces in the media. As for dodecaphonism itself, it had already lost its vitality in Europe, becoming an academic discipline within the walls of music departments. It continued to thrive at the University of São Paulo, where composer Oliver Toni unambiguously practiced "the Vienna School and nothing more" (Martins, 1988: 98). This hard line of Toni's was not without its motives. Indeed, it may be explained as a defensive position against the increasing domination of the culture industry in all media – the music department of the University of São Paulo openly stated that "possibility of critique and mass culture cannot join hands". The department, then, became, under the guidance of Oliver Toni, a place of avant-garde music, of elitism, which offered courses of composition and performance of orchestral instruments (piano, violin, viola, cello, percussion, clarinet, flute, oboe and bassoon), and did not allow entrance to popular instruments, not even the guitar. According to maestro Toni, "anyone can play the guitar" (Martins, 1988: 103). Given the rigid lines adopted by the music department of the University of São Paulo, the most significant student productions happened precisely in the field of popular music, of that kind of guitar music that "anyone can play".

By the end of the 1970s, a number of musicians from the underground music scene of São Paulo aggregated around the *Teatro Lira Paulistana* and eventually became what was known as the *Vanguarda Paulista* (São Paulo Avant-Garde). Arrigo Barnabé, Luiz Tatit of the *Rumo* Group, Mário Manga and Clauss Petersen of *Premeditando o Breque*, among others, were or had been students at the University of São Paulo. Instead of merely following the dictates of the Music School, they decided, individually, to apply their musical knowledge to the field of popular music. Among these composers, Arrigo Barnabé stands out for his inclusion of dodecaphonism *strictu sensu* in the popular song. Self-conceived as a direct descendant of *Tropicalism*, Barnabé's musical project pushed beyond the limits of the experiments carried out in the 1960s. If *Tropicalism* completely changed the notion of the arrangement of the popular song by introducing several techniques originating in so-called erudite music, and opened up song lyrics to literary influences such as concrete poetry, the next step, for Barnabé, was the introduction of atonalism and the twelve-tone row in popular music. *Clara Crocodilo* (1980), his first and technically most accomplished album, mixes twelve-tone compositional procedures with such defining features of the popular song as a regular beat, intonational singing, and a tendency to theatricality. Of its eight pieces, three make use of free atonalism (*Diversões Eletrônicas*, *Sabor de Veneno*, and *Clara Crocodilo*), and five are strictly dodecaphonic (*Acapulco Drive-In*, *Orgasmo Total*, *Instante*, *Infortúnio*, *Office-Boy*).

His work includes transpositions, retrogressions, inversions, rotations, multiplications, fragmentations, derivations, and partitioning. Integrated into and appropriated by the popular song, these compositional procedures create an aesthetics in which the rhythm and pulsation of the megalopolis resonate. At the same time, Barnabé transforms its ever-more automated inhabitants into characters of his songs by means of different tempos, overlapping pulses and polyrhythms (Fenerick, *Façanhas às próprias custas* 152). The characters appear as dehumanized beings, who are disintegrated or disintegrating. They are, in short, "monstrous" creatures. The song "Clara Crocodilo", for instance, tells the story of a harmless office boy who sells his body to "a powerful multinational lab", and has his frail, anonymous human body accidentally transformed into a mighty mutant, "the dangerous criminal, Clara Crocodile, public enemy no.1". This is how the lyrics begin:

> [spoken] São Paulo, December 31st, 1999. There is little, very little for 2000 to come. And you, absent-minded listener, who in the coziness of your home has carelessly placed this record on the player; you who now eagerly wait to open your champagne and hear the clinking of the glasses; you, mortal enemy of anxiety and despair, be prepared... the nightmare has started. Yes, I know, you're going to say that's only your imagination, that you've been reading too many comics lately, but why is it that your hands started to shake, shake, shake so much when you went for that cigarette? And why did you become so pale all of a sudden? Would that be just your imagination? No, my friend, go to the bathroom now, before it's too late, because in this old record you bought at a second hand store there has been imprisoned for more than

twenty years the dangerous criminal, the delinquent, the terrible public enemy #1: Clara Crocodile
[The song starts]

- Silence gives consent, I don't silence
I'm not dying at a cop's hand
Silence gives consent, I don't consent
I'm not dying at rat's hand!
I'm not staying in this hell
Nor going to a cemetery
Machine guns don't reach me
I'm no longer staying in this ring.

[Speaking/singing]
- Hey you listening to me,
Do you think you're going to catch me?
So take this...
I see that you want to go on.
Let's see if you can take this one...
Gee, girl, do you guys think that they want more?
- Yes they do!
- You're such a smarty, let's see if you can follow me in this labyrinth.

Dodecaphonism is the unifying force in the song: it joins together a poor melodic line, at times indistinguishable from plain speaking and shouting with very colloquial lyrics. Without the technique these elements would hardly manage to constitute anything noteworthy, but welded in/through the dodecaphonic arrangement, the song acquires a *sui generis* identity allowing one to argue that it expresses crudely and realistically the neurotic and dehumanizing life in contemporary Brazilian metropolises. In order to integrate the text with serialism and free atonality, Arrigo Barnabé carried out a distortion and disintegration of the tonal center, thus bewildering traditional listeners of urban popular, tonal music, those to whom the LP is explicitly addressed. (Cavazotti, 2000: 8-9)

Despite Barnabé's efforts to see himself as heir to *Tropicalism*, and of his insight that the historic advance in Brazilian popular music could only come by means of atonalism and dodecaphonism, the utilization of dodecaphonism in popular music did not take place as if occurring in a continuous historical continuum, as had happened in Europe with Schoenberg. In other words, Barnabé introduces dodecaphonism in Brazilian popular music "as an apocalyptic sign, an outrage, an explicit rupture with tonalism" (Cavazotti, 2000: 11). Thus, the adoption of the technique and its introduction into Brazilian popular music are characterized by a clear confrontational sense *vis-à-vis* the mainstream or the commodified music of the culture industry of the 1970s and 1980s. Ultimately, Barnabé's dodecaphonism can be viewed as a gesture of resistance to the increasing homogenization and standardization promoted by the culture industry. And that open challenge to the market naturally had a price: the systematic exclusion of Barnabé's work from the mass media (Fenerick, 2007).

It is important to point out how unique Barnabé's case is in the history of Brazilian popular music (maybe even worldwide), due not only to the originality of his appropriation, but also to the fate of his efforts which ultimately did not prove to be economically feasible, and did it lead other composers to make use of the technique. Furthermore, according to Cavazotti, "by stating that after *Tropicália* the next step would be the utilization of atonalism and serialism, Arrigo Barnabé made a direct transfer to Brazilian urban popular music of another kind of music, which belonged to another cultural universe, determined by other forms of social relations" (2000: 12). Thus, Barnabé's feat was eventually as frustrated as the experiments carried out in serious music. Now inserted into the field of popular music, the twelve-tone technique once more failed to find fertile ground for its full development, becoming more of an exception or curiosity than a fountainhead from which other creations could originate. Barnabé today sees himself as a classical composer in his own right: his last work, *a Requiem* (2005), has no traces left of popular music.[49] This should not, however, be interpreted as an indictment of Barnabé's earlier work, which did manage to reinvigorate Brazilian popular music like the *Vanguarda Paulista* did as a whole. But it should not prevent one either from viewing their experiments as failures.

To explain why, it is necessary to recall Roberto Schwarz's words when he argues that it has been noticed that at each generation Brazilian intellectual life seems to start from scratch. The appetite for the recent production of advanced countries has frequently as its counterpart the lack of interest in the work of the previous generation and the ensuing lack of continuity in thinking (Schwarz, 1987: 30).

49 Indeed, in a recent email exchange he denied that *Clara Crocodilo* is made of songs [*canções*] in the formal sense of the term, as A-B-A constructions. We can only see this as an attempt to distance himself from the popular field.

To be sure, the passage should be not be read as implying that sheer continuity would be in itself desirable, as opposed to the frenzied import of cultural artifacts and techniques. Its validity is contingent on the analysis of concrete experiences such as that of dodecaphonism in Brazil. From its inception with Koellreutter, it did not manage to become a generative organic form, nor did it prove itself capable of being integrated objectively into the classical or popular Brazilian music scenes. But rather than merely viewing this as a failure, it is more productive to consider it as a result of the contradictory and ambiguous character of Brazil's modernity. Resembling a pendulum, it cannot firmly define itself as either cosmopolitan or nationalist, as fostering the arts or the culture industry, and thus it presents itself as essentially contradictory. Dodecaphonism exemplified this to perfection. On the one hand, it proved unable to create a self-regulated movement in Brazilian serious music; on the other, Brazilian modernity did not obstruct dodecaphonism's circulation within several spheres of Brazilian society as a whole. The twelve-tone technique did not stagnate as a musical language of the past, as a result of "specific historical necessity", nor did it function as a basis from which further musical experiments could develop. Its trajectory was not a necessity but was rather the agent of *a possible newness* in a given time and within determinate fields. The adventures of dodecaphonism in and through Brazil made it possible for musicians to break with the past, for a small view of the future to open, and for the creation of fundamental movements in the history of Brazil's culture, but the technique itself was never converted into an effective rationality, for traditional Brazilian modernity did not afford it this opportunity. Here again everything was lacking that should materially support a successful cultural practice: sponsorship, audiences, government funding, and concert halls. Interpreting the history of dodecaphonism in Brazil as a representative case of transnational exchange, it is tempting to posit a parallelism between its fate and that of national projects of modernization, as Robert Kurz so cogently argued for in his *Der Kollaps der Modernisierung* (1999). The conclusion which imposes itself on the impartial observer is that if the twelve-tone technique was a frustrated experience in Brazil, it did demonstrate, conversely, how much it could *circulate* in the country by mobilizing nationalists and avant-gardists, and involving both the popular and the erudite. Brazil's porosity regarding dodecaphonism is the flipside of its lack of sedimentation. This reflects the ultimate ambiguity of this transnational encounter: on the one hand, the failure of dodecaphonism to take root as a living manifestation of Brazilian culture; on the other, the ease with which it penetrated different spheres and was welcomed by different artists. This can be read, on the one hand, as the bleak fate of a peripheral country trying to catch up with so-called advanced or developed countries; on the other hand, Brazil's openness towards new kinds of appropriations in a promising, fruitful kind of conviviality, reflects its alternative modernity. This force field, here obtained through the history of dodecaphonism's reception, deserves to be investigated in broader terms. We suspect that the adventures of the twelve-tone technique could stand as a microcosm forlarger dilemmas.

Appropriation in reverse; or, what happens when popular music goes dodecaphonic. (with José Adriano Fenerick)

The problematic current situation of music can be detected in its propensity to generate misnomers. "Classical music" is at best a metonymy, the part for the whole; "erudite," a falsification; "serious," a neutralization; "popular," the greatest untruth. Perhaps only "folk" music corresponds to a minimally accurate denomination, but this may be because its referent, unmediated collective composition/singing no longer really exists – for its "living" counterpart the infamous "ethnic" was coined. This difficulty to name is also present in the single instance where it should actually obtain, namely, in mixed artifacts, whose origins include apparently incompatible, often contradictory, trends or traditions. This is exactly the case of Brazilian "popular" composer Arrigo Barnabé, the most formally oriented member of the so-called "Vanguarda Paulista" (São Paulo Avant-Garde), a term that, taken rigorously, represents yet another misconceptualization. First of all, because its members did not constitute a self-proclaimed movement: Língua de Trapo, the Grupo Rumo, Premeditando o Breque, Itamar Assumpção and Arrigo Barnabé knew each other and often collaborated among themselves, but their own projects were conceived autonomously, without any preexisting agenda or overall plan.

The epithet was given, rather, because of an unprecedented degree of compositional self-awareness in the field of popular music, which could take the form of ironically quoting from different popular genres, often with critical intent, stylistic mélange and pastiche, or a heightened sense of the theatrical in the performance of the popular song.

Detachment from any given musical/dramatic material, the fact that everything lay at one's disposal to be worked on, was a sign of increasing rationality, but it was in Arrigo Barnabé's case that this reflexive stance, the possibility (and the daring) of questioning anything, reached its fullest.

His was an appropriation in reverse, for with him the exchange between the popular and the erudite took the opposite direction of what has normally been the case. In the history of "serious" music one finds various examples of composers turning to popular musical manifestations as a way of reinvigorating an exhausted tradition, or as an important means in their search of the new – not to mention the often less laudable, extra-artistic at- tempts to foster nationalistic sentiment. A telling, indeed early instance of the former is that of Bach's suites, of the latter those of Bartók and Kodaly, and, in Brazil, Villa-Lobos, especially his *Choros.* But Barnabé inverted the direction: from within the field of "popular" music he incorporated several of the techniques belonging to repertoire of modern "erudite" composition such as polyrhythm, multitonalism, and dodecaphonism, thus producing sui generis pieces.

The meaning and implications of this practice, however, can only be properly treated once the notion is dispelled that "popular" music is something derivative or inferior to what would be its "classical" counterpart. Granted, it is possible to argue that there is a high degree of standardization in popular music, as was so well done by Adorno and Simpson (1941). However, that does not mean to say that such standardization may not be studied, and profitably so, either in its own right or as a force against which some trends of popular music struggled. For in one way or another, for better or worse, the contemporary popular song is the privileged field for the study of the most central transformations in the faculty of hearing that have been taking place for the last decades. It is only within the framework of increasing harmonic patterning, melodic conventionalism, and rhythmic repetition that Barnabé's project of popular music's technical modernization becomes fully meaningful.

In order to describe how this works, a few preliminary comments on the nature of the popular song are in order. To use Adorno's terminology, the popular song mobilizes the two most fundamental coordinates of listening, the "expressive-dynamic" and the "rhythmical-spatial" (Adorno 2006: 144), which correspond to the melody and the beat; it is to these elements the verbal material is added. These three layers are structured so as to produce less an artifact in its own right than an instrument of inducement. It is in the nature of the popular song that it addresses the listener in a process that under the name of interpellation (worked out by such authors as Althusser, Butler, and Laplanche) has acquired a wide theoretical currency. Either as an invitation to dance, or a trigger to cry, popular songs cannot be viewed as self-sufficient entities, but rather as half- or quasi-objects, tone/word composites inciting that *something* be done by those who listen to them (even if just talking). This embedded performativity, as it were, one that constitutes the "popular" song as such, is both the result of and precondition for what is central to it: a feeling of closeness and intimacy, of concrete interaction. As a technique, *Bel Canto* had its own natural determinants. In order to be able to play along with the other instruments, the human body had to be made one by utilizing the thorax as a resonance chamber, thus resulting in greater volume of sound and precision in the emission of notes. Electric means made amplification unproblematic thus allowing for a whole new dimension of natural intonation to emerge, something the *Sprechgesang* both anticipated, mirrored, and resisted. It is a clear dialectic whereby technological development, domination over nature, released potentialities for the enactment of the human voice in all its naturalness, the appearance of the singer as a person, *both* a singular, special individual and someone just like you and me. And herein lies the fundamental contradiction, for this sense of intimacy corresponds to what is most utopian and infamous in the popular song: its capacity for the creation and strengthening of com- munities on the one hand, and for the manipulation (even conditioning) of affects, on the other.

In Brazil, this tension has been all the more dramatic due to the absolute supremacy of the popular song since the second half of the 20th century, which has relegated other musical manifestations such as "erudite," and the folk music to a quasi-nonexistent, statistically negligible position. The "popular" song, conceived in its present state, as a commodity like anything else, emerged in Brazil in close association with the rise of urbanization and technical developments in recording (Napolitano 2002: 11-15). In its mainstream form, it shared the same fate as other branches of the culture industry; its success bears witness to the victory of the project of conservative modernization in the country brought about by the military dictator- ship from the mid-1960s to the late 1980s, a process that consolidated at an incredible pace and with the highest competence an effective technological infrastructure, which for the first time managed to encompass the whole of the Brazilian territory within its reach (Ortiz 1999: 182ss).

And yet, it was precisely during the hardest, most dismal period of the military dictatorship in Brazil, from 1968 to 1972, that the field of popular music underwent its deepest transformations. Since a good deal of it in the 1960s was closely connected to political-ideological debate, increasing repression and censorship radically interfered in the production and consumption of music. With the Institutional Act 5, which suspended civil rights and authorized unlimited official control over the media, musical movements and events situated between *Bossa Nova* (1959) and *Tropicalismo* (1968) could then be conceived as forming a cycle which, as it seemed to be the case, was about to end. This then became known as the period of Brazilian popular music, MPB in Portuguese, characterized by attempts at so forging the popular song as to express the country as a coherent entity, the result of a meaningful national project. Its grounds was a political culture informed by national-popular ideology and by industrial development that had been taking place since 1950 (Fenerick, 2005: 157).

The years 1968-1972, also known as the golden age of the popular music festivals, coincide with the modernizing/ developmentist project that had been carried out by the military regime since 1964 in conjunction with repressive political action of the *Estado de Segurança Nacional*. As Ortiz points out (1999: 116), the State of National Security was not only concerned with the curtailment of liberties; it also had its own positive cultural agenda. It was at that period that such fundamental agencies were founded as the *Conselho Federal de Cultura*, *Instituto Nacional de Cinema*, *EMBRAFILME*, *FUNARTE*, and *Pró-Memória*, among others. In sum, as far as cultural policies go, the military dictatorship was both time repressive and supportive (Dias, 2000: 51).[50] The concept of "conservative modernization" captures well the state of affairs; it calls attention to the establishment and consolidation already in the late 1960s and early 1970s of a musical market, which would greatly influence the production and distribution of popular music. It was only during the military regime that the market became sufficiently organized so as to play the role of a determining force directing cultural production in Brazil; since then, potential consumption has been the main yardstick to measure the relevance or importance of a given cultural product. The formula is a simple one, and has become ever more valid in Brazil ever since: If it sells it is good, otherwise it is of no importance. However, one should not confuse this logic with simple sameness or self-identity, for from the 1970s on the culture industry started to implement an increasing segmentation of the market. Reliable infrastructure and the consolidation of stable and competent casts in recording companies allowed for the manufacture of MPB songs, deemed more intellectualized and which targeted layers A and B of the market. Even if it did not yield immense profits at first, MPB guaranteed steady returns given the prestige surrounding several of its great names such as Chico Buarque, Elis Regina, Maria Bethânia, Caetano Veloso, Tom Jobim, and so on. On the other hand, segmentation ascribed to layers D and E so-called *música brega* (kitsch or camp), which, as opposed to MPB, was despised among more cultured circles but widely consumed by the poor.[51]

50 The supportive aspect of the military government's cultural policies became much more apparent in the recent period of economic deregulation and liberalization from 1989 to 2003.

51 Only very recently has this division started to break down through the logic of camp conceived as good taste about bad taste. But even here

Hence, the importance of figures like Roberto Carlos, who managed to circulate in both spheres, recording with Maria Bethânia and Caetano Veloso, for instance, and at the same time composing over-saccharine songs; he then performed the role of a cultural mediator of sorts between MPB and the brega spheres.[52]

But the field of popular music was not monolithic; it proved rather to be elastic enough to turn into the stage for alternative, often contradictory and polemical movements. The Vanguarda Paulista itself must be regarded as an offspring of Brazilian modernization (Fenerick, 2007). Its emergence would be unthinkable without the consolidation of the Brazilian public university system, which made formal knowledge of advanced compositional techniques available to musicians steeped in the tradition of the popular song. Groups as the Língua de Trapo, Rumo, Premeditando o Breque, and musicians like Itamar Assumpção brought to the popular song an unheard of degree of formal elaboration and stylistic self-consciousness. Arrigo Barnabé was the sharpest case of this clash between rigor and spontaneity. Following the lead of the Tropicália movement, he wanted to carry out a transformation in popular music he saw as incomplete, for *Tropicália* revolutionized the lyrics, making them more complex and "literary"; it also drastically modified compositional arrangement, including techniques such as *Pop Art* collage and even elements of concrete music. This came as a result of a more total view of the song, which now comprised a theatrical-philosophical sense in itself, enhancing the notion of stage performance and cultural intervention. In fact, Tropicalism's seemingly all-inclusive aesthetics, in which the

---

social division and aesthetic preferences are still at play.

52 On *brega* music, see Araújo (2002).

archaic and the modern were mixed as in Gilberto Gil's famous "Geléia Geral" or melting pot (literally "General Jelly"), may be viewed as both an *implosion* of the Brazilian popular song, the end of a cycle beginning with the first popular composers of the 20th century, and as an *explosion* that splintered in all directions and which opened new possibilities for the development of the popular song in Brazil (Hollanda, 1992; Favareto, 1996; Cyntrão, 2000). These contradictory tendencies would have a crucial effect on Barnabé: the explosion would lead him to try the limits of the popular song in albums such as *Clara Crocodilo* or *Tubarões Voadores;* the implosion would account for his eventual abandonment of popular mu- sic altogether and his turning to erudite music.[53]

Barnabé's early music was conceived as an attempt to carry further Tropicalist ambitions by modernizing the musical material itself, which Arrigo saw as lagging behind transformations in the other aspects of the popular song. Barnabé's project was to further musical experimentation without abandoning the conception of the song as a multiple event, or the oppositional substratum that pervaded a great deal of the Brazilian tradition. Having appeared in 1980, *Clara Crocodilo* remains Barnabé's most ambitious and important album; all of the eight songs in it have serial elements, four

53 This transition deserves to be studied, not only because of its sui generis nature but also because it was apparently motivated by economic failure. Barnabé prepared the album Suspeito (1987) with a broad audience in mind. He launched it through giant Continental Records, which made it play in radio stations; however, the songs were still too complex to become immediately popular and the project floundered. Even though two other LPs appeared in the 90, Façanhas and Gigante Negão, both equally financially unsuccessful, the decade witnessed Barnabé's gradual withdrawal, which is now complete, from the field of popular music. His last work released, a Missa in Memoriam Itamar Assumpção (2006), is to be firmly placed in the field of erudite music.

of which – "Acapulco Drive-in," "Orgasmo Total," "Instante," "Infortúnio," and "Office-Boy" – use partially or fully the 12-tone technique (Cavazotti, 2000: 9). And in terms of the appropriation of dodecaphonism, the opening song of the album, "Acapulco Drive-in," is exemplary.

The song may be fruitfully analyzed in three different layers. In the first one, that of the beat, the tension between rhythm and pulse is worth discussing. For even though significant changes in measuring take place throughout "Acapulco Drive-in" (4/4, 2/4, 3/8, 6/8, 9/8), one cannot say that polyrhythm in its strict sense is being employed. To be sure, such alternation of measures is quite unusual in the popular song (albeit not in the recent tradition of instrumental music in Brazil, as in Hermeto Pascoal or Egberto Gismonti); nonetheless, they do not happen vertically, that is, simultaneously, but rather in the flux of sounds, which is constantly interrupted. In the first 18 bars of the song, for example, Barnabé composes an asymmetrical rhythmic structure based on 3 blocks of 6 bars each, varying rhythmic patterns with 3/8, 4/4, 2/4, 3/8, 4/4, 2/4. However, a "poly- rhythm effect" does emerge when he makes use of the 4/4 bar in order to create a repetitive, regular, and constant rhythmic nucleus on the bass (followed by the drums, which are not marked in the score). This regular pulse remains through all rhythmic variations in the song, giving it a sense of "stability," even if a tense one, for there is an unavoidable clash between the pulse and the song's rhythm. By means of this "effect," Barnabé manages to keep the song within the field of popular music – the pulse makes "Acapulco Drive-in" regular and fit for dancing – at the same time that rhythmic asymmetry breaks the normal pattern of repetitions typical of the popular song. In short, it is a hybrid that combines constant pulse and continuously interrupted rhythm.

But it is when one turns to its harmonic procedures that the mixed nature of "Acapulco Drive-in" becomes even more apparent and interesting. According to Cavazotti (1993), the 12-tone row of the song is (0 X C) 0 3 5 11 6 4 1 2 8 10 7 9. In the first 24 bars, which make up the introduction, the original series is presented as a 5-note motive (0 3 5 11 6), which is repeated three times, corresponding to "Boca da Noite," and is interspersed with atonal musical blocks played by Arrigo Barnabé's Band Sabor de Veneno. The 5-note motive, then, performs a role that is similar to that of introductory short melodies beginning the mainstream popular song. But since its atonal character causes a suspension in the harmonic direction of the song, it converts the section more into a disturbing beginning for the ear than a peaceful introduction to memory. The dodecaphonic fragment introduced in the beginning of the song, which opens *Clara Crocodilo,* already creates in the listener the sensation of estrangement, for even if parts and variations of the main melody may be detected ("Boca da Noite"), as is normally the case in the introduction of tonal popular songs, it does not point to any harmonic direction in the traditional sense of tension and relaxing, dissonance and consonance. The 12-tone technique abolishes such harmonic sense, for it proposes another direction and way of listening (see Menezes, 2002).

The initial effect of suspension is only resolved (but not in the tonal sense of the term) at measure 25 onwards, when the 5-note motive becomes a musical phrase in its own right. It is at this point that the series is presented in its entirety, in 5 measures corresponding to "Boca da Noite/ Boquinha de Gata/Chupando, Mordendo" and completed by a small 7-note mirroring in "Bala de Conhaque." But the whole phrase is interrupted by a *breque* (the "break" transliterated in Portuguese), when "Colored. Color na garoa" is uttered, not sung. Again, expectations are frustrated. Since at least the 1930s, the *breque* has been a common element of the Brazilian popular song, especially in the traditional samba-de-breque, in which the sambista interrupts the melody with the *breque* and starts to talk, to improvise on the topic of the lyrics.[54] Estrangement here is not a result of the *breque* itself, but of its unexpectedness; for the accustomed listener the break is expected, it is even dictated by harmonic progression and stanzaic development.[55] This is not what happens in "Acapulco Drive-in." At no point in the song does the series announce anything and the *breques*, for there are several others, take place as if suspended, in a void. Indeed, this indeterminacy draws the *breque* close to "pure" sprechgesang.

Further, the tense relationship between European avant-gardes and the tradition of the Brazilian popular music can also be witnessed in the A-B-A form of the song. Cavazotti (1993, 36) argues that the 12-tone row in "Acapulco Drive-in" appears in inverted, retrograde, transposed, and rotated forms, fragmented in ditones, trichords, tetrachords, pentachords, hexachords, and heptachords. Nevertheless, still according to Cavazotti (1993: 36), the first (A) and third (A') parts of the

54 Moreira da Silva was the most emblematic samba de breque singer, a variety which has traditionally been associated with the figure of the malandro – indeed, it is tempting to posit a parallelism between song and breque on the one hand and the law/order and its infringement on the other.

55 Note the name of a group already alluded to: "Premeditando o Breque" means exactly this, premeditating the break. Even if the signifier, the succession /pr/ – /br/, may have been the main reason for the group's choice, the idea therein contained clearly points to mixture of compositional rationality, popular inspiration and performatic irreverence.

song are composed on inferior sequences of notes starting with S0 (C) and S7 (G), which reproduce a similar relation to that of tonic-dominant-tonic typical of the A-B-A' structure of the song. Such implicit harmonic construction results in an ambiguous sense of the piece, which seems to hover over tonalism and atonalism, a tension involving fields and traditions of western music, the tonal/popular and the atonal/vanguard. This tension is not resolved, but exposed as such, and not by chance concluded with an improvisation.[56]

The analysis of the series points to a strong contradiction. The complexity of the work on the musical material just alluded to is in tension with the constant nature of the beat, thus producing an ambiguity whereby the melodic aspect may figure as criticism of the pulse, or, on the contrary, the beat may obscure note differentiation. In this latter case, variations of sound become just a jumble of noise; they are simply not heard. Further- more, the tension between the option for the 12-tone series, on the one hand, and the basic, A-B-A' form of the song, on the other, encourages a potentially critical listening, dialectically oscillating between the recognition and estrangement of the musical material used by the composer. This may be one of the reasons why the São Paulo media, without fully grasping the implications of Barnabé's work for the field of popular music, has labeled him together with other musicians of his generation as *Vanguarda Paulista,* "avant-garde" here meaning both appraisal

56 In a recent exchange of emails, Barnabé denied that "Acapulco Drive-in" or any other item of Clara Crocodilo, with the exception of "Instante," could be characterized as a song (canção) as such. We can only interpret this as a sign of willingness to distance himself (even retrospectively) from the field of popular music.

for creativity and rebuke for the failure to communicate with a mass audience. As was already mentioned, musicians and composers of the so-called Vanguarda Paulista had such a great variety of projects and interests, from the introduction of dodecaphonism in the Brazilian popular song to parodic re-readings of traditional genres as samba and *chorinho*, that one should be cautious to apply one single name to all of them. They never really put forth a coordinated and coherent musical movement. What they brought about was a great cultural renewal in the São Paulo musical scene of the 1980s (Fenerick, 2007). But even though their work was different in so many ways, some strong common features seem to give validity to the overall label. The urban, underground, and artisanal character of their work, their lack of adjustment to the culture industry of the time is one such aspect.

The use of the sung speech (*fala-cantada*) is another. In one way or another all groups of the Vanguarda Paulista availed themselves of speech in singing (or singing in speech) in their compositions and Arrigo Barnabé was no exception. This aspect becomes even more relevant in Brazil as the popular song is characterized by the drawing together of speech and singing. According to composer Luiz Tatit, former member of the Rumo group and currently professor of linguistics at the University of São Paulo, "In the world of the singer [*cancionista*] it is not so important what is said, but the way of saying, and the way of saying is essentially melodic. On this basis, that which is said oftentimes becomes magnificent." For "in the juncture of the melodic sequences with the linguistic units, the kernel of tension, the cancionista always has an elegant oral gesture available, in order to smooth things up and eliminate residues that might otherwise hamper the song's naturalness. Her main device is the intoning process that extends speaking to singing. Or, in a more rigorous process, that produces speaking in singing" (Tatit, 1996: 9).

Arrigo Barnabé's work may thus be understood as the one of a *cancionista*; and however strange that may sound, the utilization of dodecaphonism only strengthens this tendency. Throughout the song, the use of the dodecaphonic series and its implicit chromatism allow the singer to search for the most convincing intonation and the truest intertwining of singing and speech, what one is singing and what is being sung, what one is saying and what is being said, which in the last instance characterizes the Brazilian popular song, according to Tatit.

Indeed, the verbal meaning contained in the lyrics is closely related to all that. The song's text adds yet a new layer of sense and tension in all this. Its dramatic character comes not only from the action described, the meeting of a prostitute and her client, but also from the intonation adopted. The words of "Acapulco Drive-in":

(female voices) Night starts [*Boca da noite*] (3x) "Acapulco Drive-in"

Night starts, pussycat's mouth [boca da noite, boquinha de gata] sucking, biting, cognac sweets colored color in the dribble (3x) + in a Maverick car with jasmine smell (male voice) the old man comes (female voices) Waving his hand (male voice) ps, ps, hey, ps, ps (repeat but go to) (male voice) ps, ps, ps, hey princess Have you already been to the Playcenter? (female voices) Hum, what an extravagant idea . . . (male voice) So, what about a movie? (female voices) Not that, come on . . . (male voice) How about a drink at a drive-in? (female voices) My fees are high, darling . . . (laughs) (male voice) For you I do everything. For you I go crazy. "Acapulco Drive-in"

(female voice, imitating operatic style) Take it off, I want your brown [parda] skin

carmine lips. (male voice, pedal on) Brrr . . . Naked temptation. (female voices) Bends on the steering wheel In the zipper (male choir) The surprise waiting too long (male voice) Panties imitating (female voices) Leopard skin (male voice) But how cute (female voices) Leopard skin

(male voice) Good to know (female voices) Leopard skin (male voice) Panties imitating (female voices) Leopard skin (male voice) Acapulco (female voices) Drive-in[57]

The Acapulco Drive-in actually existed; it belonged to Barnabé's brother, Paulo, and it may very well be the case

57 In the original: (female voices) Boca da noite (3x)/"Acapulco Drive-in"/boca da noite, boquinha de gata/chupando, mordendo, bala de conhaque/colored/color na garoa (3x)//dentro de um Maverick/cheirando a jasmim/(male voice) passa o coroa/ (female voices) Fazendo sinal/(male voice) ps, ps, ei, ps, ps/(male voice) ps, ps, ps, ei princesa/Você já foi ao Playcenter?/(female voices) Hum, mas que idéia estravagante.../(male voice) Então, que tal uma tela?/(female voices) Ah, essa não, vai!/(male voice) Topas um drinque num drive-in?/(female voices) Meu preço é alto, viu, bem?/(laughs)/(male voice) Por você, eu faço tudo./Por você, eu perco o juízo.//"Acapulco Drive-in"/(female voice, imitating operatic style) Tire, quero sua pele parda/lábios de carmim./(male voice, pedal on) Brrr . . . Tentação nua./(female voices) Empina no volante/No zíper/(male choir) A surpresa que já tarda/(male voice) Calcinha imitando/(female voices) Pele de leoparda/(male voice) Mas que gracinha/(female voices) Pele de leoparda/(male voice) Bom saber/(female voices) Pele de leoparda/(male voice) Calcinha imitando/(female voices) Pele de leoparda/ (male voice) Acapulco/(female voices) Drive-in.

that the exchange described between client and prostitute actually took place there. But for all its appearance of reality, the *meaning* of what is being said/sung is far from clear. Cavazotti's claim that the text "evinces the 'reification' of sex, reduced in the lyrics to a sheer object of commerce" (1993: 40), thus expressing "the decadent character of humanity" (41) is not supported by the song. Because the voices do as much acting as singing, intonation becomes unreliable and it is impossible to determine the song's stance vis-à-vis what it presents. One cannot really know if the scene represents a criticism of contemporary urban life is being carried out, or whether the encounter is presented for its own sake and the world of commodities consequently endorsed. The quotation marks on "Acapulco Drive-in" clearly express this: their absence would suggest taking the place at its face value, whereas the distance established by citation would allow for reflexive detachment. But the inverted commas are not transferable to the song, for there everything seems to be quoted and therefore it is possible that nothing is. The song enacts then the clash be- tween metropolitan environment and advanced compositional technique in their common origin in the process of modernization: criticism of a technologically oriented world would have to come to terms with the dodecaphonism, by implication also becoming negative; conversely, perfect agreement with a São Paulo where everything is for sale would have to justify the song's obvious ugliness.

The contradictions accumulate. Polyrhythm and the beat, work on the row and the A-B-A' form, performatic singing as critique or sheer mimetism of the status quo – as a whole, they eventually constitute an object that exposes the insufficiency of technique as such, and it is tempting to conceive of "Acapulco Drive-in" as expressing the deadlock of modernization (Kurz, 1992). The text and the technique go hand in hand. All they do is point to possibilities in the use of resources that may end up, if unsuccessful, as sheer noise and commodification. What happens when popular music goes dodecaphonic is that technique becomes what it is: the undecidability of itself, either the emergence of something else or domination, in this case presented under the guise of the virtual existence of form or sheer noise. These internal ambiguities inevitably bear upon reception, for Barnabé's mixing of popular and erudite engenders an interesting topological paradox, as it were. If viewed from the outside, that is, from the perspective of "serious" music, acknowledging and starting from extraneous technique, *then* the song becomes a living proof of the flexibility of popular music, of its openness and potential to accommodate what is foreign; conversely, when approached from within the realm of the popular itself the potential difference in the technique is absorbed and nullified: it is not felt as such and dissolves into atmosphere. Or, to put it somewhat differently: since distance is both fostered and shunned, the listener is placed in a difficult position of either connecting to the song through its pulse, voice, and theatricality, in which case the musical elaboration is perceived as noise, or conversely, resist the song's interpellation and concentrate on the organization of dissonances, thus placing herself outside the group-creating effect of the music. Or she may yet try another listening position and focus on this tension itself, the result of an appropriation in reverse, which is so revealing of what is at stake for the song as a popular genre in the age of its digitalized transmission.

Tom Zé's Unsong and the Fate of the Tropicália Movement. (with José Adriano Fenerick)

I

The strength of the concept of a "popular avant-garde" must come as the result of tension embedded in the expression itself. If the latent disagreement between the two terms making up the expression passes without comment, it easily becomes apologetic or ideological; yet if it is construed as an unlikely exception, the popular avant-garde may shake the boundaries dividing two worlds at a time when they no longer hold. For while in the arts talk of a post-avant-garde era is far from new, popular music has for decades been anything but popular since it has been increasingly dominated by a business-oriented rationality in its conception and industrial processes in its production. At least provisionally, it seems safe to argue that a true fusion between the avant-garde and the popular can only take place at specific moments, when there is a certain porosity within and between both spheres. Brazil's case, in this respect, is both exemplary and unusual. Although in Brazil, artistic institutions have not been strong enough to support a vigorous and continuous tradition, they haven't been sufficiently fragile so as to simply disappear or become unable to accommodate extraneous elements, forces or impulses coming from the outside of their canons.

As a consequence, either from internal crises or external pressures, the Brazilian art establishment has had greater difficulty in ignoring the popular than other national traditions. In the field of popular art, it is essential to keep the productive (and explosive) nature of the Brazilian population in mind. A product of the clash among native-born *criollo* Brazilians and Portuguese colonizers (joined later by immigrants from Japan and other parts of Europe) and an enormous black population – mostly composed of former slaves – Brazilian popular culture looked to the erudite to provide a semblance of unity and prestige while at the same time keeping its innermost impulses alive (Durão, 2008d).

Without a doubt, one of the clearest examples of the popular avant-garde in Brazil is *Tropicália*, a movement that not only generated a heated cultural debate, but also influenced other avant-gardist experiments in the popular musical sphere, such as the 1980s *Vanguarda Paulista* (Fenerick, 2007). It was perhaps unsurprising that music would galvanize experimentalism among the common people: in eighteenth and nineteenth century Brazil, music more than any other art form was the true medium of popular expression, and the only one to constitute a tradition that could be handed down through generations independently of formal educational institutions. This is mainly due to the kind of communication involved in the popular song, which combines verbal and melodic aspects, and mixes linguistic references with tonal ambience. The popular song can be defined as a hybrid object that satisfies the imagination while stimulating the body, and which does not require flawless technique to be performed (even if a few players did acquire the status of virtuoso). It was precisely the lack of consolidation of formal musical training in Brazil, coupled with a rich folk musical culture, which generated an unusually easy circulation between the popular and the traditional.

If *Tropicália* was the first full-blown vanguard movement in Brazilian popular music, it can also be said to have been the last, not because no other ever came into being, but because Tropicalian mixtures questioned the very idea of a movement. On the one hand, *Tropicália* emerged almost simultaneously in such different art forms as literature, the plastic arts, cinema, and the theater; on the other hand, by welcoming the products of the culture industry and adding them to the tradition of the Brazilian popular song, Tropicália went against the idea of rupture that underlined most, if not all, "conventional" manifestations of the avant-garde (Favaretto, 2000: 32)[58]. Tropicalists strived to incorporate a great deal of the popular musical repertoire, welcoming past achievements as raw material to be worked on, and a basis from which it could put forth its own agenda of unlikely combinations (Naves, 2001: 47-48). They fully accepted the contradictions of modernization and refused to hide the ambiguities and problems that went with taking sides – either traditional values or future hopes. Furthermore, their assessment of Brazilian reality differed, too, from other typical positions in the 1960s, by virtue of their self-referentiality, which allowed society's contradictions to be expressed through musical strategies. *Tropicália* included elements from diverse origins in the same new object. Because this material was withdrawn from particular traditions and lines of development, as well as from any temporal continuum, a strange effect of rupture was produced that froze time and created the effect of surprise.

The apparent paradox of an avant-garde that regarded the past as potential building blocks can be in part explained

58 For a full list of artists, see Basualdo (2007: 321-35). Here one can call to mind film director Glauber Rocha, poets Décio Pignatari, Augusto de Campos and Haroldo de Campos, artist Hélio Oiticica, theater director José Celso Martinez Correa and the Oficina group, among others.

by the cultural and political context of the period in which it emerged. The 1960s in Brazil, as elsewhere, was a period of intense ideological debate and cultural conflict. This situation was to a large extent catalyzed by popular music, which became, by means of the televised *Festivais de Música Popular*, a makeshift forum for argument about national issues, even though popular music was part and parcel of an emergent Brazilian culture industry in its process of consolidation. Tropicália started to be seen as the antithesis of the traditional popular song (simply called MPB, *música popular brasileira*), something that the Tropicalists themselves did not deny, for such a view granted them a specific slot in the market (Napolitano, 2001: 270). *Tropicália* thus presented itself as a possible stage on which to articulate the political and cultural conflicts of the late 60s' – a period of fierce repression by Brazil's military regime. It also brought about a new language in popular song, characterized by the unlikely mixture of an established Brazilian tradition, rooted in rural experience, and elements made available by a rapidly modernizing country. In so doing, *Tropicália* re-defined Brazilian culture in terms of a necessary interdependence between the archaic and the latest innovation.

Nevertheless, the Tropicalists' stance was far from unproblematic. Marxists criticized *Tropicália* for reifying contradiction as such, as if it corresponded to an ontological and atemporal essence, instead of trying to aim for a state of resolution in which opposites would cease to exist. This, of course, is the very definition of a redeemed socialist society according to classic Marxist theory. For Roberto Schwarz, for instance, the aesthetic experience created by *Tropicália* substituted melancholy conformism for the practice of changing minds. In his view, political impotence, both on the part of the artist and public, *vis-à-vis* historical challenges, would represent the real cause of *Tropicália*'s symbolic violence, above all in the theater. The Tropicalists' allegory of Brazil as a combination of old and new, regressive and progressive, would then indirectly reinforce the ideology of the country as averse to real change. At the same time, one must remember that Schwarz's main engagement with *Tropicália*, in his book *Culture and Politics* (2005), was written in 1970, in reaction to the aftereffects of the "Tropicalist surge" in Brazilian culture. Indeed, the "movement" would develop in different directions as the decade unfolded, and any evaluation of it in the twenty-first century must profit from the benefit of hindsight. In other words, new criticism must be able to incorporate development into any conception of origin, as well as characterizing what *Tropicália* was through the lens of what it became. In music, two very distinct trends can be identified in their relation to the market and musical experimentation respectively. If musicians like Caetano Veloso and Gilberto Gil opted to privilege the former, inserting the Tropicalist moment into their now mainstream careers, Tom Zé never subordinated his music making to the logic of success and stardom. It is this choice that must now be investigated, with regard to its most important presuppositions and consequences.

By operating at once from outside and within the juxtaposing of disparate components that came to constitute Brazilian culture, *Tropicália* brought about "a cultural summa of an anthropophagic nature, in which historical, ideological and artistic contradictions were gathered in order to undergo a demystifying operation" (Favaretto, 2000: 26). These disparate elements involved issues of modernization and temporality; they also articulated a rupture of the boundaries between "serious" and "popular" music. This is not to say that Tropicália managed to create a new musical genre in its own right, as *Bossa Nova* did in the late 50s (Dunn, 2001: 3). Still, in order to be able to meaningfully synthesize contradictory forces, thereby demystifying them and opening the way for critique, at its inception Tropicália conciliated musical projects that eventually would prove to be incompatible. The dissonances in Tropicalist musical trends can be illustrated through the work of Rogério Duprat and the *Mutantes* group, which just as Zé, were relegated to the periphery – the B-Side of Tropicália, as it were, with "Side A" represented by Gilberto Gil and Caetano Veloso.

A conductor and composer, Duprat had been an important name in the restricted circles of Brazilian "serious" contemporary music before he met and began working with soon-to-be *Tropicália* musicians. Two principal reasons may account for their improbable approximation: first, Duprat was disillusioned with the institutionalization of contemporary music's avant-garde, which in his opinion had become a "new academicism," especially with the ossification of dodecaphonism; and second, popular music at that particular moment seemed more full of life and open to innovation in light of the academic leanings of the musical vanguard. *Tropicália*'s initial stirrings offered the opportunity for introducing most, if not all, of the achievements of the post-World War II avant-gardes into popular music (Gaúna, 2002: 97). From their perspective, the Tropicalists quickly perceived the advantages Duprat could offer to the same "geléia geral" (general jelly)[59]

59 The expression was coined by poet Décio Pignatari, inspired by

aimed at by Gil and Caetano. Duprat, together with other vanguard composers such as Julio Medaglia, Sandino Hohagen, and Damiano Cozzella, joined the ranks of *Tropicália* as the arranger of the songs that would make it known.

At this point, a specific technical issue must be dealt with. The LP format of 33 1/3 rpm was patented by CBS soon after the end of World War II, in 1948; however, the codification of the LP in circulation and production would only take place in the 60s. Once the LP became firmly established as the privileged medium for commercial music, phonographic industries redefined their marketing strategies, which were now directed more at the artist than at individual songs. Due to its greater playing time in comparison with its predecessor, the long play of the compact record altered the definition of the album to one that conceived a set of songs as a coherent whole. This extrinsic change in the means of production had deep and lasting effects on the conception of popular music.

In the Brazil of the early 60s, it became clear from *Bossa Nova* that popular music had the potential to be something more than a mere cheap commodity, and that it was not completely exhausted by its commercial value. As popular music gained in sophistication, a self- reflexive quality began to emerge, distancing it from the supposed spontaneity of folk singing, and drawing it closer to what could be thought of as art. Moreover, the LP changed the role of the studio which, having ceased to be merely a place where songs were recorded, turned

Oswald de Andrade's famous "Anthropophagic Manifesto." It was used too as the title of a manifesto-song by Torquato Neto and Gilberto Gil, in their programmatic LP Panis et Circencis (1967). It points to the mixtures proposed by Tropicália of national and foreign, the archaic and the modern, pop and folk cultures, the erudite and popular, etc.

into a laboratory where new sounds were shaped. Perhaps the most telling example of this transformation in the 60s' was the Beatles' album, *Sgt. Pepper's Lonely Hearts Club Band*, where one finds a "sonic kaleidoscope" created by the group together with its producer/arranger, George Martin (Fenerick and Marquioni, 2008). In short, with these transformations, the arranger took on the status of a co-author of songs.

A similar type of studio system governed Duprat's arrangements of *Tropicália*: he recreated the songs in such a way as to make them constitutive parts of the album and, therefore, virtually irreplaceable. It was in the arranging of the Tropicalists' songs that Duprat's knowledge of avant-garde musical techniques was put to work. Yet as Brazilian popular music in the 70s solidified into what became known as MPB, a technologically advanced product which was fully schematized with predetermined parts and firmly established protocols, the same impulse that permitted Duprat's interaction in the field of popular music would push him gradually away from it. Inasmuch as popular music lost its capacity to incorporate new languages and techniques, it became uninteresting to vanguard musicians, who saw themselves having to subordinate experimentation to market standardization, even if that standardization only affected arrangements.

If Duprat can be regarded as a representative of the vanguard side of *Tropicália*, *Os Mutantes* would stand for what can be termed the anarchic side. The trio, made up of the musicians Rita Lee, Arnaldo Batista and Sérigo Dias, entered the Brazilian musical scene through the mediation of Duprat, who introduced them to Gilberto Gil in 1967. Their musical project centered on an idea of freedom at a time when popular music in Brazil was absorbed by the polarizing debate between supporters of the national or international, the "authentic" (folkloric) or the universal, the politically committed or the "alienated" song. No longer invested in this ideological dispute, the *Mutantes* brought to *Tropicália* a new element, namely pop music itself. Contrastingly, in the first wave of Brazilian rock music, the behavioral changes that were fostered and reflected upon by the so-named *Jovem Guarda*, were more significant than musical achievement. The joining of Gil and Veloso with the *Mutantes* was spurred by their mutual desire for a return to the musical. For the former, the *Mutantes* represented an effective instrument of intervention which could open the way for new modes of musical production and thinking about popular music in an ideologically-charged period. At the same time, the intense character and high stakes of the debates taking place in the period actually encouraged innovation, such as the inclusion of electric guitars and amplification, and a pop-rock beat. For the *Mutantes*, partnering with Gil and Caetano meant, among other things, the possibility of entering the stage of Brazilian popular song through the front door: the group could have much easier access to the media, even while it mocked the same mainstream means of communication and cherished products (Harvey, qtd. in Perrone and Dunn, 2001: 106-22).

Duprat and the *Mutantes* proved to be fundamental forces in the *Tropicália* project, although their cooperation was limited to a couple of years. They produced a kind of popular music that could claim to be innovative and experimental – formally and ideologically – and opposed to traditional – read conservative – forms of popular song. Theirs was a partnership that benefited all involved; however, it did not last long. After *Tropicália*'s initial moment of rupture with the mainstream in 1967-1968, it became clear that there were strong disagreements within the movement and that it was, in fact, split in two. Each faction supported different, even incompatible, projects which could only be brought together for a short period. The first was really experimental and radical, corresponding to what Luiz Tatit called "intense" music making, in which collaborative work played a fundamental role. In contradistinction, the second was "extensive" and had as its focus not so much musical innovation as such but market success and the tastes of a wide audience (Tatit, 2004: 213-14).

Looking back from today's perspective, *Tropicália*'s internal tensions pointed towards different directions. From its inception, *Tropicália* utilized mass communication – TV programs and televised music festivals, radio, and records – in combination with avant-garde musical languages. This strategy was, to a great extent, made possible by the still feeble development of the culture industry in Brazil, in comparison with its current level of power. However, by the early 70s, as the apparatus of cultural commercialization grew quantitatively (i.e., the number of stations and TV sets) and qualitatively (through market segmentation and production of demand), the conjunction of mass media and experimentation could no longer sustain itself. The search for invention from within the song form was relegated to the periphery, and figures such as Tom Zé, the *Mutantes*, and others became marginal. If Gil, Veloso and Lee never really ceased to be mainstream, the "Side B" of *Tropicália* carried on the original program of rupture, experimentation, and criticism.

Tom Zé came onto the Brazilian musical scene during the golden age of TV festivals and popular music contests, which mobilized the whole country. His first performance at the 1967 III *Festival da Música Popular Brasileira* was not particularly promising, however. In contrast with such watershed songs as Veloso's "Alegria, alegria" and Gil's "Domingo no parque," Zé's piece, "A moreninha," was traditionally lyrical and melodious and, in consequence, did not manage to move beyond the first round of competition. But the following year, the situation would be radically different: in 1968, Zé recorded his first LP, *Tom Zé, Grande liquidação*, which can be translated as "Big Sales" or "Great Annihilation." He entered the festival with the song "Parque industrial" (Industrial Park), which would be included in the manifesto-record of the same year, *Tropicália ou panis et circensis*, thus definitively associating his name with the movement. In the same year, he composed "2001" with Lee, a song that was recorded by the *Mutantes* and would become one of the key manifestations of Tropicalist aesthetics. Zé won the IV Festival of the TV station Record with the song "São, São Paulo meu amor," while "2001" got fourth place.[60] His vertiginous rise would lead one to believe that Zé's career was destined for success, and that he had already decided on stardom as his goal, but that was far from the case.

By the time the *Tropicália* movement reached its apogee in 1968, Zé was operating according to a logic of shock rather than a well- delineated aesthetics, as part of his career plan. Winning Record's Festival[61] meant, in this sense,

60 The original 1968 recording of "São, São Paulo meu amor" is available online.

61 In the 60s in Brazil, the song contests promoted by several TV

both glory and the beginning of his reclusion. In spite of the Tropicalists' criticism of the festival structure, they welcomed the 1968 results as the arrival of *Tropicália* on the national musical scene. Yet at the same time, the need to sustain a radical stance, as well as an attitude of shock and rupture, counterbalanced the euphoria generated by the movement's popular acceptance. Entering into mass circulation and the culture industry at a moment when the commercial apparatus was willing to propagate a certain kind of newness offered a way of making a difference and winning one round in the fight against traditional MPB (Napolitano, 2001: 276-77). *Tropicália* and MPB were fighting over the same market share, which, while quickly growing, was still too weak to accommodate such different musical tendencies. Conditions would change in the following decade when the opposing trends drew together – almost to the point of fusion. Zé refused to take part in precisely this compromise. Even though he was considered by the commercial musical establishment as the next in line for media success, he would not join the mainstream or cooperate with its demands. As he has insisted in recent interviews, from this point on, he started to sabotage his work, thus jeopardizing his own career.[62] The idea of conscious self-sabotage should of course be taken with a grain of salt, since it would be much more fruitful to consider it part of Zé's musical project, which took on mature form only when musical innovation was no longer so welcome. In the 70s, in an attempt to escape both an institutionalized MPB and an increasingly sold-out *Tropicália*, Zé's songs turned noticeably personal in character and experimental in technique: they then became "unsongs."

---

stations, especially by Record, became immensely famous and helped shape much of the culture of the time.

62 See the documentary Tom Zé, ou Quem irá colocar uma dinamite na cabeça do século? (2002), directed by Carla Gallo.

Zé's musical project became clearer (even to the composer himself) when he abandoned the traditional song form and began systematically developing what could be called a negative process of music making–or rather music's unmaking. Unsongs have as their starting point musical imperfections, either in the writing, arrangement, or performance. Working with these imperfections allowed Zé to obtain a privileged perspective from which to invert and subvert the social values crystallized in the song form. As Tatit argues:

> [O]ne can say that instead of the traditional procedure of song makers to aestheticize the quotidian, Tom Zé made aesthetics a daily affair: he inserted imperfections, insufficiencies, defects. [. . .] Therefore, this had nothing to do with the extensive (or implicit) Tropicália project, which ended up engendering the radio song of the 70s and opening the space for the Brazilian pop song of the end of the millennium (2004: 237-38).

Zé brought to the universe of the popular song compositional elements and techniques from the so-called classical music Avant-guards, such as polyrhythm, the inclusion of noise, research on new instruments, and performances that verged on happenings. Such methods, however, were used less as techniques for making songs than as means for their undoing. The parallel with deconstruction is almost unavoidable, with the difference, however, that his point of departure was not metaphysics, but the concrete song form. His emphasis on dismantling differentiates him from Duprat or Arrigo Barnabé, who introduced dodecaphonism into the popular song. In spite of Zé's formal music training – rare among popular composers – or perhaps precisely because of it, he adopted an apocalyptic position vis-à-vis the Brazilian popular song. His compositions were utterly devoid of the beauty and melodiousness prized in traditional songs, which generated two important effects. In the first place, it is important to point out that the beauty associated with traditional popular music eventually became connected to ideas of national identity. Musical styles like *samba, frevo, baião, chachado,* and *chorinho* emerged as popular forms, but soon enough attained a second layer of meaning that imbued them with a regional character, which was part of the dialectics of part and whole, region and nation. Secondly, beauty, when expressed in terms of consonance and regularity, becomes the means through which the listener identifies with the song, both in its linguistic content as well as rhythmic patterns. *Tropicália* disturbed the process of listener identification by bringing to the song a heightened level of musical and verbal self-consciousness, even if later on Veloso and Gil would bring back the ideal of beauty that they once helped to destabilize.

Debunking the idea of beauty was a result of Zé's practices of undoing. Perhaps the degree zero of his strategy can be fixed at the composer's first album, *Grande liquidação*, in the clash between rhythm and lyrics. In the carnival march "Não buzine que eu estou paquerando" ("Don't honk because I'm looking at the girls"), whose style is normally an unambiguous conveyor of joy, turns into a criticism of capitalism's takeover of leisure. The case of "Sabor de burrice" ("A Taste of Stupidity") is even more ironic. Consider the lyrics of the song, which take their form from the Brazilian country music, *música caipira*, a genre associated with folk wisdom and authenticity of the land:

Tem diversas cores
Veja que beleza
Em vários sabores
A burrice está na mesa (1968)

It has many colors
See how beautiful
In many flavors
Stupidity is being served

Another compositional strategy is that of nonsense – for example in "Dodô and Zezé." Since the song is a question-and-answer dialogue between two narrators, it becomes impossible to know if the replies are unfathomably stupid or, on the contrary, extremely smart. Be that as it may, nearly the whole second half of the song is composed of phonological variations on the phrase, "é porque é que é" 'it is because it is': "é porque a que purcá, é porque é que porqué, é porque i qui porqui, é porque oh que porcó," etc.

In the song "Se o caso é chorar" ("If it's a matter of crying"; 1972) of the eponymous album, Zé makes use of a procedure that he would again adopt in the 90s, that of overt plagiarism. Zé's aesthetics of plagiarism, which he would later term "plagi-combination," raises important issues. To begin with, if "plagi-combination," cannot properly be called intertextuality, it is because the market forces governing production render the song less a text than a product. Yet even more significantly, the borrowing of existing material not only calls into question the idea of originality, but also interferes in the way one listens to the original music. According to Zé, in his "Se o caso é chorar," the harmony is the same as a Chopin piano study, but it is also shaped by Tom Jobim and Vinícius de Moraes's well-known "Insensatez."[63] Further, the form, theme, and diction of the song are based on the kitschy songs of Antonio Carlos and Jocafi, which were popular in the 70s. Zé creates a collage of Brazilian popular songs in the second part of the song's lyrics:

Hoje quem paga sou eu
O remorso talvez
As estrelas do céu
Também refletem na cama
De noite na lama
No fundo do copo
Rever os amigos
Me acompanha o meu violão. (1972)

Today I'm the one who pays
Maybe remorse
The stars in the sky
Also twinkle in bed
At night in the mud
At the glass's bottom
See friends again
My guitar accompanies me.

The whole passage is plagiarized: "Today I'm the one who pays" is the title of a tango by Herivelto Martins and David Nasser; "Maybe remorse (is the cause of your desperation)" imitates a line from "Vingança" ("Revenge") by Lupicínio Rodrigues; "At night in the mud" makes a joke on Veloso's "At night in bed" (in which "cama" is replaced by "lama"); "At

63 See especially "Tom Zé appropriates Chopin" on You Tube and http://www.tomze.com. br/ent22.htm.

the glass's bottom" appropriates Ari Barroso's work; and "My guitar accompanies me" is part of Adelino Moreira's "A volta do Boêmio" ("The Bohemian Comes Back"). In this fashion, Zé at once dismantles and rebuilds the tradition of Brazilian popular music by means of collage. Collage was a common technique among Tropicalists, but in Zé, it exchanges its shock value to become an enigma.

It is with his 1973 album, *Tom Zé todos os olhos* (Tom Zé all the eyes), that Zé's methods of experimentation turn increasingly personal. Zé begins to conceptualize what he terms "small bottle openers to be deciphered by the listener."[64]

From 1973 on, the rejection of beauty and regularity acquires a programmatic character; a good example would be Zé's "re-composition" or, better yet, "decomposition" of Dolores Duran's 1950 "A noite do meu bem" ("My darling's night"). Instead of reproducing the original drama- ridden atmosphere, Zé half speaks the lyrics, while an organ's pedal notes and a guitar intervene independently. There is a sharp contrast between the absolute lack of expressivity in Zé voice and seeming attempts by the guitar to bring sensation back, which constitutes an inversion of the voice-instrument relationship common in popular music. The result is one of a tense series of dichotomies: singing and speaking, expression and blankness, song and unsong.

Another example of unsong is "Epic Complex," also from *All the Eyes*. Here the repetition of sounds endows the song with a minimalist character; a rhythmic base composed of percussion

64 See Tom Zé, "O Gênio de Irará: Tom Zé" (1999: 34).

and voices is repeated indefinitely with only a few subtle alterations of timbre. Once again, singing borders on speech, but the violation of this traditional limit becomes radicalized when syllables are spelled out separately, as if the singer or listener were learning to read. The synthesis of song and speech in "Epic Complex" satirizes Brazilian popular composers:

> (speaking-singing)
> Todo compositor brasileiro é um complexado
> (spelling-speaking)
> Por-que en-tão es-sa ma-nia da-na-da, es-sa preo-cupa-ção de fa-lar
> tão sério
> (speaking-singing)
> de parecer tão sério
> de ser tão sério
> de chorar tão sério
> de se sorrir tão sério
> de brincar tão sério
> de amar tão sério?
> Ai meu Deus do céu, vai ser sério assim no inferno! (1973)
> Every Brazilian composer has a complex
>
> Why-this-damn-ma-ni-athis-pre-oc-cu-pa-tion-to-speak-so-se-rious-ly
> to seem so serious
> to be so serious
> to cry so serious
> to smile so serious
> to play so

serious
to love so serious
Dear God, only in hell to be so serious!

In the 1975 LP *Studying Samba*, Zé plays with *samba*'s rhythmic 2/4 pattern, which he decomposes and reworks using polyrhythm and counterpoint – putting all three styles together is unusual in the samba tradition. In "Toc," for instance, he sets counter-metrical pulses in counterpoint to the constant of the rhythmic-harmonic base. In addition, interspersed in the song are electro-acoustic sounds such as horns, moaning, and senseless speaking; the song ends abruptly, without the expected repetition. Incorporating noise is characteristic of Zé's work during this period. In a 1978 television program, one of the last times he would appear in the mass media for a long time, he "plays" a waxing machine (which he called a "enceroscópio" [waxcopium]), saws, emery with an *agogô*, an Afro-Brazilian percussion instrument, and what he termed *Hertzé*, a kind of sound sequencer; all of them had their sounds recorded and were replayed at random.[65] Zé thus goes beyond what Tatit conceives as rendering aesthetics quotidian, for he also brings to the stage an unexpected performative element by utilizing all these instruments and recordings. By introducing "homemade noises" and such devices as the Hertzé, which he considered to be a forerunner of the sampler, Zé moves in the opposite direction in relation to the technologizing of Brazilian popular music.[66] By means of all these procedures, Zé not only decomposes the popular song, but also highlights its limits. His speaking-singing, is both a beginning and

65 See especially Os Alquimistas do Som. On the waxcopium and the Hertzé, see also the DVD *Tom Zé. Jogos de Armar.*

66 See *Tom Zé. Jogos de Armar*: "'Sonhar' ao vivo" and "Passagem de Som ao vivo" on You Tube. The latter, a song that imitates the testing of equipment before a show (passagem de som), is particularly interesting.

an end to song. When he mixes musical and nonmusical sounds, they contaminate each other, which draws attention to the musicality of common objects and the machine-character of electronic instruments, as well as creating an indeterminate gap between them.[67] Zé also exposes, through his "aesthetics of plagiarism," minimalist interventions, and inclusion of vanguard compositional techniques in popular song, the contradiction at the bottom of a significant strand of Brazilian music: the desire to be something more than sheer amusement or pastime; to stand out as something serious, autonomous, and solidly anchored in culture. By stretching these limits, Zé proposes an aesthetics of the song based on defect, noise, lack, and on the negation of finished, "round" beauty (Zé, 2003). In the 70s, Zé's project would become incompatible with MPB pieces that were technically and technologically well-made songs – supported by an increasingly strong culture industry that was quickly abandoning the unconventional and experimental. Zé's project of the unsong, or insufficient song, took shape precisely at a moment when mainstream popular music was consolidated as such, which explains the composer's long internal exile in Brazil, until his rediscovery by David Byrne in the early 90s. Zé's music had become too advanced for what the apparatus of music had become.[68]

With its cultural legitimacy and solid commercial footing, MPB survived with all its strength until the early 80s, after which time phonographic industries would turn to the emergent Brazilian *pop-rock*. It was at this point, after 15 years

---

67 It is worthwhile here to compare Tom Zé to Hermeto Pascoal, who also uses all kinds of everyday objects (and animals as well) to make music. Their use of objects is complementary: whereas Zé plays mechanical utensils, Hermeto creates music from things rural. See, for instance, Pascoal's "Música na Lagoa" on You Tube.

68 See "David Byrne Fala sobre Tom Zé" on You Tube.

of ostracism, that Zé reappeared on the music scene. His most recent work must be seen in a different context: not that of the growth of MPB, but instead, of the crisis of the song tout court. These new circumstances caused Zé to turn his project of the unsong upside down, for today's Brazilian popular music has distanced itself from its original harmonic roundness and melodiousness to become more repetitive and aggressive. Be it Rio's funk, São Paulo's rap, or Bahia's *axé music*, what is at stake is no longer MPB's "good taste," but a pervasive standardization. From Zé's perspective, melodies have become mere excuses for beat patterns; harmony has been reduced to a bare minimum; lyrics are ever more repetitive; and sexualization has reached an apex. Rather than samba, Zé now centers his critical interventions on *pagode*, *samba*'s pop-globalized mutation, and polemicizes against funk and rap. His focus and compositional procedures may have changed, but the creativeness and daring of his critical stance in music have lost none of their force.

FILM

Fernando Meirelles' City of God 14 years later. (with Charles Ponte and José Carlos Felix).

I

In *City of God* (Meirelles, 2002, BR) scene: 20, 1h10min00sec to 46sec, Lil Zé beats Neguinho for having killed his (Neguinho's) girlfriend inside the favela. The problem here was not the deed, but the location; in Rio's shantytowns a monopoly on violence belongs to the drug dealers, hampered only by occasional raids of the police or attacks by enemy gangs. Blood in this scene is literally revealing because it encapsulates a very complex question: that of realism and reality in Third World art in general and in film in particular. But before we can interpret how these images comprising but a few tens of seconds may prove to be so significant, a good deal of contextualizing is necessary

II

When reality is harsh and society clearly unequal, realism appears as the privileged means to portray injustice and mobilize people for change. Suffering reinforces the sense that truth exists; it acts as a gravitational force attracting representation to exhibit things as they really are, as though the impact itself of apparent unfairness were enough at least to start abolishing it. As far as the history of film is concerned, two opposing trends must be mentioned here as basic sources for *City of God*. The first one comes from Sergei Eisenstein's early and groundbreaking experimentations on film montage, which laid bare the inherent artificiality of the medium and showed that realism is not a synonym for spontaneity. Realism is not an enemy of technique; on the contrary, film is a privileged vehicle for social change precisely insofar as it possesses an almost unlimited potential for montage.[69] An opposing position comes from Italian neorealism, however historically contingent and relatively short its duration as a movement might have been. This was a pivotal chapter in the history of film, which set the tone of much of the progressive cinematic productions after World War II. The cinematic and the aesthetic accomplishments of directors such as Roberto Rosselinni, Vittorio de Sica, and Luchino Visconti derived to a great extent from their refusal to resort to standard narrative codes and their adoption of a documentary-like style, which included low budgets, shooting on location, and, most importantly for us here, sole use of non-actors, and which would subsequently be incorporated as intrinsic features of guerilla or counter-cinema. In addition, their films were based on the fundamental assertion that realistic films should not be limited only to an accurate *exposé* of reality's unfairness, but should above all prompt viewers to cross-examine their own lives in society and how they helped social life to be reproduced.

In Brazil, an emblematic expression of realism in film emerged in the 50s with Nelson Pereira dos Santos' influential *Rio 40 Graus* (1955) and *Rio Zona Norte* (1957), which acted as harbingers of the country's most widely known film movement: the *Cinema Novo*. The most concise expression of its aims can be found in Glauber Rocha's famous 1965 manifesto "Aesthetics of Hunger," which advocated cinematic representation of the real Brazil, as opposed to ages-old alienated images of natural plenty, and an amicable folk – an

69 See Eisenstein's discussion on the method to produce a working class film (2003).

alienation that continues to this day in a multitude of films where poverty cannot be seen.[70] In the fifties, this idealized construction of the country was best exemplified by the production of the Vera Cruz Company, which closely followed the Hollywood standards of the time. Thus, instead of self-created idyllic clichés, instead of the bland life of the rich, the works produced by *Cinema Novo*'s iconoclasts challenged other filmmakers to face Brazil's constitutive primitivism and be true to the violence the country both produced and required for its reproduction. The antidote against quotidian, but unseen, aggression should be of the same kind: the representation of existing violence, which would also be necessary to the overthrow of the economic and social system. The irony, however, was that nearly five decades later the issues of social inequality and harshness of the lives of the dwellers of Rio's *favelas* would be met in a film impressively devoid of any critical, let alone revolutionary inclination in the sense proposed by the *Cinema Novo*. After twelve years of its release, Fernando Meirelle's *City of God* deserves to be considered a watershed in the history of Brazilian film, for it stands as an emblematic illustration of a new kind of realism: the conspicuous appropriation of revolutionary cinematic forms by the machinery of the mainstream film industry.

In spite of the presence of much suffering clearly caused by social exclusion, the film bears little relation to any kind of artistic expression aiming to be thought provoking. Its unprecedented combination of the film trends mentioned above produced a type of film that demanded reflection

70 In Bruno Barreto's Bossa Nova (2000), for instance, all apartment windows face Rio's beaches and an English teacher lives in the most expensive neighborhood of the city.

and analysis. Any hasty and careless observation of this film resulted in praise by critics and audiences for the filmmakers' treatment of reality beyond the realm of sheer entertainment. Such viewers lauded, on the one hand, an utterly realistic representation of a traditionally neglected, but culturally immensely important sphere of Brazilian urban reality of drug dealers and the oppressed inhabitants of a *favela*, and, on the other, perfect cinematic technique, which managed to follow the high (and costly) standards of "Hollywood" idiom[71].

Indeed, at first sight, realism in the diegesis is overwhelming and there is absolutely nothing that could be deemed extraneous to the community filmed in particular. Firstly, this was made easier because of the eponymous novel by Paulo Lins, on which the movie was based. The work of fiction started as an ethnographic research (Lins himself was a dweller of the City of God shantytown) and ended up as a breakthrough in realism (Schwarz, 1999). In this sense, considering the 1990's Brazilian cinema context, it is conspicuous that the first responses to *City of God* would

71 The "Hollywood" idiom is defined as a series of conventional codes and stylistic conventions established by the North American film industry in its first decades, which eventually encapsulated its modus operandi. The conventionality of style and production in this kind of film aesthetics, perceptively pointed by Adorno in his critique of the cultural industry, sets a number of restrictions to individual expression (in opposition to Glauber and Espinosa's claims to a freer, more artistic and a less compromised filmmaking). The norms that govern this dominant cinema production are commonly presented in two levels: i) technical devices, which involve the technicalities that are characteristic of mainstream cinema such as continuity editing and soundtrack composition; ii) systems of narrative logics, namely the framework of the classical story, for instance, as a consequence of the characters' psychological motivations and system of cinematic space and time at the service of narrative. These two previous systems are interrelated in a hierarchical order where narrative logic determines time and space. This ranking also accounts for variations in the model, which can be evaluated in terms of their purposefulness once they serve the narrative function.

be entangled by a general understanding that the film would take on the mission of filling the void of cinematic narrative with a social inclination, for, with a few exceptions restricted to small audiences, few films since the two Nelson Pereira dos Santos' aforementioned ones reproduced from the inside the language of the excluded population of a large metropolis such as Rio. Secondly, its apparent precise treatment of the *favelas'* reality is delivered in a modern film aesthetics which makes use of an array of cinematic techniques such as camera virtuosity, a "genuinely Brazilian" sound-tracking in its diversity, soothing and eye-pleasing cinematography, and a non-linear, overwrought editing, synthesizing main-stream and avant-garde cinema elements in a type of neorealist narrative hardly seen before in Brazilian film history. Its outcomes were quite cogent for they created a stir in the audiences and critics alike. While the former embraced the film as an utterly 'artistic' expression of everyday violence commonly depicted by media, hinting a certain familiarity with it (thus it is no wonder that the pattern was soon explored in numerous TV and film productions), the latter shared a relatively similar view that its frenetic rhythm and hyper-exposition to violence would shake off one's apathy and therefore a critic thought a response on the part of audiences would be corollary[72].

Yet, with regards to the favorable and immediate reception of both Brazilian and worldwide audiences, one cannot forget Meirelles' previous and longstanding experience in the advertising market. *City of God* was also recognized for its video-like style in a sense that Meirelles' mastery of a genre known for comprising both 'artistry' and persuasive elements in one single 'product' could subdue both audiences,

72 See City of God reviews in: http://cidadededeus.globo.com/.

who regarded the film as rather accessible, despite its highly aesthetic sophistication for Brazilian's film standards, and critics (notably Nagib, 2006) who praised its aesthetics innovations and its capacity to evade the scheme of mainstream film.

Questions of realism are again central to *City of God* with respect to its adaptation of the source material. Screenwriter Bráulio Mantovani manifests a tendency that has been in play since the beginning of *Cinema Novo*: the attempt to represent the shantytown inhabitants in their self-contained identity, unlike the previous examples of such Brazilian contexts as Nelson Pereira dos Santos' *Rio Zona Norte* (1957), in which the contacts between both the inner and outer spheres are more constant, though both cry out the desire to leave this overwhelmingly uneven context. In that tradition, there is a significant shift in the image of the Other, and its identity counterpoint: in *Rio Zona Norte*, the main characters' feelings towards the outer characters, a somewhat conformist feeling for their inability of transforming completely into the mirrored counterparts[73], whereas Meirelles' depiction reduces the difference between them, implying a naturalistic view that leaving the place and social status attached to it would suffice to make a clean break.

The novel's ethnographic spirit was adequately mirrored in the film's cast. Meirelles declared in several interviews that from the beginning of the production he was aware of the kind of realism he aimed for, one that could rival the novel's, could

73 The inability of Brazilian films (such as the Vera Cruz studios in the fifties) to mimic the American cinema was considered its most original trait (cf. GOMES, 2005), as in the substitution of cowboys for cangaceiros in Carlos Manga's Matar ou correr (1954; To kill or to run, a parody of Fred Zinnermmann's High noon, title translated in Brazil as To kill or to die). This feeling permeates the Brazilian cinema as well as its criticism up to City of God, when Brazilian cinema shows the funding to utilize most of the mainstream cinema techniques.

only be achieved on the screen through spontaneous acting: a mode of acting that, in his opinion, no performer with previous formal dramatic training could accomplish. When asked the reasons to use this casting strategy, Meirelles stated: "I wanted audiences to see Lil Zé, and not an extraordinary performance of Lil Zé"74. Thus, except for a few cases, all actors were members of favela communities. Producers needed over a year to come up with a suitable cast. They first selected 400 hundred people out of 2,000 candidates from community-based drama schools to attend a theater workshop; from them, the 60 main actors and 150 secondary ones were finally chosen.75 However, in spite of Meirelles' observation that the endemic talent of the chosen actors was responsible for the film's success, it is questionable that ethnographic precision could be attained without the collaboration Fátima Toledo, a Brazilian acting coach who developed an original method to extract realistic performances out of non-professional actors – in short, to teach them to become themselves on screen[76]. This mixture of spontaneity and dramatic technique in the actors' preparation also took place in the shooting.

74 Cidade de Deus, commentary on the DVD.

75 For the actor's lives after the film, see Cidade de Deus: 10 anos depois (2012). This documentary shows what happened to some of those who participated in City of God; even though the impulse to convey a sense of variety of destinies is palpable, as if each had just a different one, the gravity of social class can be clearly felt. Most of the actors didn't manage to build a career and some reverted to crime – being true to their characters in the film; the exceptions are Seu Jorge (Mané Galinha), who was already struggling as musician by the time of the shooting, and Alice Braga (Angélica), Sônia Braga's niece, who became a Hollywood star, and came from a solid white, middle class milieu.

76 Afterwards, the film's success also capitalized Toledo's work within Brazilian mainstream film industry; her method became synonymous of realistic performances and a number of recent Brazilian films that were extensively debated for drawing upon similar issues and themes of City of God, such as Elite squad (2007), and Linha de Passe (2008), all had their leading actors coached by her. Not to mention, they were also box office success and internationally awarded.

Meirelles explained that the most effective the way to check out the screenplay's accuracy to a given situation was to observe the actors reaction to it: if for any reason they did not respond positively to what was proposed, the scene had to be rewritten. In this sense, Meirelles concludes that Montonvani's Oscar-nominated script was greatly shaped by the sense of accuracy derived from the cast's intimacy with its own milieu.

Nevertheless, the film's ethnographic precision of criminality coupled with avant-garde shooting and editing did not lead to progressive representation, but to its opposite, the absorption of possible nonconformist energies into the reaffirmation of the *status quo*. It is this apparently contradictory outcome that must be carefully explained. At least five features of mainstream film appear notable in *City of God*:

a. the lack of self-consciousness on the part of the camera. In spite of (or precisely because) of masterful editing, the camera never calls attention to itself, to the fact that it is shooting, that it is a tool: it masterfully erases itself and thereupon shuns any thought of editing manipulation, enhancing the illusion of the wholeness of the reality portrayed. What once had been the result of radical perspectivism is now incorporated in the flow of images. A good example is the 360° camera rotation around Rocket at 4 min 43 sec to 50 sec, which ends the masterful introduction of the film with the runaway chicken. The procedure is symbolically effective in portraying Rocket's in-between position the drug dealers and the police, crime and legality. In this sense, it could lead to reflection – perhaps showing the similarity between both spheres – and the camera could literally be its instrument. Nonetheless, this potential is not actualized, for the same rotation that offered a full, simultaneous viewed of opposed forces, also provides the link for the past as it encircles Rocket with increasing speed. In sum, the whole work of camera movement and editing is daring without being really challenging, innovative but not revolutionary, eye-pleasing but not eye-opening.

b. the nature of music. In *City of God,* the sound underlines the image and does not produce any tension in relation to it. And yet, as in the case of the camera, the music is highly competent. One cannot reproach the film for choosing an inaccurate musical medium, for the samba performed is really one of the kinds of music produced and consumed in the peripheries of Rio de Janeiro. The problem is that samba, or chorinho, or even the later funk is associated with happiness and joy, which can be observed for instance during the flashback to the sixties (23min50sec to 24min30sec), which brings a discontinuity between the nostalgic song about the happy life in the *favelas* and the police's periodic violent raids. Again, that which could generate criticism by means of the clash between a barbaric world and reconciling sound is neutralized, and music in the end helps shaping the images so as to make them more enjoyable.

c. photography. *City of God* is a film in which, for all its unbridled violence, mercilessly shown, the colors in themselves are not aggressive. In most of it brown and grey are the prevailing tones, and only very seldom do vivid red or any other shocking pigment is dominant. Almost all hues are welcoming to the eye, especially in interior locations. Once again, the temporal leap into the sixties serves as a good example to examine the choices of color, which dissolve the tension in a time represented with some nostalgia, as becomes clear with the very agreeable change of palette, from the cold bluish present to a nostalgic ocher past.

d. identification with Rocket, the main character, who narrates the story, eventually manages to get out of the *favela*, and becomes a reliable worker. The good fortune of the individual here overshadows the fact that for the community everything continues to be the same. Identification is a result of a narrative strategy of focalization, which has been a trademark of "Hollywood" film and has been incorporated by most so-called independent productions[77]. It works by means of a narrowing of focus into an individual, thereby detaching him or her from the rest, which becomes a background, and creating empathy between the character and the audience. In *City of God*, chapter 32 of the DVD is emblematic. Having photographed the policemen receiving bribes, Rocket decides to send to the newspaper instead the pictures of Lil Zé's corpse perforated by tens of bullets. In his words: "The picture of the hood will get me the job. This one will make me famous. It'll even make the cover of a magazine. I won't have to worry about Lil Zé anymore. But the cops?" The choice is presented as one between fame and self-preservation, dangerous ambition and prudent conformism. But this is a dilemma as projected by Rocket's eyes, which then tend to become the viewer's. For the real issue at stake is not professional success or even security

77 No wonder that Danny Boyle's Slumdog Millionaire (2008) was immediately compared to City of God. Ironically, despite the resemblance between both, what critics failed to notice was that such similarity reveals a powerful and inescapable process of standardization which, within the logics of cultural production, even the so-called independent films cannot possibly escape.

in itself, but the option for an *individual* project. Exposing the policemen could have been part of political action aimed at changing reality. This possibility is simply repressed in the film and the following scene, where Buscapé is talking to his friend Barbantinho serves only to strengthen it. There, the hero confirms that he managed to get a job as photographer at a newspaper:

Not a job, an internship/
It pays a little, doesn't it? /
A little. /
What about the lady journalist? Was she a good lay?

The change of topic from work to sex, with all its chauvinism, is appeasing; it helps to end the question of Buscapé's choice, which is dissipated in male bonding. The pattern may be seen as an adaptation of Horatio Alger for the peripheral reality of Rio's shanty towns.

d. the production of shocks and the imposition of a high-speed rhythm. It is true that in *City of God* a lack of camera consciousness and identification with the main character would not in principle exhaust the film's critical potentials. It could be argued that the film is complex enough not to take clear sides and not avoid dissonance, conflict and ambiguity. But this is true only insofar as the film's tempo is not taken into account. Once one pays attention to the fast cuts, frenzied camera movements, one realizes that perfect color and sound are here united to hyper-slang and explicit violence in a homogenous whole that fosters reactions of enjoyment somewhat akin to those of any American thriller. *City of God* would then be sufficiently close to allow for identification, but distant enough to provoke excitement, the thrill of shock. There is simply no time left, no holes in the narrative, to allow for thinking or critical judgment[78].

The film then can be seen (literally) as an inverted tour de force, as it were. It is not the case that it manages to create a masterpiece from an unwelcoming setting; quite the opposite, it manages to produce, from the most blatantly dystopic reality, an object of leisure, amusement and diversion (or any word for comfortable cultural consumption that you may find). And this was not achieved owing to faulty technical means, which would distort representation, but by unheard-of technical expertise in the history of Brazilian cinema. Thus the importance of that which would escape the rule of perfected realism.

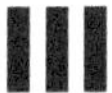

It is precisely the film's technical perfection which calls for a close reading of it as an attempt to find revealing details that could contradict it from the inside. There is an interpretative program in this. Non-computerized films by definition contains in itself more than what it can master: the absence of some post-production touches-up brings to light that no filmmaker, no matter how perfectionist, can control all aspects of a shot.

78 In her very good reading of the film Lúcia Nagib agrees that "Violence, be it in the plot or language, in the end generates the same result aimed at by American commercial film, that is, that of illusionist catharsis. The hallucinating rhythm of the novel is here translated into the fast cuts of digital montage, in the manner of advertisement and the video clip." Nonetheless, she claims that "the film, as well as the novel, evades the scheme [of commercial film] by the importance the narrative acquires." (Nagib, 2006: 150) She can only reach this conclusion because of her positive idea of form, based on the "narrative potential of myth" (150), whereas the history of late modernity could be told as the sustained attempt to reject the organicity and conciliatory aspect of the well made form.

Slowing it down radically in order to show what was always there, visible but unseen, may be a source of inspiration for other media – either slower ones like literature, or faster ones like TV or the internet. The fragment is made of three parts. After the beating starts and Lil Zé kicks Neguinho, we see him from the frame of another room, with his shirt already marked with blood.

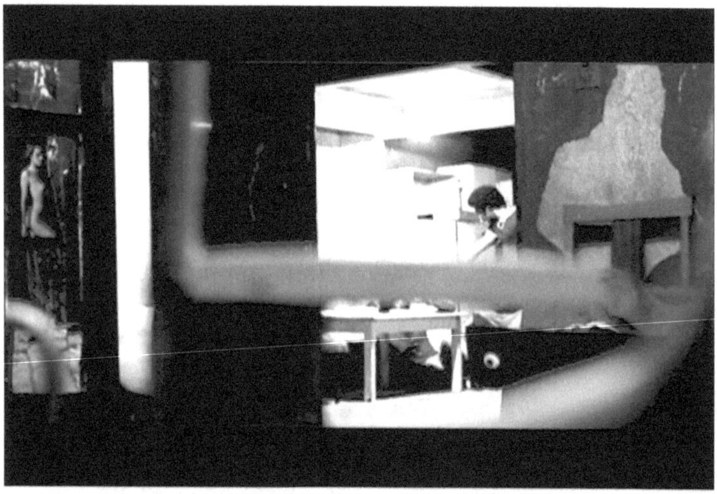

Then the camera comes back to a close up and the cut on the forehead is open.

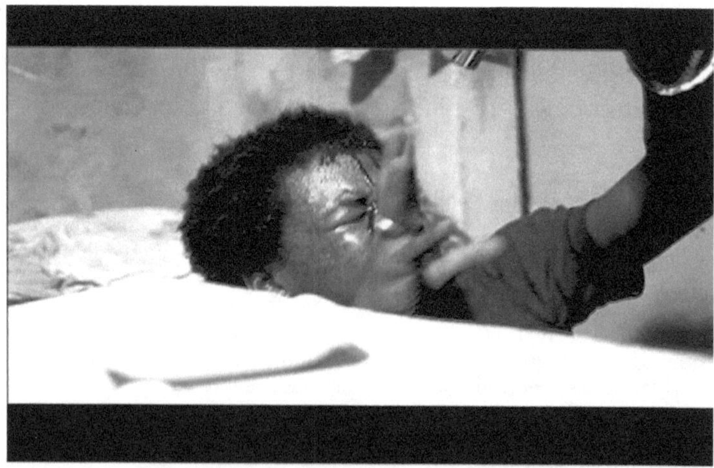

When just some seconds later, viewed again back from the outside room, he leaves the shanty, no blood can be seen either on his forehead or his shirt.

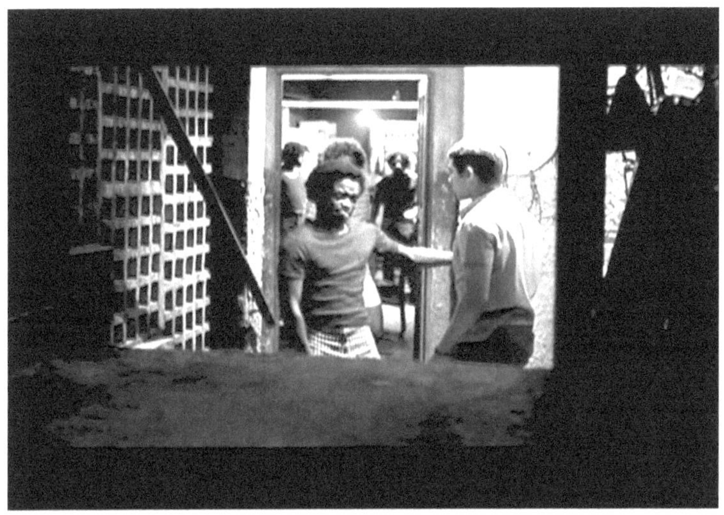

Thus the dialectic of blood in the scene: on the one hand, there is the perfect construction of a cut on Neguinho's forehead, starting with a darkened frame with the camera on frantic motion, but which lets one discern a revolver strike before several kicks. Only after this does Neguinho appear at the center, and a little blood can already be discerned. In the next frame, one sees Lil Zé and Neguinho from a more distanced perspective of a darkened room, through a door, and when the camera returns blood flows generously on the contorted face in a quasi close up. But the virtuoso-like timing of the cut is undermined just a few seconds later, for when Neguinho leaves the shanty, the formerly clearly visible blood stain on his shirt and on his forehead has already dried up and can no longer be seen.

Now think about the loophole that the goof reveals, a seminal flaw a in the most perfect technical rationality. By laying bare the device (as the Russian Formalists would put it), it shows more than only holes in the whole. To be sure, goofs are far from belonging to the nobler elements of film theory; the claim that they can be cognitively relevant would more likely than not be met with surprise, if not suspicion, by critics. At least two main reasons can be thought of here. First, goofs are generally seen as the pastime of obsessive viewers, who perhaps want to prove their superiority regarding the object they have in front of themselves, an object in relation to which they may entertain love-hate sentiments. Second, goofs are normally not emphatic by virtue of their sheer commonness. Virtually all films have something in them that went wrong, to the point that the obsessive viewer may eventually rightly see as a goof something that was not.

And yet, two other reasons may be adduced to argue for the relevance, at least a partial one, of goofs. In the first place, they imply a different kind of seeing. Anyone who has spent time looking for them (or even trying to verify them), is acquainted with the speed they impose on the viewer. The absurdly slow movement of the frame-by-frame pace generates another kind of object altogether, something in between a painting and moving pictures. This experience as such is one that deserves to be pondered. Furthermore, however, one should be able to differentiate goofs according to the kind of meaning they engender, for if in many cases they are but a curiosity – only revealing, say, the incompetence of an actor who does not stop breathing after being dead – in other instances they may produce a kind of sense that is relevant to what is at stake in the film itself. It is exactly in this sense that the goof above allows us the following interpretation which may be regarded as a true dialectics of blood.

In a film highly praised for its meticulous technical care, the juxtaposition of the three frames discovers more than a simple imprecision regarding verisimilitude and editing cohesion. Indeed, the three planes are themselves revealing in their screen formats and the particular fashion with which they represent violence. In terms of framing, no doubt, all three captures can be read as oppressive, considering the fact that the screen is not used in its entirety, which suggests that violence of the gangs, personified by Lil Zé, must be seen from a hidden position, that it is ubiquitous and thus oppresses the whole community. An attentive look reveals that the first frame capture inverts the conventional dimensions of the screen established by the Hollywood mainstream cinema, for the traditional horizontal axis is reframed by the door into an extreme vertical, making the actual violence a central, but not exclusive place in the background scene. Meanwhile, the foreground occupies a prominent position not only by framing the action as in a portrait but by adding a number of set-establishing elements, such as the pictures of a naked woman (which, framed by horizontal and vertical lines, resembles a piece of film regularly cut out from daring scenes during the editing process or, in many cases, requested to be excluded by censorship), a shattered wall and scattered debris all over the place. An extreme balancing between brightness and darkness also corroborates the picture's sense of realism. The contrast of light produced by the use of *chiaroscuro* in the scene's photography, in which the excessive white light coming from the light bulb is restricted to the background room, produces a sense of realist three-dimensionality and reminds one of the kind of spotlight used during torture sessions. Equally noteworthy is the pipe tube placed conveniently in a position that prevents any view of the gun, working somehow as a band, covering certain eyesore parts, frequently imposed by censors onto those films/scenes considered morally inappropriate or too wanton and obscene. In a nutshell, in view of all these elements comprised in this single frame, it is tempting to read it as alluding to the daring guerilla anti-cinema aesthetics for which *City of God* was widely and mistakenly taken.

By contrast, the second capture points to the opposite direction as it stands as a typical instance of mainstream film screening: the white table flattens the image, bringing about a characteristic widescreen frame[79]. The immediate outcome of such radical inversion exposes one of the major efforts of "Hollywood" aesthetics: the manipulation and control of any repulsive or shocking scene to maintain a certain level of tolerance to viewers. On one hand, the extreme close-up projects the core of the violence to the screen as a whole, which would free the audience's attention from any other visual distraction, leaving therefore no other option but the rawness of the scene; on the other, it produces an opposite effect compared to the previous capture inasmuch as the cleanliness of frame with its extensive whiteness and brilliance encircling the Neguinho lessens the brutality of the action by stripping down the all the peripheral debris of visual information

79 The cinema, spawning from nineteenth-century photography, presents the horizontal axis bigger than the vertical by no accident, in convergence to both social infrastructure (the family size and city architecture) as well as aesthetic tendencies (the modernist characteristic horizontality).

which composed the first frame. The extreme close-up thus creates a misleading effect regarding the development and enhancement the scene's violence, reinforcing *City of God*'s dialectics between realistic and conventional film aesthetics. Its abrupt approximation to the core of the action can be easily mistaken as a movement towards the paroxysm of the violence. However, the use of a standard screen format such as cinemascope, though brief, does no more than assuage the impact and realism of the action represented in the previous frame – confining then the harshness of the violence within the limits of a screen format familiar to the viewers.

Finally, in the third frame the composition of the viewpoint reaches a middle-ground angle between the two previous and extreme divergent captures. Once again, the screen format reveals a good deal of the means in which the bloodshed is depicted. Here the mitigation of violence resides not only in the aforementioned and unprecedented vanishing of the blood from Neguinho's T-shirt, but mostly by the symptomatic manner in which the image resembles a screen composition much closer to TV-like framing. What immediately draws attention about this image in particular lies in its succession of "a frame-within-a-frame", displayed in *mise en abîme*. Its disposition produces a new rearrangement of the pictorial elements that constituted the two previous ones. Likewise, each of these frames, in turn, encloses each character (Neguinho, Bené and Lil Zé) in an order rightly in accordance to their position regarding the scene's resolution. Thus, Neguinho, in the foreground frame, escapes practically uninjured, but is banished from the *favela* by Bené. The second frame is delimited by the shanty's door and, in it, we can see

Bené standing right in its center. This midway position between the foreground frame (Neguinho) and the background where Lil Zé stands also corroborates Bené's position and role in the scene's unfolding of events for, in the confrontation between the two other characters, he is the one who intervenes in the course of the beating and prevents Neguinho from being killed by Lil Zé. Finally, the third frame right in the background displays Lil Zé left "powerless" after Bené takes over the situation and decides what is best to do with Neguinho. In the same way which his menacing presence loses power in the course of the action, the composition of the three frames *en abîme* relegates him to the very back of the picture where he can only be recognized by the contour of his body since it is mostly out of focus.

In addition to that, the juxtaposition of these three frames is yet encapsulated by a larger and much more far-reaching pattern of screen format, namely, that of television. In contrast to the axis inversion of the first caption to extreme vertical or even the flattening horizontal axis featuring the cinemascope format of the second one, the disposition, arrangement and length of the frames in the third caption reveals, in a series of compositional elements, an unprecedented resemblance to a conventional television screen. Again, in comparison to the two previous ones, it is a midway in which the two vertical edges, created by the lighting effect, slightly covering the right and left sides of the screen. It is not by chance, then, that such screen format seems the most suitable to conclude this sequence, because the resolution of the conflict in a "happy ending", after the realist representation of violence through the guerilla-aesthetics of the first frame, could not be better met and transmitted than in a medium well-known for its striking capability for accommodating anything within a reified schema. Such an assertion becomes even more conclusive if we take into account the imperative power that television has in the lives of Brazilians: it is by far the most important and sometimes the only means through which information (factual or fictional) can be accessed by the people.

In this sense, the progression of the three frames from the daring anti-cinema guerilla aesthetic to TV-screen format can be read as an instance of the film's internal logic in its capacity to absorb a variety of film codes and conventions. This is supported by a design that constantly favors a sense of the audience's immediate and straightforward contact with reality in its wholeness. As the action unfolds, however, any cinematic device, composition or arrangement that was first introduced in the film narrative as a novelty or in a non-conventional fashion is rapidly, or eventually, adapted and adjusted into a standard pattern. And *City of God* impresses for its striking ability to manipulate such transitions and skillfully perform such adjustment both in terms of form and content. To sum up, the series of frames starts with the impact of an image marked by the irregularity of all elements of the *mise-en-scéne*, as way to convey the ideia that reality's harshness resides not only in the cruelty of the action itself (the beating of Neguinho and his potential death), but it is endemic to its surroundings as well (the disarray and disorder of the decadent setting captured by the viewpoint of the frame); it then progresses to the standard symmetry and cleanliness of mainstream film codes in which the enhancement of the action leaves little or no room for the sense of realism previously established by the conjunction of action and setting; it finally reaches the balance and the adjustment of the far-reaching TV-like-format where the portrait of daring issues such as violence and brutality operates according to particular pre-established conventions based above all on bourgeois moral values. As in the sex scenes in erotic films regularly exhibited on cable TV, cruelty in this media format can be ever suggested and fully exploited but never shown in its entirety. Likewise, the third frame stands as an impressive example of such logic not only due to its similarity and conformity to the TV-screen format, but by the way that the symptomatic (and mistaken) vanishing of the blood corroborates the idea that any overt manifestation of cruelty/violence ought to be immediately eliminated.

The sequence's content can also be interpreted as a restaging of the form of the frames. The beginning of the sequence subverts a traditional order of action development by placing the climax of the action right in the first scene, thus suggesting to the audience that there might be few or no limits in the treatment of violence. Nonetheless, such promise does not last long, for what first appeared to be another daring portrait of gratuitous violence is rapidly softened by Bené's interference in favor of less drastic resolution for the conflict. In the course of the action, therefore, Bené plays a meditative role much similar to the TV-like frame configuration. If the outburst of overt, overwhelming violence and accurate sense of realism that Lil Zé impersonates is much analogous to the guerilla aesthetics described in the first frame, Bené's interference in the action and mediation for its "good-for-all" resolution is also akin to adjustment attained by the third frame, emulating the mediation of culture by capital[80]. Furthermore, the vanishing of the blood alongside the TV-like configuration of this frame fits perfectly the standard narrative pattern of famous Brazilian soap operas in which the relief of tension is always followed by a happy and well-adjusted ending.

But here is our point: the blood presented was realistically manufactured, and perfectly so, mobilizing as it did, avant-garde editing. But that was not the blood of reality; the blood of reality cannot be represented as such and that is why its *absence* on the shirt of the favela inhabitant may stand as a sign for what would be real thing. Since, as we now saw, the actors recruited for the film have come from favela communities, including City of God itself, in the errors of the film they *emerge as they really are, in such a way that they could never do, if one tried to represent them directly.* In other words, it is the eruption of reality in realism that can only take place through this manipulation, that otherwise would not appear as such. When one places the goof at the center, the *absent* blood points to the unreality of realistically contrived bleeding. The real is not there, or, better yet, it makes itself felt by a lack indiscernible to the eye, which can only emerge in the utmost effort of vision.

80 It suffices to argue that this mediation favors the mere *survival* of guerilla formats when confronted with the Hollywood mode of production; conversely, closer to the climax of the film, as Neguinho tries to revenge his humiliation by killing Lil Zé, and Bené's attempt to revert the mediation ends up with his own death, in a moralistic outcome pro media standardization.

THEORY

Towards a Model of Inclusive Exclusion: Marginal Subjectivation in Rio de Janeiro.

I

One does not have to be a fierce advocate of dialectics to consider the claim that the exercise of dystopic imagination may represent a necessary stage to think a better world. If it is good to know the worst, that does not mean, however, that cognition of the truly bad is immediately accessible or unproblematic. Such knowledge demands rather that one walk the tight rope between turning the object of scrutiny into an example, thus weakening it of its impact, diluting the pain it generates in a chain of causality; or granting it the status of the absolutely singular, which approximates it to the ineffable (always so dangerously close to the religious) or the monument (solidified history ready to be sold). The idea of the model, as developed by T.W. Adorno in *Negative Dialectics* and *Critical Models*, for instance, offers a fruitful way out of this dilemma. For just as constellations or force fields, two other of his favorite figures of thought, models are ad hoc constructions, "not causal examples for, or explanations of, critical theory. They *are* that theory, but always at the same time reflection, objective discussion and intervention in consciousness, which needs to be criticized when it is no longer a reflex of reality, but just comprehends and affirms what merely happens." Models furnish, in other words, the illustration of a thesis they themselves only suggest; they constitute the "extension [*Ergänzung*] of a theory that only in them is unfolded" (Demirovič, 2003: 7).[81]

81 See also my review of this interesting book, "Uma Iniciativa a ser Emulada" (2004). Also available online.

This methodological framework is particularly adequate for dealing with such hazy notions as that of subjectivity, a category that is at the same time both too broad and too narrow, too general to be handled in abstract, but also too specific to be immediately extrapolated. The case here, however, is less that of subjectivity as such than of subjectivation, the *production* of subjects under determinate conditions. This stress on process rather than constitution allows one to eschew the false opposition between determination and freedom, structure and agency, for the production of subjects is both a precondition for and the result of the dynamics of *social reproduction*. Only through the incessant engendering of determinate subjects, in other words, is society able to continue to exist as such; on the other hand, subjectivation is never truly seamless, domination is always incomplete and countered by resistance (perhaps even ontologically preceded by it).[82] The tension involving these two drives, which may be translated, *mutatis mutandis*, into the contradiction of forces (resistance) and relations (domination) of production, or re-inscribed into a dialectic of nature (as in Adorno & Horkheimer's *Dialectic of Enlightenment*,[83] where subjectivation is produced through the interiorization of sacrifice, a practice of exchange) – this tension is responsible for social change and transformation.

That the social process of reproduction is ultimately both acephalous, and non-teleological – no matter how

82 To demonstrate this is one of the greatest achievements of Hardt & Negri's bestseller Empire (2000), a strong influence underlying this text. The reader will notice, however, that the main difference, the one allowing for the tense mediation of the Frankfurt School lies in the handling of the notion of lack, which Hardt & Negri's Deleuzian ontology refuses to take into consideration.

83 See also Alfred Schmidt's clear exposition of this in his Der Begriff der Natur in der Lehre von Marx (1993).

sophisticated or advanced systems of policy making may be, or how forcefully ideology may try to impose itself giving a meaning to life – is but a consequence springing from all that. It represents one of Marx's greatest achievements, and has inspired all traditions of Marxism ever since.[84] But such "acephality" and lack of a telos at hand has reached an extreme degree today, for when the crisis has become endemic and war (in its diverse forms) a perennial state (Hardt & Negri, 2004: 1-96), much if not all of the controlling powers, both governmental and ideological, are devoted solely to maintenance of the status quo, the sheer administration of turbulence, with no predictable exit in sight. In Rio de Janeiro, the raging coexistence of domination and resistance, repression and revolt can no longer be concealed; it fills the daily news and seems dangerously to trigger the opposite reactions of either proto-fascist aspiration for total oppression, or sheer resignation in anomie. Marginal subjectivation play a fundamental role in all this – "marginal," indeed, in its useful double meaning in Portuguese as both "peripheral" and "criminal," an adjective that most appropriately links the logical/topographic to the juridical. In its two senses, then, marginality in Rio did not originate in a plan; on the contrary, it was the result of a long history of failed attempts at planning the city and its environment – but one more illustration of the Third World's curse of eternal beginnings and miscarried projects.[85] I would like to approach marginal subjectivation in Rio as the product of three intersecting vectors combining into a dynamic model. The first one concerns the withering

84 An up-to-date, masterful exposition of it can be found in David Harvey (2003).

85 For a recent good overall description of Rio's history see Lessa (2001).

away of the performative effect of the law's universality. That all are equally subject to the law represents one the greatest achievements of the Enlightenment in its struggle against privileges of birth; underlying it is an assertion of immanence against transcendent justifications for the structure of the world, as, say, totemic narratives or theories of divine right. The coming into being of the law's abstract nature corresponds to the transition from closed to open societies, as it was influentially developed by Lukács in his early *The Theory of the Novel* (1971). This seemingly far-fetched trans-historical observation is justified here inasmuch as Brazil's partial insertion in modernity, its preservation of colonial pre-/non- /anti-modern social traits, has long been a familiar *topos* in Brazilian critical theory, where they were either blamed for hindering modernizing efforts, or lauded as the other of capitalism. It so happens, however, that in this case no residues are to be found anymore: the law's claim for universality can no longer be ignored by anyone; its former strength, that is, its potential to approach, summon and mobilize subjects to transform an unjust reality has been completely exhausted. For as a result of increasing social interaction generating a totally socialized society,[86] with the transformation of Rio into a metropolis, the spreading out of systems of communications and the like, the call of the law is no longer a novelty, and the subjective effects it once certainly generated are no longer available. It is important to emphasize this because of the somewhat different valence of the law in Brazilian theoretical discourse, for here, where

86 The expression (vergesellschaftete Gesellschaft) comes from Adorno's sociological writings and designates a social formation totally mediated by the principle of exchange. In my reading below I substitute the concept of interpellation for it, which seems to me to be particularly relevant in a situation of material scarcity and symbolic overabundance.

the institutionalized struggle for equality has a quite recent history, its positive side is more easily seen, whereas in the so-called First World the oppressiveness of the law's universality may be more immediately apparent (hence the emphasis on transgression an so forth). In sum, then, the claim for equality – its currency – is by now so widespread that no matter how distorted or mediated it has lost the power to liberate subjects, it has become a commonplace.

Of course, taken at face value, this is not something to be regretted. It represents rather a social achievement; it is one face of progress, insofar as it conceptualizes citizenship as *formally* all-inclusive. Nevertheless, it is in sharp contrast to actual social exclusion, the second vector to be considered.

Be it in terms of access to welfare, to education, public health, housing programs, or in relation to the consumption of goods, the marginal population in Rio has very little or no access to them. To be sure, privation is a complex concept to handle, for it is always mediated by culture and the specific degree of development of the forces of production. Calling attention to the former, Adorno remarks that hunger, "considered as a natural category, can be satisfied with grasshoppers and gnats, a repast to many wild animals. To satiate the concrete hunger of civilized men, it is necessary that they received something that does not disgust them, and in disgust and its contrary the whole of history is reflected" (Adorno, 1972: 392; see also my "Adorno in Brazil", in this volume). This means that needs, however deep and rooted in psychological/physiological impulses, are never merely natural (one may die of hunger surrounded by grasshoppers and gnats), but it does *not* mean that they are merely cultural. Since, as Adorno claimed very early on, history is natural and nature is a historical category,[87] particular needs must be measured against the background of the total development of the forces of production, which always points to a dialectics of nature. It is very different to starve in a tribal, "primitive" society during a drought than to do so under the rationalized control of nature – hence, of course, the absurdity of capitalist crises, where privation is caused precisely by overproduction.

In Rio de Janeiro, need must be considered in the context of successive failures in development projects, of industrial modernization and "catching up" with developed countries.[88] Resulting from the coexistence of these two vectors, the exhaustion of the performative force of legality claims and the incomplete, probably already doomed inclusion of the country in the so-called First World, a baleful kind of enlightened skepticism takes shape. Since the ideology critique of equality is immanent to life itself (people experience it every day), and since the claim for equality is ubiquitous, the latter can be neither ignored nor really believed in. Since legality becomes that which is foreign, and no overall social project can really be envisioned, any political plan of action not emerging inside the community of the excluded – including those genuinely alternative or progressive political projects – are likely to be met with disbelief if not with animosity.

---

87 Cf. Adorno, "The Idea of Natural History" (1984).

88 In this context, it is worthwhile to call attention to Robert Kurz's O colapso da modernização (1999), which had a particular strong impact in Brazilian critical theory, especially through of Roberto Schwarz's review of it (1999). The vicissitudes of Brazilian developmentism have been exhaustively analyzed by Celso Furtado.

The third vector is related to the discourse of commodities, which here generates an interesting case of inclusive exclusion. This is produced by means of the clash between the universality presupposed by advertisement, ever more inseparable from all commodities,[89] and the very restricted access the poor have to them. The language commodities are structurally formed in that it does not differentiate addressees, but summons all within its reach; again, modernization plays a fundamental role here, insofar as semiotic overproduction occupies all available social spaces in Brazil. Thriving on a tradition that never fully separated the public from the private,[90] the audiovisual sector found no barriers to its expansion. In Rio, but also in almost all populated areas of Brazil, all interstices can be accessed by any of the means of transmission of signs, radio, TV, or outdoors advertisement.[91] Even (or especially) the dispossessed cannot help being bombarded by signs; semiotic silence has increasingly become an expensive commodity.

The fundamental category to deal with this state of affairs, an overwhelming proliferation of messages in a context of material scarcity, is that of interpellation. Originally theorized by Althusser in his famous "Ideology and Ideological State Apparatuses" (1971), the concept has been widely criticized by both social scientists and (Lacanian) psychoanalysts.[92]

---

89 See here Christoph Türcke's discussion of the formula esse est percipii, being is being seen, as the fundamental ontological tendency in postmodernity, in his pathbreaking Erregte Gesellschaft. (2002).

90 The reference here, of course, is Sérgio Buarque de Hollanda's characterization of the homem cordial in his fundamental Raízes do Brasil (2003).

91 TV in particular occupies a central position in Brazil, much more so than elsewhere. Its role in Brazilian culture is fruitfully investigated by Kehl and Pucci Videologias (2004).

92 It would be beyond the scope of the essay to reproduce the whole

Althusser's focus on the state seems outdated in times of neoliberalism and governmental deregulation, while his concern with disciplinary procedures achieved their most refined form in Foucault, who furthermore, theorized the passage from discipline to control as the dominant feature of social domination. On the other hand, however, Judith Butler's *The Psychic Life of Power* (1997) has rehabilitated the concept for the process of subject formation. According to Butler, there is a logical impossibility involved in the constitution of the subject: through the call of the other it is established by means of a self-referential movement, a turning to itself that in the same gesture inaugurates the self. Discussing a passage where Althusser describes a policeman hailing someone, Butler observes: "It is important to remember that the turn toward the law is not necessitated by the hailing; it is compelling, in a less than logical sense, because it promises identity" (108). Now, this description can be easily adapted to describe the pragmatics of commodification, for by means of advertisement commodities simultaneously approach and shape subjects.

Their "hey, you!" is rigorously universal and increasingly inescapable. Moreover, this partial reformulation would not be unfaithful to Althusser's own intention, for with the publication of his notes under the title of *Sur la reproduction* (1995), of which "Ideological State Apparatuses" is a part, two points become clear: first, that the project was a tentative one, open to different re-elaborations; second, that the emphasis should fall on the process of social reproduction, and should likewise have society as its core. This would be a proper rebuke

controversy involving the concept. Reference should be made however to Pêcheux (1997), Žižek (1989; 1999) and Butler, Laclau & Žižek (2000).

to Dolar (1993), who argues that Althusser fails to account for a remainder in the process of subjectivation, that "little bit of surplus" (92) or excess that would correspond to the presence of the Lacanian Real.

The problem here is one of focus, for due to its own theoretical framework, its concerns and not least its own past and scope, psychoanalysis must *somehow* be related to the individual and her symptom. It is by definition unable to treat society as a changing whole and to explain how, by being self-contradictory, it can *reproduce* itself. In order to do this it would have to acknowledge that the remainder and eventually the Real is a product of society in its dialectical relationship with nature, a heresy to the Lacanian creed. The performative, subject-creating interpellation of commodities can be fruitfully inserted into an "actantial" framework *à la* Greimas. Patrick Charaudeau discusses it in an unpretentious work (1983) that presents important and unexpected resonance for marginal subjectivation. For according to him, "advertisement sets up a narrative organization in which the addressee occupies the place of an actant endowed with a Lack, in such a way that becoming aware of his or her lack incites him or her to become the Agent of a Search (to overcome the Lack) in which the Object is presented through that which the Product offers. The Product thus functions as the Helper in this Search" (Charaudeau, 1983: 122). "Incite" ("*inciter,*" in French) could be translated here as "summon," or "enforce an interpellation," in a kind of discourse that subjectifies in the process of multiplying lack(s), and inserts/includes the subject in a narrative where it only exists in the process of consumption, from which it is excluded.

Summing up, then, these three vectors – first, the weakening of the performative equality-claim of the law; then, material privation, poverty, and lack of access to welfare and the like, and, finally, the overwhelming summoning of commodities – frame a situation in which the pair inclusion/exclusion presents itself as multi-layered. In its formal character, the law includes all (for one thing, the police and the judicial apparatus do not let one forget that); on the other hand, material exclusion is a social fact; the appeal of commodities, finally, is ubiquitous. The explosive nature of this combination should be obvious, deriving as it does from the interaction among abstract/formal legality, concrete need and the universal, even coercive stimulation of desire carried out by commodities. Its utterly dystopic nature should also be clear: in sharp opposition to Leftist hopes of the past the excluded prove to be, not revolutionary subjects, but their opposite, precisely those who are the most included inside a capitalist logic of desire.

What is less evident is that such a dystopic picture also poses important problems for (literary and political) representation, which are in fact related to the question of handling two contradictory tendencies. On the one hand, approaching scarcity and poverty groups is no easy task; it requires an inside view on the part of the author/writer, who normally belongs to another social class. In order not to project his or her own desires onto the excluded (there are so many such projections: naiveté, purity, spontaneity, revolt, authenticity, solidarity etc.) the researcher must find ways of bridging the gap and of speaking naturally a language that as a rule is not his or her own. What is more, unlike traditional ethnographic research with indigenous groups, working on/ with the socially excluded may involve a clash of classes, sometimes being even dangerous for the middle class scholar. The other difficulty is of a different nature, namely that of discovering procedures to deal with an abundance of messages and signs constantly bombarding subjects. In this case, in other words, the kind of language needed is not that of the ex-centric, but that of the negative itself, a kind of language that in the process of countering semiotic overproduction becomes aware of its own semiosis, of the fact it cannot but reproduce that which it is against: how to deal with excitement in writing, which is the fundamental aim of advertisement, without reproducing that which should be shunned.

II

All these remarks could be taken as a preface to Paulo Lins' path-breaking bestseller *Cidade de Deus* (2002), which in turn must be viewed as working them out. Indeed, the book is a perfection of mixtures, more the result of the tense cohabitation of opposites than of the celebration of hybridity or difference. The first of them concerns the precariousness of the opposition of reality and fiction. Originating in a project on cultural anthropology supervised by Alba Zaluar at the State University of Rio de Janeiro (UERJ), the novel is made of "true" stories that circulate in the apartment complex *Cidade de Deus*, properly named a *neofavela* by Lins. The housing project itself stands as a perfect example of a failed attempt at modernization. Originally planned to be a workers' heaven to house the victims of the 1966 floods, which destroyed several favelas in Rio, the place very soon became a no man's land where the State (read police) had only intermittent control.

This poses interesting questions as to the text's status, its right to be literature and to be called a "novel." *Cidade de Deus*' claim to literariness comes actually from a compellingly original interaction between form and content, where the latter stands for oral raw material collected and the former for its narrative structuring, the organization of the tales and the development of a proper style of presentation, sometimes endowed with a puzzling lyrical quality. The sense of fictionality is derived from this combination of elements into a totality, whose precise nature will be discussed below, but which appears intentional and gives the text the semblance of an artifact; the sense of reality comes with the undaunted exhibition of the stories told, so unlike anything else in the Brazilian literary tradition: a mixture of local-color typicality with unheard-of violence, at first only imaginable at the highest degree of urban depersonalization. Given the absurdity of reality, this is one of those typical cases when its faithful rendering coincides with a seemingly delirious working of the imagination.

A second interesting case of blurring of boundaries is to be found in the relationship between literature and criticism. The traditional representation of it sees the latter as dependent on the former; as the expression goes, it is "secondary literature." In the case of *Cidade de Deus* the opposite is true. Were it not for the support of prominent Brazilian critic Roberto Schwarz it is doubtful whether the manuscript would have found an editor, but it is certain that it would never have been published by *Companhia das Letras*, the most prestigious publishing house in the country. Furthermore, much of the rancorous character of the ensuing debate (see Mello 2000) would be unthinkable without Schwarz's review in *Folha de São Paulo* on Independence Day (Sept. 7th, 1997) praising the work.[93] Regardless of the merit of novel and essay (the former a breakthrough, the latter an impeccable analytical piece), criticism in Brazil now seems to outweigh literary production; it looms sovereign even before literature is produced, let alone after it is published.[94]

Finally, the third case involving a mixture of opposites is a consequence of what was said above, and it concerns the reliance of recent Brazilian fiction on science and scientific methodology for working out its raw materials (Camenietzki, 2000). However, this revitalizing source of inspiration and dialogue should not be considered a purely cultural phenomenon, a stylistic feature in the periodization of the present, for it is anchored in a material situation in which public universities play a fundamental role. Being really public, in the sense of being free, and in Brazil not (yet) completely destroyed by neoliberalism, they allow for the frequent encounter of the popular with the cultivated, especially in the humanities, where, due to low salaries, competition to enter the universities is very low. It is the sheer precariousness of the job market that makes it difficult for the social whole to maintain symbolic capital in the hands of the upper and middle classes. One just needs to remember that before joining Zaluar's project, Paulo Lins studied literature at the Federal University of Rio de Janeiro (UFRJ) for the following equation to become suggestive: neofavela dweller + ethnographic

---

93 The essay was republished in Schwarz (1999).

94 I owe this insight to Marcos Natali, whom I thank.

methodology + literary ambition = *Cidade de Deus*.[95] All these features point to a very complex stage for the production of marginal subjectivities. Critics have already repeatedly called attention to the most obvious constitutive element in the text, its overwhelming realism, the verisimilitude to the real *Cidade de Deus*. For the novel does manage to naturally inhabit the neofavela's universe, to the point that it "becomes a discursive event of a new – political and literary – subject of enunciation" (Ribeiro, 2003: 128). The text is keen to exhibit a whole gamut of popular traits, including kinds of food, beliefs, and patterns of behavior that at times on the verge of the fantastic, thus uncannily blending merciless naturalism with quasi magic realism. The ghetto's language becomes most conspicuous, beginning with the names themselves, always nicknames, always given, most often in the diminutive form: "Inferninho," "Pardalzinho," "Zé Miúdo," the main characters after whom the book's chapters are named, but also "Barbantinho," "Busca Pé," "Tutuca," "Passistinha"... In the City of God, proper and last names never designate legal persons. Nouns and verbs, too, are so faithfully reproduced that even for native speakers of Brazilian Portuguese the novel demands the kind of work required by foreign texts, in which the meaning of certain words has to be derived from their occurrences and repetitions. This amazing immersion in the language is coupled with an equally faithfulness of point of view. The worldview of the *neofavelados* is never transcended, for one never feels the intrusion of a foreign voice raising itself above the

95 It would be interesting to compare the kind of subjectivation proposed here to a strictly middle class one, in which case the work Mirian Goldenberg could parallel that of Alba Zaluar as a source of ethnographic inspiration. In fact, her recently edited *Nu & Vestido* [Naked and Dressed] (2002), a coherent pun on Lévi-Strauss' famous book, *The Raw and the Cooked*, provides the intellectual "raw material" for the description of middle class subjectivation in Rio through corpolatry.

narrative material to pass judgment, moralize or analyze. The degree of immanence attained is nothing short of stunning.

But the cogent reproduction of the local is here coupled with an intriguing universal-negative impulse. First, because of the undeniable inclusion of the illicit: drug dealers in *Cidade de Deus* are in fact part of a full-fledged capitalist system linked to both legal and illegal branches of production. As pawns of a system they are disposable, being either killed or arrested before long. This accounts for the radical lack of any teleology in the book; strictly speaking, the text can have a beginning but not an end, for in spite of all inside material and the excitement of particular stories they are all interchangeable in the sense that they are part of an open-ended chain of violence where motivation cannot be really differentiated from randomness. To be sure, there is a spiraling effect in the text since as the narrative progresses drug dealers become ever younger and die sooner, at the same time that criminal organization/rationalization seems to increase (Schwarz, 1999: 166). Nonetheless, this is never theoretically worked out by the text and it behooves the critic to reach a satisfactory conclusion or to speculate about the possible limits at stake. The narrativization of chaos leads to a strange configuration, with negativity depriving terror of its initial impact and posing urgent ethical problems for the reader. For even the most shocking scene in the text, a detailed description of a jealous husband sawing, hammering and dismembering his newborn, does not stay for long in the reader's mind, being succeeded by several other atrocities in eventually almost boring repetition.

The cinematographic nature of the writing, its vivid images and dialogues (no doubt in part responsible for the success of Meirelles' film) is undermined by a recurrent structural marginal pattern, reiterated ad nauseam: initiation of person "x" in crime → stealing, robbing and/or killing → being killed → initiation of person "y" etc.

What is the import of all that for marginal subjectivation? It is fair to say that *Cidade de Deus* offers both less and more than ethnographic or sociological research. Less, because the novel's strength, its confinement to the community of *Cidade de Deus*, prevents it from establishing links with the world outside the apartment complex, in particular with other social discourses, legal or political. Even the effects of the media are but obliquely alluded to.[96] To understand fully how drug dealing is inserted in consumerist society one should turn instead to Zaluar's latest book (2004). But in spite of that – or rather because of it – *Cidade de Deus* exhibits something that analytical writing cannot by definition transmit, a utopic impulse at the very kernel of a dystopic structured chaos: the overwhelming nature of desire (*male* desire, to be sure). It is not only the desire for power, which, as all drug dealers in *City of God* know deep inside, eventually it leads to prison or death, but also sexual desire, as in the many (quasi) pornographic descriptions in the text, and above all a desire for happiness. This is perhaps the most remarkable feature of *Cidade de Deus*: the absence of boredom and the *unproblematic* nature

96 E.g. "The Block Thirteen gang split up when they got to the Rec and headed up the river's edge. Tiny's gang split up and took Middle Street and the alleys. The youngest enjoyed that feeling of war, thinking they were TV heros." City of God, translated by Alison Entrekin. New York: Black Cat, 2006" (Lins, 2013: 352).

of pleasure – no *ennui* or *Weltschmerz* is to be found here. Enjoyment has no side effects and in four hundred pages of narrative no guilt or melancholy is to be found.

Characterized as it is by the conflict between scarcity and abundance, modernization and tradition, inclusion and exclusion, the environment both depicted and transformed by *Cidade de Deus* may be regarded in one sense as decisive. The unbridled, ferocious nature of the desire therein (re)presented corresponds to a radical process of subjectivity, which responds whole-heartedly to an incitement to pleasure and enjoyment and that spurns that most cherished of bourgeois psychological traits: self-preservation.

In *Counterrevolution and Revolt* (1972), Marcuse argued that the multiplication of needs, without which capitalism could not reproduce itself, could eventually prove to be destructive to the system. He had in mind, of course, the relatively affluent society of the 60s and early 70s; the people of *Cidade de Deus* are witnesses of the truth of this claim in a situation of social disintegration. "Destruction" in this context, however, is a rigorously dialectical concept. As Marcuse was very well aware, it could mean intransitive destruction, sheer annihilation of life through violence, at the same time that it could represent a necessary step in the emergence of a better world. This is something that theory cannot resolve, although it can point out that such living/deadly desire is produced at a time when the conditions for the overcoming of need have long been objectively given.

T.W. Adorno in Brazil.

From May 13th to May 17th 2002 a conference took place in Pi- racicaba, São Paulo, with the title "Tecnologia, Cultura e Formação ... Ainda Auschwitz." Organized by two multidisciplinary study groups, of the Universidade Metodista de Piracicaba (UNIMEP) and of the Universidade Federal de São Carlos (UFSCar), the four-day meeting represented the consolidation of something new in Brazilian cultural and academic life. This novelty, which was only to be made even more visible in the numerous events celebrating Adorno's 100th birthday last year, helped in the first place to confirm the emergence of a numerically significant school of interpretation of Adorno in Brazil. Attendance at the conference was very mixed; at peak times it totaled more than three hundred people, while the presentation of papers involved members from all strata of the academic spectrum, from undergraduates, through master and doctoral students, to young professors and senior scholars. Panels dealt mostly with issues of technology in its relation to education (in the ample German sense of *Bildung*), aesthetics, and the culture industry, while keynote talks elucidated diverse aspects of Adorno's works and its relation to more distant philosophers, such as Nietzsche, and fellow thinkers, such as Marcuse and Horkheimer.

Noteworthy was not only the extremely comfortable atmosphere, which permitted the circulation of ideas among people of so many different places and ages, but also the fact that in one way or another participants were talking the same language, managing to communicate by means of a shared code, inhabiting a common thinking space. One would have to turn to Jacques Lacan to find a theorist with such a similar broad audience in Brazil, but in his case the number of interpreters and commentators has been supported by a highly organized, and reasonably bureaucratized, institutional apparatus, the psychoanalytical, both inside and outside the university. Conversely, what is remarkable about the current reception of Adorno in Brazil is that it has taken place within a minimum of underlying structures, academic or otherwise, while at the same time it managed to overcome regional differences and perennial political disagreements in what is now a coherent set of theoretical questions and approaches. This concordance, which may strike North Americans as restrictive or even repressive, was a real achievement in the Brazilian context, for there the recurrent problem intellectuals saw themselves confronted with in the last decades was the difficulty to form a critical tradition, a common ground from which discussions could gain momentum. Even though the Brazilian university apparatus, especially its graduate system, is one of the best in Latin America, it is not strong enough (especially after a decade of neoliberalism) to absorb the increasing availability of imported theoretical goods, now much enhanced by the Internet. This led to a situation in which assimilation of interpretative systems proved to be impossible. There was simply no time to digest what was brought from the outside, no time to verify, not even to experience, the productivity, tensions and contradictions a given theoretical framework could offer when transplanted to the Brazilian context.[97] This

97 That direct importation of theories can prove to be disastrous is

is why one should see with good eyes the solidification of an interpretative community around such a multi-layered and far-reaching thinker as Adorno.

In fact, the history of the reception of the Frankfurt School in Brazil is not a really recent one. In 1969 José Guilherme Merquior had already published his *Arte e Sociedade em Marcuse, Adorno e Benjamin*, which was to a great degree responsible for the stereotype of Adorno as an "anti-modern terrorist of art" (Duarte, 1997: 122), in contradistinction to a revolutionary Benjamin. This early assessment was followed by a series of works that appeared in the 80s and 90s, both translations and by native authors, which competently dissected the difficult philosophy of the Frankfurt School, presenting its main ideas and central concepts, articulating its aims and at times proposing reformulations for supposed deadlocks.[98]

But what makes the Frankfurt School in general, and Adorno in particular, so interesting for Brazilian intellectuals *today* is his cultural criticism of capitalism, especially of what became known as the culture industry – a mixed term that conceptualizes those artifacts that are *cultural* (i.e. not fitting for "concrete" purposes, as clothing or pans) and yet are produced industrially, in mass quantities and for profit. For in Brazil is to

made clear, for instance, by the bizarre reception of Bahktin's theory of carnavalization. By uncritically adhering to it, Brazilian critics ultimately offered what turned out to be indeed a noxious contribution. For in Brazil, there is nothing so institutionalized (and commodified) as carnival itself. When being happy becomes a social imposition and moral obligation following the calendar, the critical gesture must go in the other direction, in the struggle for the individual's right not to hide his or her sadness. See Durão (2004a).

98 Among the extensive bibliography of works written by Brazilian scholars, one could mention, chronologically: Klothe (1978); Rouanet (1983); Freitag (1988); Matos (1993); Duarte, (1993); Gagnebin (1997); Nobre, (1998); Zuin, Pucci & Oliveira (2000).

be found one of the most monopolized systems of mass media in the world, epitomized by the all-powerful Globo Network.[99] More than theorists of the new media like Bourdieu, Baudrillard or Deleuze, Adorno furnished Leftist intellectuals with a set of conceptual tools and a framework that linked immanent criticism of cultural goods to a solid and comprehensive philosophy that encouraged interdisciplinary work, thus enabling both scholars and activists to establish a link between their lived experience and their practice of thinking. Derived from Marx's description of capitalism and Weber's account of rationality, Adorno's strong concept of totality functioned perfectly as a heuristic instrument to conceptualize a totalitarian system of communication and cultural production, one that allowed very little space for what differed from its pasteurized products. Thus, from and through the critique of the culture industry, a door was opened to the recent carrying out of research in the most diverse fields, such as pedagogy, literary theory, sociology, music, anthropology and even physical education.

And yet Adorno's reception in Brazil was not immune to a certain dialectic of light. Precisely because of its difficulty, of the challenge it presents to readers, his texts begged to be explained, dissected, analyzed, paraphrased, in short, to be *illuminated*; they encouraged, in other words, the proliferation of the secondary literature and of philological work that keeps

---

99 See Lopes (2001) and Herz (1987). These otherwise overly denunciatory and somewhat propagandistic books are here useful, inasmuch as they call attention to the narrow connection between mass media and conservative politics, which tends to be overlooked by Adorno's more epistemological/formal approach. It is perhaps the first great irony of the twenty-first century in Brazil that Rede Globo saw itself obliged to support Lula's left-wing government, due to its overwhelming debt of some billions of dollars. Such support, however, would soon disappear after Dilma Rousseff's election in 2010.

the academic industry going. This explains the title of the conference in Piracicaba, especially the "still Auschwitz" (*ainda Auschwitz*) in it. For most of the papers presented there were devoted to the elucidation of determined aspects of Adorno's theory, which, given the general approval it enjoyed, ended up by enthroning the philosopher and turning him into an infallible Master. This led to some disheartening results: since Adorno deploys concepts that point beyond their sheer content and strive to exhibit (*darstellen*) something other, it was not uncommon to find analytical definitions of "constellations," self-identical commentaries on "nonidentity," intellectualized categorizations of "experience," rationalistic assessments of "mimesis," or intentional descriptions of "exact imagination." While this might elsewhere generate, at most, boring results, in Brazil it gives birth to blatant contradictions, for the obsession with conceptual clarification, an otherwise necessary step in intellectual practice, is in Brazil at best repetitive and stifling (how many times can one recapitulate the argument of *Dialectic of Enlightenment*?), at worst radically at odds with the experience of the concepts themselves. What should shed light on a form of thinking reverts into obscurantist acceptance.[100]

What follows is an initial attempt, tentative and limited, to be sure, in the opposite direction: not to pledge an oath of filiation, but to venture into a dialectic of fidelity, whereby the emancipating impulse underlying a given theory can only

100 It is interesting to observe that the exact opposite happens in relation to the greatest living Brazilian literary critic, Roberto Schwarz, whose theory of misplaced ideas (1992) shares an undeniable Adornian inspiration. It so happens, however, that Schwarz (whom Shierry W. Nicholsen acknowledges in her translation of Prisms for introducing her to the Frankfurt School) has systematically avoided mentioning Adorno in his work as well as approaching his relationship to him.

remain the same once it is made different by turning against itself. This is signaled in the double meaning the preposition "in" may have in the title above. If the text's first part focused, however briefly, on the reception of Adorno in Brazil, mainly emphasizing its laudable consistency and questionable subservience, a second step should follow, now suggesting a description of what could result from the clash of his theory with a reality he could have had no inkling of. In order to do this, a short detour is necessary.

II

In a short text, "Thesen über Bedürfnis" ["Theses on Need" (1979f)], Adorno presents an important argument concerning the irreducibly social character of human needs. Far from being universal, or even constant, they vary according to the specificities of particular societies. Even those utterly biological necessities, such as eating, he says, cannot be taken as natural, but must be considered as functions inside a totality in which its parts are interrelated, and in a process of mutual determination. For hunger, "conceived as a natural category, can be satisfied with grasshoppers and gnats, a repast to many wild animals. To satiate the concrete hunger of civilized men, it is necessary that they receive something that does not disgust them, and in disgust and its contrary the whole of history is reflected."

Eating is not a sheer natural phenomenon; menus are determined by a cultural framework dictating what counts as edible. But if human needs are socially configured, it is also possible to argue that "the differentiation between deep and superficial needs is a socially produced semblance [*Schein*]"

(Adorno, 1979f: 392; see also Adorno, 1979c: 220-222). That is, since the social whole, the ever-more socialized society [*vergesellschaftete Gesellschaft*], is a total space, one that does not allow for any kind of exteriority, the mediation between biological and psychic needs (as manifested in symptoms of neuroses, psychosis and the like) must be carried out precisely through the fundamental category of semblance.

A dialectical figure of thought, it acquires in Adorno's sociological writings the opposite valences it exhibits in his texts on aesthetics. In art, *Schein* is a false appearance that conveys truth; as a sociological category, it is a given, a fact, that in itself leads to error. Needs that are in fact the result of a complex process of socialization appear as immediate and evident, as natural. This is why "to judge about what would be true and false needs it would be necessary to take into account the structure of society as a whole, with all its mediations" (Adorno, 1979d: 365-366).

However, the presence of the social in the most apparently organic functions, in the very structures of drives (*Triebe*) themselves, should not be taken as an endpoint for thought; it should not turn into a slogan. Even though for Adorno there may seem to be only one synchronic social whole, the capitalist system in its monopolistic phase, it is fair to ask whether his kind of totality can really bear the mark of universality. Now, one main feature that characterizes late capitalism for the German philosopher, the nodal point for the analysis that follows, is the assumption of a partial, at least precarious, fulfillment of basic human needs. Indeed, once this unacknowledged *Bestimmung* of the Adornian concept of society in advanced countries comes to the fore, it is possible to realize to what extent capitalism's restrictive abundance lies in the background of Adorno's sociological writings.

To be sure, he considers this trait to be heteronomous to capitalism as a purely economic system, for the fulfillment of urgent needs can only be brought about by some form of non-economic organization, such as the State, through welfare programs, or institutions of charity and the like. Nevertheless, it is precisely this intervention in the "free" workings of the market that characterizes Adorno's idea of monopolistic capitalism as opposed to its earlier, liberal stage. Much of the novelty brought about by monopoly capitalism, in fact, can be fruitfully approached through the lenses of a typically Marxian contradiction, which is properly adapted by Adorno, namely that of overwhelming human needs in a situation without scarcity. Differently from Marx, who saw in capitalism the *potential* for the overcoming of privation through the already-attained development of the productive forces, Adorno had to work with a state of affairs in which suffering persisted hand in hand with the at least partial fulfillment of material necessities.

This lack of fundamental needs can even be used as central point around which much, if not all, of Adorno's sociological texts may be interpreted. Once the Marxian prognosis of the proletariat's ultimate absolute impoverishment (*Verelendung*) is proven wrong, it becomes important to acknowledge that "the proletariat has more to lose than its fetters. In comparison to the situation in England a hundred years ago, as it stood before the eyes of the authors of the *Manifesto*, the proletariat's standard of living has not worsened, but improved" (Adorno, 1979e: 384; see also Adorno, 1979d: 358-361). Precisely because human needs are social and in constant historical mutation, it is possible for Adorno to argue that classes continue to exist, even if their for-itself becomes blurred in a false egalitarianism. From another perspective, relative abundance is also responsible for salient changes in the realm of culture. Two of the most central targets of Adornian analyses, homogenization and standardization, with all the consequences they bring about in terms of subjectivization, would prove to be impossible if need were overwhelming, which would thus force subjects to act more spontaneously and autonomously to counter it. His theory of semi-formation (Adorno, 1979a: esp. 110-111), would be unthinkable without the availability of symbolic goods adapted for the masses, which now occupy the position of consumers. Even the fundamental philosophical *topos* of administration (*Verwaltung*, see e.g. Adorno, 1979b) is logically connected to the radical reduction or abrogation of basic needs. From a quite simplistic point of view, indeed, it is possible to argue that the un- comfortable presence of utter need would lead to revolts that would threaten rational planning and coordination. In other words, for social control to work under ideal conditions, a certain degree of stability is welcome, if not required. And if we remember that in capitalism, it needs become a function of the market, and not the other way round – i.e. the commodities "pick up" their consumers and not the other way round – then psychological urges and the functioning of the psychic apparatus itself become intertwined with the sociological determination of the suppression of absolute need. Finally, in a last step, when one is reminded that through the logic of exchange (*Tauschprinzip*) subjectivity and the commodity form are dealt with by Adorno and Horkheimer in the *Dialectic of Enlightenment* as sharing the same functioning as the concept itself, the model of a totality based on the overcoming of basic necessities may be extended to epistemology and metaphysics. It may indeed look like a far-fetched claim to argue that a link exists between Adorno's close totality and its immanent criticism of concepts, on the one hand, and the satisfaction of basic, concrete needs, on the other. This suspicion could start to dissipate once two observations are taken into account. In the first place, the separation between philosophy and sociology in Adorno can only be brought about at the critic's own expense; for him, the two disciplines always mediate one another. Secondly, historical depth (which in the *Dialectic of Enlightenment* becomes a *reductio ad absurdum*) can only be worked out from the point of view of the present, which illuminates what came before it, but remains blind to suppressed possibilities, unrealized potentials time did bury, but which could reemerge in a different future. The abrogation of immediate necessity and the totality matching it, in other words, project their own genealogy in a history that could have been otherwise.

All of this, it is important to emphasize, does not mean that need is *the* most fundamental category in Adorno's philosophy. To say so would be tantamount to claiming that it represents a firm ground, a first principle from which a conceptual system could be reconstructed by deduction. The argument here runs in a different direction, namely, that need is a border-concept that, just as many others in Adorno (e.g. nonidentity, experience, suffering, constellation, or even dialectics), may be used as a lens to interpret the whole of his philosophy, one side of the prism light can go through. Once this is granted, the next move must be to determine to what extent a different configuration of need might restructure and transform Adorno's characterization of totality and the theoretical practice attached to it.

III

It should be clear by now that what is at stake in this reformulation is nothing but the simple question: what happens to the Adornian notion of totality when it exhibits a strong version of need, when the most fundamental requirements for the sustenance of human life cannot be taken for granted? Underlying this question there is the suggestion that Adorno's concept of totality can only imperfectly function in Brazil, where massive need and privation are grafted in a country completely colonized by capitalism.[101] The coexistence of material scarcity, on the one hand, and capitalist structures of desire and intersubjective action, on the other, point to the formation of a kind of totality that cannot be sustained without the formation of *constitutive margins*. The challenge for thinking Adorno in Brazil hinges on how to theorize the relationship between inside and outside, core and periphery in a satisfactory way. That this must be done in a dialectical fashion can be seen in the insufficiency of two opposed positions, when taken in isolation. Brazil cannot represent either a pure and simple sameness, or a perfect alterity, in relation to the so-called First World. By arguing that Adornian categories function perfectly in the Brazilian context, the first position leads to an always-doomed project of mimicry, which,

101 Recent estimates say that 50 million Brazilians live in utter misery, 29.3% of the population, making less than US $ 25.8 a month. See http://www.rebidia.org. br/novida/FGV_MFOME.htm.

as was claimed above, enters in sharp contradiction with the experiential content of concepts themselves. On the other hand, inasmuch as it posits the total incompatibility between periphery and center, the second perspective almost as a rule generates mediocre theories of a strongly resented tinge. A refocusing of Adornian lenses to Brazil demands a kind of structure capable of thinking difference and sameness within the same theoretical framework. Below, the attempt will be made to demonstrate that the kind of totality exhibited in the Brazilian context, which could *mutatis mutandis* be expanded too much, if not all, of the Third World, is itself in dialectical tension with the Adornian one. The suspicion informing and underlying this comparison is that, when transplanted to the margins of the world-system, the concept of totality exhibits a peculiar dialectic of inside and outside, according to which an idea of openness tends to force itself, only to be proven wrong as it is closely scrutinized.

To be sure, there are a number of Adornian philosophemes begging to be examined from the ex-centric Brazilian point of view, sensuality as semblance (*Schein*) and the problematic nature of aesthetic autonomy being, perhaps, the first ones to come to mind. Here, however, two other themes will be dealt with: first, what could be called the phenomenology of the commodity form. The expression refers to the interaction between commodities, as scrutinized by Marx in the beginning of *Capital*, and the mental set generated by them. The second topic concerns the concentration camp of *Auschwitz*, which represented for Adorno a concrete philosophical problem, as we will see, a nodal point linking epistemology, metaphysics, ethics and political praxis. These two issues could function as a proper starting point, not only because, as will be shown, they present strong connections in the Brazilian context, but also because they belong to two fundamental broad areas of research from which much complementary work could be carried out.

Adorno's criticism of the commodity form in monopoly capitalism can be fruitfully approached by his theorizations regarding obscurantism (see *The Stars Down to Earth* [1975] and "Theses against occultism" [1974]). This important philosopheme answers for a complex of problems that unite politics in its broadest sense, here in the guise of administration and domination; economy, as the production and circulation of commodities is always implied; and psychology, since obscurantism as a social practice strongly interferes in individuals' structure of drives. For our present purposes, it is important to emphasize that the mechanisms worked out by Adorno, in his *The Stars Down to Earth*, regarding astrology can be very satisfactorily applied to the world of commodities in general.[102] Just as the Freudian characterization of the drive involves the inseparable link between an imagistic, representational content, and a physiological impulse, so *all* commodities in today's late capitalism combine a semiotic element (the process of signification it fosters), and a material character. In astrology, Adorno argues, two social spheres, severed by an increasing division of labor, are brought together, namely, those of astronomy and psychology. The astrologist, that is, has to possess at least a minimal knowledge about the

102 Interestingly enough, Adorno sees his reading of the horoscope column in the *Los Angeles Times* as a contribution to a general theory of totalitarianism. If the comparison with commodities proves right, then a very disturbing image indeed of an economic oppressive totality emerges, within liberal democracy itself.

planets' movements, on the one hand, and a fairly acute sense of his readers' anxieties and desires, on the other. Obscurantism arises from the incapacity to question the arbitrary nature of this joining together of planets and people; the question readers of the *Los Angeles Times* did not ask was simply: what proves that the movements of celestial bodies interfere with human lives? Adorno calls this kind of superstition secondary, because "the individual's experience of the occult, whatever its psychological meaning and roots or its validity, rarely, if ever, enter the social phenomenon to which our studies are devoted. Here, the occult appears rather institutionalized, objectified and, to a large extent, socialized" (*Stars Down to Earth* 16). At play in this case is a dialectic of rationality and irrationality. Reason is made obscure, insofar as facts are hypostatized and cannot be related to a meaningful whole; subjects "feel that everything is linked up with everything else and that they have no way out, but at the same time the whole mechanism is so complicated that they fail to understand its raison d'être" (Adorno, 1975: 110), and that is why they are prone to somehow accept irrational explanations such as that of astrology. On the other hand, that "somehow" is crucial, for in an enlightened society (in the strong sense of *aufgeklärte*) it is hard to *really believe* such improbable "theories" as astrology. What is constituted, rather, is a structure of partial disbelief, since "so many followers of astrology do not seem quite to believe but rather take an indulgent, semi-ironical attitude towards their own conviction" (Adorno, 1975: 109).

Now, this posture is the one that most accurately accounts for the relationship between consumers and commodities in late capitalism: they *know* that the association of a product with a given image is not true, but they conceal it to themselves and enact a kind of "suspension of disbelief" that is not so easily distinguishable from that involved in aesthetic experience, except, perhaps, that it involves a good deal of bad faith. In Brazil, the contrary happens; the situation here is a paradoxical one, insofar as the principle of exchange is both present and absent: absent, because a great part of the population (from 20 to 50 million, depending on how one calculates and interprets statistics) lies outside exchange, has no buying power; present, because the desire structured by the commodity form is ubiquitous. And since there are so many people concretely outside the market but with their desires ruled by it (what Robert Kurz once termed "monetary subjects without money"), a certain literalism prevails. Whereas in advanced capitalist countries, those inside the market have to try to pretend they are not, in Brazil, those outside it represent perfect capitalist subjectivities. Precisely because they suffer need in a society that fully eradicated pre-capitalist structures of life, they completely believe the promises made by that which they do not have. The expensive car *really* brings beautiful women; the cigarette *really* takes one to the old West. In the closed totality of central capitalist countries, "there is no place anymore outside the machinery, from which one may name the phantasmagoria", for "only on its own incoherence should the lever be set" (Adorno, 1979d: 369). That which lies outside has to be found within; the potential for change, what is other, has to be sought inside the system of exchange. In Brazil, since the principle of exchange is a fiction for so many subjects, otherness is present in that interior "outsideness". It is precisely because of that literalism, that belief about the face-value character of commodities that the excluded may constitute revolutionary subjectivities. It is true that this structure of desire can lead to the most barbaric acts of violence (e.g. killing someone for a pair of tennis shoes), but when compared to the detached posture of postmodern cynicism, i.e. *knowing* the truth and perpetuating the false, taking things to the letter may generate action. By demanding that commodities be equal to what they communicate about themselves, a typical practice of immanent critique, subjects may, under propitious conditions, *act* in a way directed to radical difference and continue to maintain what they know is bad.[103]

A second term of comparison can be fruitfully investigated by means of the confrontation with the problematic of Auschwitz. For Adorno the concentration camp became both the example and the symbol for what is best approached as a nightmare of reason. There, the most advanced technological means were deployed to exterminate human beings who were thereby deprived of their humanness. In order to eliminate as many individuals as possible, everything should work as a clock: arrival and departure of trains, the process of selection of those who should go to gas chambers, disposal of bodies, collection of belongings and organic leftovers such as hair. People were thus turned into numbers; they ceased to be viewed even as objects: they became abstractions. This perfectly corresponds to the culmination of a long tradition in philosophy, that of disenchantment with the world, the struggle against animism and geometrization of the universe. Auschwitz was a closed space within which control over

103 Slavoj Žižek has repeatedly been making the same argument for some time now, stressing that the self-distancing embedded in irony, rather than representing a resistance to capitalism, brings about the most effective way of adapting to it (e.g. 1994: 1-33, 296-331).

inmates was total (Sofsky, 1997) and extermination could be carried out in the most cold-blooded and calculated fashion. Dying, as a result, lost any meaning it could once have had; it became the function of an unpredictable system under which all individuals were fungible and replaceable (Adorno, 1998: 166-213; 1973: 361-408). For the survivors a universal context of guilt (*Schuldzusammenhang*) came into being, since there was no justification for their remaining alive in face of the others' deaths.

From a temporal perspective, Auschwitz represented a caesura in history that questioned not only any discourse based on the idea of progress, and its accompanying conception linear time, but it also led to the imposition of a categorical imperative for the future: that it may never be repeated (Adorno, 1973: 365). As an object to be criticized, the concentration camp poses a challenge to language, in what could be called a dilemma of naming. To utter or write "Auschwitz," to *represent* it, is an act of vulgarization and un- faithfulness towards the terror and suffering that cannot be conveyed through language; to deal with it rationally is an insult in view of the utter irrationality underlying it. On the other hand, maintaining silence about Auschwitz, not evoking it, is itself barbaric, for it encourages forgetfulness, thus ultimately facilitating its repetition.

The Brazilian version of Auschwitz is the daily miniature pogrom, the recurrent urban massacre, in Portuguese called *chacina*, an everyday word. Its best characterization would be that of routine terror without catastrophe – or, in a different formulation: their catastrophe (for they must be named in the plural) is none other than the absence of catastrophe, the fact that they cannot be turned into it. Inconceivable without the structure of desire described above, it exhibits a peculiar kind of coherence when put side by side to the concentration camp. First of all, the point of contact: the *chacina* can also be interpreted as a nightmare of reason. At the bottom, the dehumanization and barbarity are the same, but the kind of rationality has changed. Instead of the centralized and totalitarian space of the concentration camp, the *chacina* is mobile and may take place anywhere anytime in the margins of Brazilian big cities, occasionally at the center. It is a system in the most rigorous sense (indeed its anonymity only proves it), for, since both victims and perpetrators are mostly excluded from society, they are interchangeable. In their ongoing war with the law and opposing gangs, the latter know that their life expectancy is extremely limited; they also know that, waiting for their death, there is an unemployed reserve army eager to occupy their position. As for the victims, there is an undeniable element of un-decidability in their choosing, both in the choice on the part of the leader as to who should die, and as a result of chance encounters in the megalopolis. If underlying Auschwitz there was a pseudo-theory vilifying the Jews, the *chacina* is deprived of any ideological justification whatsoever, but involves whoever happens to be available. And if in the concentration camp anonymity was a function of total regulation, in *chacinas*, it is the result of economic deregulation, the withdrawal of the State from all welfare areas and massive unemployment. In both cases, non- subjects appear: in Auschwitz, the number tattooed on the forearm; in the periphery of Brazilian megalopolises, individuals with no IDs, non-citizens.

But also temporality and the dialectic of naming are also inverted. If Auschwitz poses a dilemma surrounding the name, the *chacina* remains unnamable. Due to its size and iterability signifiers cannot be made to apply to larger contexts or further occurrences. Two of the most representative instances, the Carandirú massacre (where 101 penitentiary inmates were killed by the police during a revolt), or the Candelária incident (when 16 street children were murdered at the steps of Rio de Janeiro's most important cathedral), could not be turned into symbols or extrapolated to represent other cases of daily murder. The categorical imperative that Auschwitz be not repeated reverts into its opposite: that the *chacinas* stop, that for one single day they cease to take place. And yet, precisely because of this difference the universal context of guilt remains the same; or, better, it becomes even more visible and cogent, both morally and epistemologically. Sacrilegious though it surely is, the idea that, in its total form of control over the "material" at hand, one finds the same kind of rationality at work underlying Auschwitz and Schoenberg's dodecaphonic technique is true. If in its orderliness, Auschwitz offered the underlying truth of modern rationality; Brazilian miniature pogroms, quotidian terror without catastrophe, open our eyes to the truth of postmodern micro-narratives, so dear to a Lyotard.

The inverted phenomenology of the commodity form and the logic of the *chacina* are only two theoretical *topoi* that come to the fore when Adorno's philosophy is confronted with the Brazilian context. As was said above, several others could be dealt with – one could think of the role of sex and carnival, constituting a politics of happiness, as a means of political domination; or the difficulty of presupposing aesthetic autonomy in art and literature, under conditions of social disintegration, as Paulo Lins' recent path-breaking bestseller *Cidade de Deus* attests. Adorno's importance for all this is that of furnishing a libertarian impulse, a posture of nonconformity and the strength to question that which would otherwise go without saying. It does not matter if his philosophy becomes utterly modified in the end: that would be the only way for it to remain the same. And if the project is to retain the impetus in different contexts of application, the challenge becomes to expand all this to the Latin American horizon. What form would these issues take where indigenous populations are prevalent? Where U.S. presence is overwhelming, or where the national context taken in isolation is insufficient? These are questions that, of course, cannot be answered here, but must be left to the reader, as an invitation.

Monologism of the multiple.

Concepts are not simply tools, nor are theories mere edifices of thought. In both, changes of time and space crystallize. These changes are sometimes linked to the transformations concepts undergo either through their period of formation (which often coincides with the life of their author); to their process of ageing (their collision with history); and sometimes to their migration to other regions (their confrontation with other traditions and forms of existence). To account for these processes, the critic must become an archaeologist: she must identify the layers of meaning, the traces left by these alterations within ideas and systems. Subsequently, however, she must metamorphose into an engineer and turn her attention to the *uses* that concepts and theories can take on at *their* specific moment of enunciation; their "here and now". These uses are the ultimate parameters for the authentication of organized thought, not just in terms of its *validity*, but also its *value*.

When considered as something in movement, Bakhtin's[104] œuvre can be seen to involve various spatial-temporal coordinates; it has a chronotope of its own. For beyond

104 With regard to the classic problem of authorship, I consider Volosinov and Medvedev's texts as part of the Bakhtin cluster, a nucleus above the individual. However, I believe it less important to determine the authorship of his works than to remember the tension involved in the effort of determining the author involved in an often collective project – the tension, in other words, between a collaborative practice and the present-day academic's wish for individuality. The flagrant contradiction between the description of a dialogical principle and the search for the definitive determination of individual authorship generally goes unnoticed. In fact, Bakhtin's original circle can be inserted in the scope of the early twentieth century's modernist groups (cf. Durão & Williams, 2008).

Bakhtin's intellectual biography and beyond its links to such a troubled time in history, there is the process of its discovery and adaptation to the post-Cold War Western world. Although the first introductory publications were issued in the 1960s, it was only in the 1970s, at the end of the author's life and more than forty years after the publication of his first works, that they came to earn recognition in Europe and the United States. It was only then that Bakhtin came to join the ranks of literary theory's great authors. This hiatus was decisive, for, despite having been translated into other languages little by little over the years, his œuvre arrived in the West as a complete whole; that is, as something that demanded explication and commentary. Ironically, this lack of dialogue made it possible for Bakhtin's writings to be configured according to parameters and conditions that were specific to different situations of reading, namely according to the contexts in which interpretation took place. In other words, these circumstances interfered in the very *internal* constitution of his books. As such, it was very easy for the West to "de-Marxify" Bakhtin, to see in him a victim of an oppressive system (which he was) and to identify in his writings a systematic, if veiled, resistance to authoritarian communism.

In Brazil, the political-intellectual climate in which Bakhtin's meteoric rise took place preserved much of the European and North American enthusiasm, but with one fundamental difference. Because the Brazilian reception only began in earnest in the 1980s, the context was not so much that of the Cold War as that of the country's political re-democratization as it emerged from a long and painful military dictatorship. This belatedness gave the Russian thinker's texts a unique timeliness: from one day to the next, an œuvre of considerable volume emerged against the horizon, imbued with a spirit that could only be seen as *democratic*. A theory that, unlike the French currents that were in vogue, strove to be communicative; that kept a progressive impulse, in some shape or form; whose writing was clear; that was based on concepts drawn from common language; that would give to the popular a central and determining role. Moreover, because it was centred on notions like dialogism and heteroglossia, it was a theory that opened itself to difference, but in concrete form, situated, and not conceived as a result of a system of binary oppositions or of an atemporal phenomenological substrate. Such a theory could receive nothing less than a warm welcome in a country that was leaving an oppressive regime. Indeed, Brazilian society was more than ever in need of a dialogue between its different voices; to come to terms with the past, to reconstitute a social pact on new foundations, to rewrite its history and to adjust its outlook on the future. It is still worth noting that Bakhtin's circle's work was welcomed in a wide spectrum of disciplines in Brazil, a spectrum that included not just literary studies but also history, communication sciences, and to a lesser degree architecture and law. Nevertheless, it was in linguistics that Bakhtin's presence made itself felt most clearly.[105] Its emphasis on enunciation, which linked linguistic material to the material conditions of its production, contrasted positively with the structuralist descriptions that prevailed in the 1960s and 1970s. With their abstraction and predominantly quantitative nature, as well as their desire for a scientific spirit, these were well accepted by the authoritarian regime in place at the time.

105 This can be verified by comparing, for example, the introductory books published in Brasil (Faraco, 2003; Fiorin, 2006) and in the United States (Holquist, 2002).

This initial reception reached its apogee at the turn of the last century. Although there is still work to be done – there remain works to be translated into Portuguese and not all the translations have been done directly from Russian – the author has been consecrated. Not only are many of his texts easy to find, a vast secondary bibliography is readily available too. This bibliography includes, among others, introductory books (Fiorin, 2006), long-form monographic studies (Tezza, 2003), conference proceedings (Brait 2005a), essay collections (Faraco, Tezza & Castro, 2006) and dictionaries of concepts (Brait, 2005b, 2006), not to mention other genres of academic writing like theses, dissertations and journal articles, which are innumerable. It is interesting to note that most of the available works on Bakhtin are written by Brazilian authors, despite the fact that a translated secondary bibliography exists (e.g. Holquist 2004). This makes it possible to conceive of a national reception for the author, at least on principle. One should also underscore the very high level of most of these texts (a rare level in Brazil) as well as their interpretive acuity and their philological precision (even though Russian is unknown to many of the commentators). Something of the singularity of Bakhtin's presence in the country will then begin to become evident. The pages below propose to investigate a phenomenon that follows from this reception and that could possibly be productively contrasted with other national contexts. It involves **a.** a process of reading; **b.** resonances in a national tradition; **c.** relationships with specific conditions of knowledge production; **d.** a concordance with a spirit of the present moment. All of this crystallizes in the concept of *monologism of the multiple*. More than a simple descriptive tool, the term points to something that demands critical reflection: not in the spirit of negating Bakhtin, but rather affirming him in another fashion, using him against himself; responding to Bakhtin's proliferation with Bakhtin himself.

II

The monologism of the multiple has as its precondition a simple reading mechanism. As inevitable as it is noxious and as ubiquitous as it is desirable, this mechanism consists in extracting Bakhtinian concepts from the context in which they originally emerged, from the textual economy in which they find themselves, only to transpose them to a great variety of writings. Such transposition occurs through two principal modalities, both equally contradictory in themselves: those of *explication* and *application*. The first occurs as much in complete works – like introductory texts devoted specifically to Bakhtin or studies of isolated concepts – as in texts with other ends. The explanation of Bakhtinian terminology represents a tremendous progress, for it helps to spread and make more accessible a corpus that would otherwise remain difficult to approach. At the same time, however, the very strategy of isolating ideas and extracting them from the relationships they had with their particular objects does not just transform them, but can be seen as a move in the opposite direction to Bakhtin's. The dissection and elucidation of concepts has as a presupposition the neutral space of the one who writes, a space in which meanings are isolated, as in a laboratory; this does not mesh well with the Bakhtinian emphasis on the concreteness of enunciation – even if it points precisely to the latter, emphasizing the idea of the "concreteness of enunciation." In other words, we could be dealing here with a performative contradiction between the statement "every utterance is subject to a specific enunciation" and its enunciation in a mode of writing that, by definition, shares its scientific neutrality. As we shall see, this paradox of enunciation is fundamental for the functioning of a broader trend, one that subsumes the monologism of the multiple. At the same time, it is important to note that what is at stake is not simply opposition to dissemination, a possible elitist gesture, but the possibility that meta-discourse on the work of the Russian thinker, beyond filling the highly important role of making it known, generates consequences that ultimately go against it. The choice, in sum, is not between dissemination and silence, but between repetition and critical consciousness of the effects of meaning that result from it.

The same holds true for the application of Bakhtinian concepts. On the one hand, application is just as vital as explication, since theories, by definition, ask to be extrapolated upon: if the scope of validity of a given thought is limited to itself, thought dies and becomes a mere historical curiosity. It is only through the continuous confrontation with difference that a work can continue being what it is – precisely by not being equal to itself, a principle of non-identity that links Bakhtin to Adorno. Unlike explication, application puts the critical imagination of the one who uses the theory into play. As such, what is brought about is a dislocation that is ultimately a condition for the work's survival; a dynamic that, if successful, produces an interesting performative effect, for it can follow that the new place, generated by the transformation of theory, ends up presenting itself as the real, as that which always belonged to the work. On the other hand, however, application can easily generate a scheme similar to that of the factory production line, one that separates Bakhtinian conceptual technology from brute matter, the most diverse cultural manifestations.[106] In this case, the meanings of the concepts ossify and theory quickly succumbs to the light that emanates from it, to the repetitive intelligibility that it disseminates.

The examples of explication and application in the contemporary Brazilian bibliography are countless; those cited below were selected through a combination of both modalities. The first example comes from an essay on Bakhtin's and Benjamin's theory of translation, from the perspective of the field of education. In the conclusion, one reads:

> Lastly, *with regard to the pedagogical practice and propositions*, and with reference to the two authors (i.e., Bakhtin and Benjamin), I say *no* to homogenization, because I understand that the possible conceptions of pedagogical propositions are many and that the desirable types of action are diverse. Plurality, many paths, this is the opposite motto to that defended by an alternative that considers itself unique, that believes it carries the "right" answer – a word that is monological, and, by the same token, authoritarian, that dictates what must and must not be done, in a normative manner, full of jargon and readymade solutions that purport to carry practice forward and redeem its problems. (Kramer, in Faraco, Tezza & Castro, 1996: 220; italics in the original)

106 It is interesting to note here a reflex of international division of labor, for it is generally the so-called First World that provides the interpretive technologies, while the Third furnishes the brute cultural matter to be read.

The syntax is not the best, but the vocabulary leaves no ambiguity about marking multiplicity as something that is simply positive, in opposition to the authoritarianism of monologism (note the rapidity of the "by the same token," as if it were not necessary to explain that causal relationship). The problem is that the "very" remains abstract; by virtue of its own meaning as "more," it makes any specific characterization difficult. Such characterization would probably need to reduce it to something less, to a unit, to make some sense of it. Like a loose screw spinning out of control, a passage like this one says much, and correctly, to say very little. It is certain that this passage does itself have a didactic quality, insofar as it thematizes multiplicity itself; however, something of this valorization of the multiple as such, something of the de-specification of theory in relation to the object, is recurrent in a wide range of studies on Bakhtin.

It is important to acknowledge that the Russian thinker's writings invite both types of appropriation. Firstly, due to the variety of his approaches, which submit the same concepts to different functions; secondly, because many of these concepts have an active life in everyday language, interfering with the most rigorously analytical meanings (something that Bakhtin does not disapprove); finally, because of his writing, which is everything but concise. Because the repetitions and recapitulations abound, they make the reiterated concepts acquire relief and appear to lead a life of their own. Moreover, Bakhtin's phenomenal erudition, by its very magnitude, discourages the reader from retracing the bibliographical trajectory already completed; the immense literary baggage that supports the analyses of Rabelais and Dostoyevsky, for example, remains as a mere background and not as a live corpus, discussable and subject to specific appropriations.[107]

107 The American edition of the Dostoyevsky book implicitly

On the other hand, Bakhtin's texts do make it difficult to reduce or simplify his ideas. With regard to the concept most suited to explication, the concept of dialogism, it is always worth remembering the precaution with which it is introduced at the beginning of *Problems*: "We consider Dostoevsky one of the greatest innovators in the realm of artistic form. We believe that he created a completely new type of artistic thinking, a type of thinking that we have *provisionally* (my emphasis) called *polyphonic*" (Bakhtin, 1984a: 3). On top of this, the coexistence of diverse voices intelligibly woven together in the text only became possible thanks to their genre: polyphony is, in great part, a tribute to the novel-form – and to a specific type of novel, no doubt, one that emerged with Dostoevsky and that has been reproduced only a few times since then. In this sense, it is important to read *Problems* side by side with the essays from *The Dialogic Imagination*, especially "Epic and the Novel." These leave no doubt as to the specificity of the novel: namely, its specificity as a form that is capable of incorporating the different within the self without thereby ceasing to be an organizing principle; in other words, its specificity as a structure that is precisely based on the incorporation of alterity.

The same holds for another important concept, that of carnivalization, one of the most easily applicable in the author's corpus. Here too the concept's scope of validity is not unrestricted, for Bakhtin emphasizes that Rabelais' greatness derives from the particular conjunction of his vast erudition and his openness to popular demonstrations and events. If one of these elements is missing, one deduces that carnivalization loses its emphatic meaning. This is important to emphasize

---

acknowledges this as it provides an appendix explaining the authors and works mentioned in the text.

so that a facile populism can be avoided. The latter would see an immediate accessibility of carnivalization, deprived of any relationship with what we call the literate world – at worst, as if it were a philistine, simply anti-intellectual position. Bakhtin himself repeatedly observes (1984a: 130 passim; 1984b: 101) that the insertion of the carnival in literature reaches its climax precisely with Rabelais, only to gradually retreat; the carnival would then stop fuelling literary writing, to be transmitted simply through works of fiction, and no longer in direct contact with communal celebrations. Even though Bakhtin asserts that genres have a life of their own, preserving in themselves traces of a remote past, it is necessary to recognize that something of the force of the encounter with the popular got lost in history, and this loss merits critical reflection.

It is from the proliferation of commentaries and applications that the monologism of the multiple emerges, the result of a clear dialectical movement. Through repetition, several Bakhtinian *topoi* revert to their opposites: for example, the reiteration, under the most diverse circumstances, that dialogism is constitutive of language, that it is present in each and every enunciative phenomenon, results in something that is ultimately monological. The same is true of application: identifying polyphony in the most diverse novels, in movies, songs, etc., transforms the supposed variety of voices into its opposite. This is valid for all the Bakhtinian concepts, to the point of suggesting a rule: any concept that holds a content of alterity transforms into its negative when it is channelled in abstract form – independently of its author's original intention, and even if it serves such laudable purposes as the dissemination and application of progressive thought.

This is the mechanism that needs to be investigated in its general characteristics and effects; but first, it is necessary to say a few words regarding the suitability of multiplicity for the Brazilian context.

III

The Bakhtinian theory of carnivalization finds strong resonances in Brazilian culture, as it calls to mind an entire modernist tradition that has the concept of anthropophagy at its heart. It is not possible to dwell on the concept here; it suffices to stress that the concept of anthropophagy delineates a cultural politics of appropriation of the foreign by the national that comes through the appeal to a barbaric indigenous practice. If primitivism represented an artistic finding in early twentieth-century European modernism, in Brazil it was a daily reality. The "being together" of opposites thus became undeniable: cultural anthropophagy celebrated Brazil's contradictory reality as though it were an epistemological gain. The coexistence of the archaic and the modern became the definition of *brasilidade* ("Brazilian-ness") *par excellence*. This particular mixture, which extended to religious syncretism, to language, to cultural practices, has had a consistent history, reaching its climax with *tropicalismo* in the 1960s and 70s. Brazilian hybridity was revisited in a celebratory manner, as a national singularity worthy of pride and praise. Carnival has a central role in this tradition. It represents that moment in which, as Bakhtin characterizes it, the distinction between the participant and the spectator is undone, the moment in which the hierarchical ordering of society is subverted. Furthermore, the representation of Brazil as a happy country, as the opposite of violence, as the country of racial democracy, the country of the successful melting pot finds an important crutch in the ideology of celebration.[108] In sum, the ideology of multiplicity lives a life of its own in the cultural history of twentieth-century Brazil.

Thus emerges the possibility of bringing together the two conceptions of carnival, which come from very different contexts but share the same name. It is precisely this attempt (and this temptation!) to appropriate that must be fought. The reasons are obvious: firstly, the subversion of social structure is not occurring in Brazil, where the law of money has not been abolished, having at best been a bit loosened; secondly, as we shall see, whatever could be transgressive in the ideas of difference, mixing and miscegenation has ceased to exist. What could be seen before as resistance to an ordered and fixedly structured world has been incorporated in the workings of contemporary capitalism. Finally, it is worth underlining – namely to anticipate an argument that will be made below – that the ideologem /party/ has a de-differentiating role that is consistent with the monologism of the multiple. For the party can incorporate everything, take everything as its own; a celebration is, by definition, that which does not allow antagonism to exist.

The majority of Bakhtin's good commentators do not agree with the direct appropriation of carnivalization for the present Brazilian context; however, they do not vehemently oppose it, thus leaving space for various articulations, which are almost always questionable. Mechanical reproduction takes care of the rest. A Google search with "Bakhtin" and

108 The term is used in the sense of Jameson (1981).

"carnivalization" as keywords, limited to Brazilian results, offered 1,600 items on August 11, 2008. A good chunk of the results correspond to academic pieces, dissertations, theses and articles in online journals, which used the concept of carnivalization in relation to an object of reading, almost always from Brazilian culture. The children's book *O Reizinho Mandão,*[109] by Ruth Rocha, the popular cultural rites of Piaui[110], the television series *Invenção do Brasil* (The Invention of Brazil), [111] the poem *Catatau* by Paulo Leminski, [112] the movie *Saturday* by Ugo Giorgetti, [113] the novels *A Hora da Estrela* by Clarice Lispector, [114] or *Macunaíma* by Mário de Andrade,[115] among many, many others – none of the above seems able to offer resistance to the idea's applicability. The very concept of carnivalization is thus carnivalized, coming closer to the limit of intelligibility, embracing everything without saying anything. It would be difficult to conceive of this dissemination of the carnival if it was not so available for Brazilians, if it did not function as a cultural magnet pulling toward it so many of the phenomena in its orbit.[116] Of course, it is possible to do away with the problem entirely if one argues that the readings that equate the two carnivals are simply wrong – which they indeed

109http://faculdade.fatema.br/tema/tema45/L%EDgia%20Regina%20Maximo%20Cavalari%20Menna.pdf
110 http://www.intercom.org.br/papers/nacionais/2006/resumos/R1821-1.pdf
111 http://www.intexto.ufrgs.br/n13/medeiros_art.html
112 http://paginas.terra.com.br/arte/PopBox/kamiquase/ensaio30.htm
113 http://www3.unisul.br/paginas/ensino/pos/linguagem/0102/20.htm
114 http://www.teses.usp.br/teses/disponiveis/8/8149/tde-05102007-145251/
115 www.unasp-ec.edu.br/biblioteca/tcc/arquivos-conteudo/arquivos-indice/tcc-letras%5Ctccsimoneeestela.doc
116 Not to mention the compensatory logic that may be at stake. The feeling of inferiority, so common in undeveloped countries, would find in carnival a source of pride: "this is something we have and they don't".

are. However, this is where a clash occurs between the idea of correction (of the philologically correct, the academically and intellectually consistent) and the very impulse of Bakhtinian prosaicness, to use Morson and Emerson's highly appropriate expression (1990). It is impossible to argue for an opening toward the people's diverse voices and everyday life on theoretical grounds while closing oneself to the meaning concretely produced in the dissemination (and banalization) of Bakhtin's œuvre. Another exit must be found.

IV

The monologism of the multiple is not an isolated phenomenon, but an important element of a general rhetoric of abundance. It is namely a result of the growing differentiation and complication of literary theory discourse. This process has been ongoing since the 1960s and has spread mainly from the United States, albeit with effects reaching the intellectual traditions of several other countries, including those from where theoretical matrices were imported. The semi-autonomization of theory (see Cusset, 2005) brought about a trend of continuous updates to interpretive language, which favoured neologisms and new concepts to the detriment of existent ones belonging to a consolidated tradition. Connected with this development has been the growing amount of discussion about concepts in themselves (as in the case of globalization) rather than about the objects to which they are supposed to refer. The result is an inflation of meta-discourses and their analyses; a development that generates meta-meta debates, which in turn cause the production of literary theory discourses to accelerate. In this context, Bakhtin's reception in Brazil has demonstrated a twofold character: while it has on the one hand shown laudable continuity, it has also adapted itself to the functioning of the academic theoretical machinery and its bibliographic superproduction, which can easily create a space of abstraction with respect to that which one is supposed to be working on.

The rhetoric of abundance can be seen as a type of common denominator for a whole series of contemporary theoretical currents and critical terms. These include the use that deconstruction makes of difference – a term that has already become commonplace and loaded with positive, almost moral, value, as though difference was necessarily something good. They also include the valorization of postcolonial hybridism; the definition of multiple identities à la Judith Butler; the forms of resistance propounded by cultural studies; and others. Bakhtinian polyphony and carnivalization thus simply appear to be two more examples – of course, with their own characteristics – of this desire for abundance, of criticism's anxiety about seeing something "more" in literature. Certainly, we are dealing with an impulse that cannot be addressed in full here and that would accordingly merit further study. It is merely possible to point to the historical conquest that was aesthetic autonomy, when the artwork ceased to be judged according to any type of transcendental parameter, any *ideal* that served as its measure, and began to be evaluated on its own terms, in accordance with the rules it imposed upon itself. In other words, as long as literature was linked with something external to it, difference could not be considered as a positive value in itself. It was only with the emergence of the text's immanence, with the romantics, that an internal richness of meaning could be illuminated as a result of the articulation between the whole and its parts.

Another chapter of the history of desire for abundance emerged with *New Criticism*, in which the search for ambiguities and polysemy came to acquire a methodological character. With *New Criticism*, the poem's richness of meanings, the fruit of its organic-ness (associated with the rural world), was brought into opposition with the disorder of the world off-kilter, of industrial society, of a poor society that was only getting poorer. This vision – a conservative one – cannot sustain itself, for it ignores the extreme order of the administered world, a world that can be considered as the dialectical opposite of chaos. The availability of the text's immanence is nevertheless highly problematic; in effect, it is more productive to think of textual immanence as an interpretive *result* flowing from what is most mediated, namely interpretation itself.[117] All the same, to give only one example of how everything can become complicated if textual immanence is conceived as something immediate, given or available, it suffices to remember that the very idea of immanence can function as a normative reading horizon; if this occurs, immanence ceases to be immanent.

This is where the strange performative effect cited earlier occurs. However, it now stems from the rushed use of the idea and ideal of abundance. The proposition "the text is multiple" (a theme that runs through an infinite number of works) has already produced, through its enunciation, a distancing vis-à-vis its object. It is as if the multiplicity postulated earlier had put itself between the text and the reader, preventing that the former negate the reader's desire for infinity. By distancing the text and ultimately de-differentiating it, this multiplicity contributes to the acceleration of the production of readings

117 This is what I tried to show in *Modernism and Coherence* (2008).

and thus facilitates the smooth running of the academic machine. It is no coincidence that its circulation is so extensive. One must note, however, that it is not a matter of defending the poverty of the literary text (although this notion, in this context, has a reinvigorating quality), but rather of calling attention to the configuration of abundance in the economy of innumerable authors' critical essays. Rather than being invoked, multiplicity should be demonstrated; rather than being considered as a starting point, it should be an endpoint; and rather than being an a priori goal of analysis, it should be its result – and not even an exclusive result.

This distancing in relation to the text's possible resistance, cause and consequence of its de-differentiation – which, of course, occurs in the name of difference – still has another effect that facilitates circulation. The rhetoric of abundance has trouble delineating an antagonist, an argumentative category that is unavoidable in any critical writing. In its extreme, such rhetoric puts antagonism itself in the position of the antagonist. The lack of clarity with respect to the distinction between friends and enemies (as it is well known, a fundamental distinction for Carl Schmitt) then begins to obscure the intra-textual politics, as well as the debate that the latter could evoke. This process facilitates the politics' migration toward other contexts – namely the private sphere, thereby perpetuating the longstanding Brazilian practice of weakening the public sphere.

One last observation must be made before concluding this section. It is crucial to emphasize the structural nature of the idea of abundance. Although there are different degrees of consciousness with respect to the idea's productivity, we do not mean to suggest that a malicious plan to promote the text's distancing (or, ultimately, the very disappearance of the object) is underway. At stake is not primordially a matter of the subject's will, but a result of the *paper*-producing academic machine. This machine functions frighteningly well in Brazil, consolidating a solid graduate system that sees 10,000 PhDs graduate every year and, in the Humanities, solidifying a satisfactory discursive field for the first time in the country's history. At this point, the contradictory nature of this process must be emphasized once more.

V

But the rhetoric of abundance is not limited to Brazil. In effect, it has already been demonstrated several times that postmodernism draws on a valorization of difference, regardless of whether it is seen as corresponding to a third phase of capitalism (Jameson, 1991) or to a new phase of flexible accumulation of capital (Harvey, 1990). As Hardt & Negri argue:

> And what if a new paradigm of power, a post-modern sovereignty, had arrived to substitute the modern paradigm and promote domination through those hierarchies that differentiate hybrid and fragmented subjectivities, those that all post-modern theories

> celebrate? In this case, the modern forms of sovereignty would not be in play anymore and postmodern and postcolonial strategies, which appear to be so libertarian, would not constitute a threat. They would in fact coincide and perhaps even strengthen, unwittingly, the new strategies of domination! (...) This new enemy is not only resistant to old weapons, but in reality prospers with them. In doing so it joins forces with its supposed antagonists, using these weapons to their maximum effect. Long live difference! Down with essentialist binaries! (2000: 138)

In other words, there is no commodity that refrains from saying "I am different"; there is no product that does not want to clear the slate left behind by those that preceded it, as the avant-gardes endeavoured to do. But to make this hypothesis more persuasive, it is worth underscoring that, like so many other times in the past, what gives strength is also what creates risk. For while difference is a crucial springboard for today's capitalism, an emphatic difference would actually defy the system, especially given that the repetitive law of profit-making is subjacent to all the commodities in the world (including, most importantly, the cultural ones). What is at stake is thus a dialectic that finds its most succinct truth in the adage: *plus ça change, plus c'est la même chose.*

The same can be said about such cherished figures as Bakhtin, who in their very being embody the presence of another. The clearest case is that of parody, which has an intrinsically contestatory and transgressive potential for many readers. It is difficult to say whether this was actually the case at any point in history; what is certain is that it no longer applies today. Slavoj Žižek has been calling attention to a change in the workings of ideology in the face of postmodern cynicism for some time: "with a disarming frankness one 'admits everything', yet this full acknowledgement of our power interests prevents us from pursuing these interests – the formula of cynicism is no longer the classic Marxian 'they do not know it, but they are doing it'; it is 'they know very well what they are doing, yet they are doing it'" (1994, p. 8). If the idea of unveiling no longer works, discursive heterogeneity loses much of its transgressive force; the incorporation of alterity loses its transgressive nature; and irony and parody can become instruments for the acceptance and strengthening of what already exists.

This development can ultimately be tied back to a new status of truth and to a new configuration of fiction. The fact that major multinationals exist first and foremost to make a profit and only secondarily to offer a socially useful service; the fact that governments lie and manipulate the masses; the fact that power and money are the engines of the world – these are no longer merely theoretical propositions, but contents that could be drawn from the trilogy *Resident Evil*. Their nature has an intermediate character, neither beyond the horizon of what is known nor sufficiently present to incite political action.

In any event, the line of thinking pursued to this point should be clear: if Bakhtinian dialogism transforms, through the explicative-applicative mode of reproduction, into a monologism of the multiple; if this is an important part of a general rhetoric of abundance, which is linked to a theory/politics of difference; and if postmodern capitalism precisely feeds upon this impoverished concept of the different; then the perspectives opened for contemporary readings of Bakhtin are not the most encouraging. But this doesn't need to be the case.

The Russian thinker's œuvre can take on a new importance if *antagonism* is placed front and centre in the workings of Bakhtinian discourse. If this is obvious in *Marxism and Philosophy of Language* (1990) (to the point of drawing attention to those commentators who do *not* emphasize it), antagonism can also be found in the rest of his œuvre: be it in the presentification of the novel in the face of epic atemporality; in the disorder of the carnival in the face of mediaeval hierarchy; in the theory of genres; in the conception of words; in interdiscursivity; and even in chronotropia. Antagonism does not need to be confused with simple contradiction, which would suggest a mechanistic dialectic. If the challenge Bakhtin poses is that of thinking the idea of multiplicity, then multiplicity should not be seen as positive, abstractly creative, but as the multiplicity of antagonism.[118] Nor should the idea

118 In this sense, it is interesting to compare the concept of dialogism to that of force field (*Kraftfeld*) in Adorno. As far as the dialectic is concerned, it is important not to mistake its impoverished, Soviet version to the rich tradition that spans from Hegel to Roberto Schwarz, through Marcuse, Benjamin, Bloch

of conflict even be opposed to the idea of creation, as if the former were inferior to the latter; on the contrary, it is fully legitimate to argue that opposition is more productive than any kind of abstract creation, which would unfold in a vacuum, isolated from power plays and articulations of power.

When conflict is made explicit and brought to the fore it becomes much easier to determine *against whom* it unfolds; and with this knowledge, it becomes possible to truly articulate an analysis of the specific conditions of enunciation. Explication and application now interpenetrate one another, for explication becomes a matter of tying what is explicated back to a specific concept, and application presupposes an adequate understanding of the concept in its new context. It is not a matter of imposing a foreign impulse on anything; on the contrary, it is a matter of retrieving a potential that is fully present in Bakhtin's œuvre. As such, the concept of dialogism now needs to be connected to a new reality, completely unknown to Bakhtin, that of the computerized world, a world dominated by large communications conglomerates, a world of semiotic super-production, of a never-before-seen proliferation of signs, that constantly call on the subject, forcing it to defend itself. This super-production of signs is inserted into a dialectics of abundance that multiplies but maintains the same, albeit ever stronger, base; a homogenization (shot through with difference) never seen before. The digitization of the world makes the latter morph into something sellable; something at once infinitely quotable and easier to dominate. Interaction gets lost in the bombardment of signs and messages; the idea of a style of life, which had once been a conquest of art in the

---

and others.

face of a hierarchized world, ceases to be an option. From there it only becomes a presupposition, to the point that the opposite is absorbed by the contrary (to speak in Greimasian terms): the lack of style comes to be seen as a style in itself, rendering the existence of mere absence impossible.

And so comes the argument: if this world is characterized both by hyper-signification and by a paucity of meaning, by a wealth of content but weak reflection, Bakhtin's conceptual apparatus has a fertile field of action. Not as the monologism of the multiple, but as a tool for the configuration of antagonism within the global capitalist system that dominates today's world. But for this development to occur, it is necessary to take real sides. While this was such an obvious assumption for Bakhtin that he did not feel the need to make it explicit, today it becomes a real objective, even for his readers; not just so that his œuvre's validity can be truly understood, but so that its value can be fruitfully explored.

REFERENCES

References

Adorno, Theodor. "Theorie der Halbbildung" *Soziologische Schriften I.* Frankfurt a.M.: Suhrkamp, 1979a. 93-121.

----. "Kultur und Verwaltung" *Soziologische Schriften I.* Frankfurt a.M.: Suhrkamp, 1979b. 122-146.

----. "Über Statik und Dynamik als soziologische Kategorien." *Soziologische Schriften I.* Frankfurt a.M.: Suhrkamp, 1979c. 220-222.

----. "Spätkapitalismus oder Industriegesellschaft?" *Soziologische Schriften I.* Frankfurt a.M.: Suhrkamp, 1979d. 354-370.

----. "Reflexionen zur Klassentheorie". *Soziologische Schriften I.* Frankfurt a.M.: Suhrkamp, 1979e. 373-391.

----. "Thesen über Bedürfnis." *Soziologische Schriften I.* Frankfurt a.M.: Suhrkamp, 1979f. 392-396.

----. *Metaphysik; Begriff und Probleme.* Frankfurt a.M.: Suhrkamp, 1998.

----. *Negative Dialectics.* Trans. E.B. Ashton. New York: Continuum, 1973.

----. "Theses against occultism." Trans. E.F.N. Jephcott. *Minima Moralia.* London: Verso, 1974. 238-244.

----. *The Stars Down to Earth. Gesammelten Schriften* 9.2. Frankfurt a.M.: Suhrkamp, 1975. 8-120.

----. "Commitment". *Notes to Literature.* Trans. Shierry W. Nicholsen. New York: Columbia University Press, 1992.

----. *Aesthetic Theory*. Trans. Robert Hullot-Kentor. Minneapolis: University of Minnesota Press, 1997.

----. *Philosophy of New Music.* Trans. Robert Hullot-Kentor. Minneapolis: Minnesota UP, 2006.

----. "The Idea of Natural History". Trans. Robert Hullot-Kentor,

Telos No. 60, Summer 1984.

----. "The Schema of Mass Culture". Trans. Nicholas Walker. *The Culture Industry:* Selected Essays on Mass Culture. Ed. J. M. Berstein. London: Routledge, 2008. 61-97.

Adorno, T.W. George Simpson. "On Popular Music." In *Studies in Philosophy and Social Science,* v. IX, ed. Max Horkheirmer. New York: Institute of Social Research, 1941. 17–48.

Althusser, Louis. *Sur la Reproduction.* Paris: Seuil, 1995.

----. "Ideology and ideological State apparatuses". In: *Lenin and Philosophy* New York: Monthly Review Press, 1971.

Anderson, Benedict. *Imagined Communities: Reflections on the Origin and Spread of Nationalism*. London: Verso, 1991.

Arantes, Paulo. *O Sentimento da Dialética na Experiência Intelectual Brasileira.* São Paulo: Paz & Terra, 1992.

Araújo, Paulo Cezar. *Eu não sou cahorro não. Música Popular Cafona e Ditadura Militar.* Rio de Janeiro: Record, 2002.

Arruda, Maria Arminda do Nascimento. *Metrópole e Cultura. São Paulo no meio século XX*. Bauru, São Paulo: EDUSC, 2001.

Assis, Joaquim Machado. *Posthumous Memoirs of Brás Cubas.* Trans. Gegory Rabassa. Oxford: O.U.P., 1997 [1881].

Bakhtin, M. *The Dialogic Imagination.* Ed. M. Holquist; Trans. C. Emerson & M. Holquist. Austin: U. of Texas P., 1981.

----. *Problems of Dostoevsky's Poetics.* Trans. C. Emerson. Minneapolis: Minnesota U.P., 1984a.

----. *Rabelais and His World.* Trans. H. Iswolsky. Bloomington: Indiana U.P., 1984b.

Bakhtin, M. (V.N. Volochinov). *Marxismo e Filosofia da Linguagem.* Trans. M. Lahud & Y.F. Vieira. São Paulo: Huicitec, 1990.

Barros, Diana L.P. & José Luiz Fiorin (orgs.) *Dialogismos, Polifonia, Intertextualidade.* São Paulo: EDUSP, 1994.

Basualdo, Carlos. *Tropicália: uma Revolução na Cultura Brasileira (1967-1972).* São Paulo: Cosac &Naify, 2007.

Bêta, Janaína Laport. *Madras: Arte e Sagrado em Arthur Bispo do Rosário*. Rio de Janeiro: Tempo Brasileiro, 2012.

Bordwell, D.; Staiger, J.; Thompson, K. *The Classical Hollywood Cinema*. New York: Columbia University Press, 1985.

Bosi, Alfredo. "Roteiro do poeta Ferreira Gullar". In: *Céu, Inferno*. São Paulo: Duas Cidades/Ed. 34, 2003.

Brait, Beth (org.). *Bakhtin; dialogismo e construção do sentido*. Campinas: Editora da Unicamp, 2005a.

----. (org.) *Bakhtin: Conceitos-Chave*. São Paulo: Contexto, 2005b.

----. (org.) *Bakhtin: Outros Conceitos-Chave*. São Paulo: Contexto, 2006.

Brito, Teca Alencar. *Koellreuter educador*. São Paulo: Peirópolis, 2001.

Bukowski, Charles. *Mulheres*. Trans. Reinaldo Moraes. Porto Alegre: L&PM, 1984.

Burrowes, Patrícia. *O Universo segundo Arthur Bispo do Rosário*. Rio de Janeiro: Editora da Fundação Getúlio Vargas, 1999.

Butler, Judith. *The Psychic Life of Power*. Stanford: Stanford U.P., 1997.

Butler, Judith; Ernesto Laclau; Žižek, Slavoj. *Contingency, Hegemony, Universality*. London: Verso, 2000.

Cadernos de Literatura Brasileira. Ferreira Gullar. No. 6. São Paulo: Instituto Moreira Salles, 1998.

Camenietzki, Eleonora Ziller. *Poesia e Política*. A Trajetória de Ferreira Gullar. Rio de Janeiro: Revan, 2006.

----. "Três propostas para o próximo milênio: *Cidade de Deus*, de Paulo Lins, *A lição do prático*, de Maurício Luz, e *Trono da rainha jinga*, de Alberto Mussa". In: Resende, Beatriz (ed.) *Literatura Brasileira Depois das Utopias*. Special issue of *Revista Tempo Brasileiro*. N. 141. Rio de Janeiro: Tempo Brasileiro, 2000.

Cândido, Antonio. "Dialética da Malandragem". In: *O Discurso e a Cidade*. São Paulo: Duas Cidades, 1993.

Cavazotti, André. "O serialismo e o atonalismo livre aportam na MPB: as canções do LP *Clara Crocodilo* de Arrigo Barnabé". *Per Musi*. Belo Horizonte, 2000. 5-15.

----. Processos Seriais na Música de Arrigo Barnabé: As Oito Canções do LP "Clara Crocodilo." Dissertação de mestrado em música. Universidade Federal do Rio Grande do Sul, 1993.

Charaudeau, Patrick *Langage et Discours; Eléments de Sémiolinguistique*. Paris: Hachette, 1983.

Corcoran, Steven. "Editor's Introduction". In: Rancière, J. *Dissensus: On politics and aesthetics*. Trans. Steven Corcoran. New York: Continuum, 2010. 1-24.

Corpas, Flavia dos Santos; Morais, Frederico (eds). *Arthur Bispo do Rosário: Arte Além da Loucura*. Rio de Janeiro: Nau, 2013.

Cusset, François. *French Theory*. Paris: La Découverte, 2005 [2003].

Cunha, Euclides da. *Backlands: The Canudos Campaign*. Trans. Elisabeth Lowe. New York: Penguin, 2010 [1902].

Cyntrão, Sylvia Helena (org.). *A Forma da Festa. Tropicalismo: a Explosão e seus Estilhaços*. Brasília: UNB, 2000.

Damaso, Tito. *Ferreira Gullar; uma Poética do Sujo*. São Paulo: Nankin Editorial, 2006.

Dantas, Maria. *Arthur Bispo do Rosário: a Poética do Delírio*. São Paulo: Editora da Unesp, 2009.

De Hollanda, Heloísa Buarque. *Impressões de Viagem: CPC, Vanguarda e Desbunde: 1960-1970*. Rio de Janeiro: Rocco, 1992.

De Hollanda, Sérgio Buarque. *Raízes do Brasil* 26ª. ed. São Paulo: Companhia das Letras, 2003[1936].

Demirovič, Alex (ed.). *Modelle kritischer Gesellschaftstheorie*. Stuttgart: J.B. Metzler, 2003.

Dias, Márcia Tosta. *Os Donos da Voz. Indústria Fonográfica Brasileira e a Mundialização da Cultura*. São Paulo:

Boitempo, 2000.

Dolar, Mladen. "Beyond Interpellation", *Qui Parle.* V. 6, No. 2, Spring/Summer, 1993.

Duarte, Rodrigo. *Mímesis e Racionalidade.* São Paulo: Loyola, 1993.

----. "Zum Rezeption kritischer Theorie in Brasilien: Der Fall Merquior". *Zeitschrift für kritische Theorie.* N. 5, 1997: 117-126.

Dunn, Christopher. *Brutality Garden: Tropicália and the Emergence of a Brazilian Counterculture*. Chapel Hill, North Carolina: University of North Carolina Press, 2001.

Dunn, Christopher; Charles A. Perrone. *Brazilian Popular Music & Globalization.* Gainesville: U.P. of Florida, 2001.

Durão, Fabio A. "Enforced Happiness; or, Domination Brazilian Style". Enforced Happiness; Or, Domination Brazilian Style. *Idea arts + society*, Cluj, v. 18, p. 141-147, 2004a.

----. "Uma Iniciativa a ser Emulada". *Impulso,* Piracicaba, v. 38, 2004b

----. "A Postmodern Paradox". *American, British and Canadian Studies.* Vol. Sibiu. 2008a.

----. "Da superprodução semiótica: caracterização e implicações estéticas" in F.A. Durão, A. Zuin, A. Vaz (eds.) *A Indústria Cultural Hoje*. São Paulo: Boitempo Editorial, 2008b.

----. *Modernism and Coherence: Four Chapters of a Negative Aesthetics*. Frankfurt/Bern/New York: Peter Lang, 2008c.

----. "Brazilian Culture". In: Juang, Richard M.; Morrissette, Noelle (eds.). *Africa and the Americas: Culture, Politics, and History*. V. 1. Santa Barbara: ABC-CLIO, 2008d: 193-195.

----. "On the disappearance of objects". In: Gilder, Eric; Mitrea, Alexandra; Scheider, Ana-Karina (eds.). *The English Connection: 40 Years of English Studies at "Lucian Blaga" University of Sibiu*. Bucharest/Sibiu, Unesco/Lucian Blaga University, 2010. 45–57.

----. *Teoria (Literária) Americana*. Campinas: Autores Associados, 2011a.

----. "De volta a Adorno na interpretação da cultura". *Fronteiraz* (São Paulo), v. 7, 2011b.

Durão, F.A. & Dominic Williams. *Modernist Group Dynamics: The Poetics and Politics of Friendship.* Newcastle: Cambridge Scholars Publishing, 2008.

Eisenstein, S.M. "Método de realização de um filme operário". In: Xavier, I. (org.). *A Experiência do Cinema:* Antologia. Rio de Janeiro: Graal – Embrafilmes, 1983.

Espinosa, J. G. "For an imperfect cinema". In: Fusco, Coco (ed.). *Selections from New Latin American Cinema.* New York: Hallwalls Contemporary Arts Center, 1998. 166-177.

Faraco, Carlos Alberto. *Linguagem & diálogo: as idéias lingüísticas do círculo de Bakhtin*. Curitiba: Criar Edições, 2003.

Faraco, Carlos Alberto, Cristóvão Tezza & Gilberto de Castro. *Vinte ensaios sobre Bakhtin.* Petrópolis: Vozes, 2006.

----. *Diálogos com Bakhtin.* Curitiba: Editora da Univ. Fed. do Paraná, 1996.

Favaretto, Celso. *Tropicália Alegoria Alegria*. 3ª ed. São Paulo: Ateliê Editorial, 2000.

Fenerick, José Adriano. *Façanhas às próprias Custas. A Produção Musical da Vanguarda Paulista, 1979-2000*. São Paulo: Annablume/FAPESP, 2007.

----. "A ditadura, a indústria fonográfica e os 'Independentes' de São Paulo nos anos 70/80." *Métis: História e Cultura.* Universidade de Caxias do Sul, v.3, N. 6, Caxias do Sul, 2005. 155–178.

----. Marquioni, Carlos Eduardo. "Sgt. Pepper's Lonely Hearts Club Band: uma colagem de sons e imagens" *Revista Fênix.* N. 5, 2008. On line at: http://www.revistafenix.pro.br/.

Figueiredo, Alda de Moura Macedo. *Manto da Apresentação: Arthur Bispo do Rosário em Diálogo com Deus.* Niterói:

Editora da Universidade Federal Fluminense, 2012.

Fiorin, José Luiz. *Introdução ao pensamento de Bakhtin.* São Paulo: Ática, 2006.

Fish, Stanley. *Is There a Text in This Class?* The Authority of Interpretative Communities. Cambridge: Harvard U.P., 1980.

Freitag, Barbara. *A Teoria Crítica Ontem e Hoje.* São Paulo: Brasiliense, 1988.

Gagnebin, Jeanne Marie. *Sete Aulas sobre Linguagem, Memória e História.* Rio de Janeiro: Imago, 1997.

Gaúna, Regiane. *Rogério Duprat: Sonoridades Múltiplas.* São Paulo: Editorial UNESP, 2002.

Goldenberg, Mirian (ed.). *Nu & Vestido.* Rio de Janeiro: Record, 2002.

Gomes, P. E. S. "Cinema: a trajectory within underdevelopment". In: Johnson, Randal; Stam, Robert (eds.). *Brazilian Cinema.* New York: Columbia U.P., 1995.

Graff, Gerald. *Professing Literature.* Chicago: University of Chicago Press, 2007 [1987].

Guelman, Leonardo. *Univvverrsso Gentileza.* Rio de Janeiro: Mundo das Idéias, 2009.

----.; Amaral, Dado; Kutassy, Mariana. (eds.). *Livro Urbano do Profeta Gentileza.* Rio de Janeiro: Mundo das Idéias, 2011

Gullar, Ferreira. "Arthur Bispo e a Arte Contempoânea". *Folha de São Paulo*, Caderno Ilustrada, 14 de agosto de 2011.

----. *Toda Poesia.* 15ª. ed. Rio de Janeiro: José Olympio Editora, 2006.

----. *Vanguarda e subdesenvolvimento.* Rio de Janeiro: Civilização Brasileira, 1978.

Hardt, Michael; Negri, Antonio. *Empire.* Cambridge: Harvard U.P., 2000.

----. . *Multitude.* New York: Penguin, 2004.

Harvey, David. *The Condition of Postmodernity.* Oxford: Blackwell, 1990.

----. *The New Imperialism*. Oxford: O.U.P., 2003.

Herz, Daniel. *A História Secreta da Rede Globo.* Porto Alegre: Tchê!, 1987.

Hidalgo, Luciana. *Arthur Bispo do Rosário: o Senhor do Labirinto*. Rio de Janeiro: Rocco, 1996.

Hullot-Kentor, Robert. "What Barbarism Is?". In: Durão, F. A. (ed.). *Culture Industry Today*. Newcastle: Cambridge Scholars Publishing, 2010.

Jameson, Fredric. *Marxism and Form*. Princeton: Princeton U.P., 1971.

----. Jameson, Fredric. *The Political Unconscious.* Ithaca: Cornell U.P., 1981.

----. *Postmodernism; or, the cultural logic of late capitalism.* Durham: Duke U.P., 1991.

----. "Periodizando os anos 60". In: De Hollanda, Heloísa Buarque (ed.) *Pós-Modernismo e Política.* Rio de Janeiro: Rocco, 1992.

Kater, Carlos. *Música Viva e H.J. Koellreutter. Movimentos em direção à modernidade*. SP: Musa Editora/Atravez, 2001.

Kehl, Maria Rita; Pucci, Eugênio. *Videologias.* São Paulo: Boitempo, 2004.

Klothe, Flávio. *Benjamin e Adorno: Confrontos.* São Paulo: Ática, 1978.

Kurz, Robert. *Der Kollaps der Modernisierung*: *Vom Zusammenbruch des Kasernensozialismus zur Krise der Weltokonomie*. Frankfurt: Eichborn, 1991.

----. *O Colapso da Modernização.* Da Derrocada do Socialismo de Caserna à Crise da Economia Mundial. Trans. Karen Elsabe Barbosa. São Paulo: Paz e Terra, 1992.

Lafetá, João Luiz. "Traduzir-se: ensaio sobre a poesia de Ferreira Gullar". In: *A Dimensão da Noite.* Organização de

A.A. Prado. São Paulo: Cidades/Ed. 34, 2004a.

----. "Dois pobres, duas medidas". In: *A Dimensão da Noite.* Organização de A.A. Prado. São Paulo: Cidades/Ed. 34, 2004b.

Lazaro, Wilson. *Arthur Bispo do Rosário.* Rio de Janeiro: Réptil, 2012.

Lessa, Carlos. *O Rio de todos os Brasis: uma Reflexão em busca da Auto-estima.* 2ª. ed. Rio de Janeiro: Record, 2001.

Lins, P. *Cidade de Deus.* São Paulo: Companhia das Letras, 1997.

Lopes, Genésio. *O Superpoder: o Raio X da Rede Globo: um Império da Ganância e da Lucratividade.* São Paulo: Ibrasa, 2001.

Lukács, Georg. *The Theory of the Novel.* Cambridge: MIT Press, 1971.

Maciel, Maria Esther. "A enciclopédia de Arthur Bispo do Rosário". In: Coutinho, Fernanda; Carvalho, Marília; Moreira, Renata. *A Vida ao Rés-do-Chão: Artes de Bispo do Rosário*. Rio de Janeiro: 7Letras, 2007. 92-106.

Marcuse, Herbert. *The Aesthetic Dimension;* Toward a Critique of Marxist Aesthetics. Boston: Beacon Press, 1978.

----. *Counter Revolution and Revolt.* Boston: Beacon Press, 1972.

Marques Filho, José Virginio. *Orgia de Exceção: um Esboço do Projeto Literário de Reinaldo Moraes*. Master's thesis, University of São Paulo, 2015.

Martins, Maria H.P. *ECA: Retrato em Branco e Preto*. São Paulo: ECA/USP, 1988.

Matos, Olgária. *A Escola de Frankfurt.* São Paulo: Moderna, 1993.

Mello, Cléa Côrrea. "O desafio crítico de *Cidade de Deus*". In: Resende, Beatriz (ed.) *Literatura Brasileira depois das Utopias.* Special issue of *Revista Tempo Brasileiro.* 141. Rio de Janeiro: Tempo Brasileiro, 2000.

Menezes, Flo. *Apoteose de Schoenberg. Tratado sobre as entidades harmônicas*. São Paulo: Ateliê Editorial, 2002.

Menke, Christoph. *Die Souveranität der Kunst.* Frankfurt a.M.: Suhrkamp, 1991.

Merquior, José Guillherme. *Arte e Sociedade em Marcuse, Adorno e Benjamin*. Rio de Janeiro: Tempo Brasileiro, 1969.

Moraes, Reinaldo. *Pornopopéia.* Rio de Janeiro: Objetiva, 2011 [2008].

Morris, Pam (ed.). *The Bakhtin Reader: Selected Writings of Bakhtin, Medvedev, Volshinov.* New York: Oxford U.P., 1994.

Morson, Gary S. & Caryl Emerson. *Mikhail Bakhtin: Creation of a Prosaics*. Stanford: Stanford U. P., 1990

Nagib, Lúcia. *A Utopia no Cinema Brasileiro.* São Paulo: Cosac & Naify, 2006.

Napolitano, Marcos. *Seguindo a Canção: Engajamento Político e Indústria Cultural na MPB (1959-1969).* São Paulo: Annablume/Fapesp, 2001.

----. *História & Música. História Cultural da Música Popular.* Belo Horizonte: Autêntica, 2002.

----. *Cultura Brasileira: Utopia e Massificação (1950-1980).* São Paulo: Contexto, 2001

Naves, Santuza Cambraia. *Da Bossa Nova à Tropicália*. Rio de Janeiro: Zahar, 2001.

Nho, Myung-Woo. *Die Schönberg-Deutung Adornos und die Dialektik der Aufklärung. Musik in und jenseits der Dialektik der Aufklärung*. Marburg: Tectum Verlag, 2001.

Nobre, Marcos. *A Dialética Negativa de Theodor W. Adorno.* São Paulo: Iluminuras, 1998.

Ohata, Milton; Cevasco, Maria Elisa (eds.). *Um Crítico na*

Periferia do Capitalismo. São Paulo: Companhia das Letras, 2007.

Ortiz, Renato. *A Moderna Tradição Brasileira.* São Paulo: Brasiliense, 1999.

Paiano, Enor. *O Berimbau e o Som Universal: Lutas Culturais e Indústria Fonográfica nos anos 60.* MA Thesis. Pontifícia Universidade Católica de São Paulo, 1994.

Patrocínio, Stela. *Reino dos Bichos e dos Animais é o Meu Nome*. Río de Janeiro: Azougue, 2001.

Paz, Ravel. A Saga dos Seres Retalhados: Impasses Auráticos e Representação Desviante na *Pornopopeia*, de Reinaldo Moraes. *Revista Olho d'água.* V. 3, n.1, 2011.

Pêcheux, Michel. *Semântica e Discurso.* Campinas: Editora da Unicamp, 1997.

Pécora, Alcir. "Moraes 'viaja' em romance com sexo, drogas e literatura". *Folha de São Paulo,* 11 de julho de 2009.

----. "Estudo busca mostrar o nexo entre poesia e política na obra de Ferreira Gullar." *Folha de São Paulo,* 5 de novembro de 2006.

Pérez-Oramas, Luis, et al. *Catálogo da 38ª. Bienal de São Paulo: a Iminência das Poéticas*. São Paulo: Fundação Bienal de São Paulo, 2012.

Ramos, Nuno. *Ensaio Geral: Projetos, Roteiros, Ensaios, Memória* São Paulo: Globo, 2007.

Rancière, Jacques. *The Politics of Aesthetics: the Distribution of the Sensible*. Trans. Gabriel Rockhill. London and New York: Continuum, 2004.

----. *A partilha do sensível.* Trans. Mônica Costa Netto. São Paulo: Editora 34, 2005.

----. *Dissensus: On Politics and Aesthetics.* Trans. Steven Corcoran. New York: Continuum, 2010.

----. *Aisthesis. Scenes from the Aesthethic Regime of Art.* Trans.

Zakir Paul. London & New York: Verso, 2013.

Resende, Beatriz (ed.) *Literatura Brasileira depois das Utopias.* Special issue of *Revista Tempo Brasileiro.* N. 141. Rio de Janeiro: Tempo Brasileiro, 2000.

Ribeiro, Paulo Jorge. "*Cidade de Deus* na Zona de Contato". *Revista de Critica Literaria Latinoamericana.* Lima/Hanover, año XXIX, n. 57, 2003.

Rocha, G. "An Esthetic of Hunger". In: Johnson, Randal; Stam, Robert (eds.) *Brazilian Cinema.* New York: Columbia U.P., 1995.

Rouanet, Sérgio Paulo. *Teoria Crítica e Psicanálise.* Rio de Janeiro: Tempo Brasileiro, 1983.

Salles Gomes, Paulo Emílio. "Cinema: Trajetória no subdesenvolvimento". In: *Argumento: Revista Mensal de Cultura*. Ano 1., v. 1, Rio de Janeiro: Paz e Terra, 1973.

Schmidt, Alfred. *Der Begriff der Natur in der Lehre von Marx.* 4ª ed. Hamburg: Europäische Verlagsanstalt, 1993.

Schwarz, Roberto. "Nacional por subtração". In: *Que horas são?* São Paulo: Companhia das Letras, 1987. 29-48

----. *Misplaced Ideas.* London & New York: Verso, 1992.

----. "Fim de século". In: *Sequências Brasileiras*. São Paulo: Companhia das Letras, 1999a. 155-162

----. "O livro audacioso de Robert Kurz". In: *Sequências Brasileiras*. São Paulo: Companhia das Letras, 1999b. 182-188.

----. "*Cidade de Deus*". In: *Seqüências brasileiras.* São Paulo: Companhia das Letras, 1999c.

----. *A Master on the Periphery of Capitalism.* Translated and with an introduction by John Gledson. Durham/London: Duke U.P., 2001.

Silva, Jorge Anthonio. *Arthur Bispo do Rosário: Arte e Loucura.* 2ª ed. São Paulo: Quaisquer, 2003.

Silva, Márcio Seligmann. "Arthur Bispo do Rosário: a arte de 'enlouquecer os signos". *Artefilosofia.* N. 3, Ouro Preto, julho de 2007: 144-55.

Soares, Ilka de Araújo. "Arthur Bispo do Rosário: a arte bruta e a propagação na cultura pós-moderna". *Psicologia: Ciência e Profissão.* V. 20. N. 4, 2000: 38-45.

Sofsky, Wolfgang. *Die Ordnung des Terrors: das Konzentrationslager.* Frankfurt a.M.: Fischer, 1997.

Tanke, Joseph J. *Jacques Ranciere: an Introduction.* New York: Continuum, 2011.

Tatit, Luiz. *O Cancionista: Composição e Canções do Brasil.* São Paulo: EDUSP, 1996.

----. *O Século da Canção.* Cotia: Ateliê Editorial, 2004.

Tezza, C. *Entre a prosa e a poesia*: *Bakhtin e os formalistas russos*. Rio de Janeiro: Rocco, 2003.

Veloso, Caetano. *Tropical Truth: A Story of Music and Revolution in Brazil.* New York: Da Capo Press, 2003.

Villaça, Alcides. "Gullar: a luz e seus avessos". *Cadernos de Literatura Brasileira.* N.6, 1998. 88-107.

Weber, Max. *The Rational and Social Foundations of Music.* Carbondale: Southern Illinois UP, 1958.

Wisnik, José Miguel. *Machado Maxixe*. São Paulo: Publifolha, 2008.

Zaluar, Alba. *Integração Perversa: Pobreza e Tráfico de Drogas.* Rio de Janeiro: Fundação Getúlio Vargas, 2004.

Zé, Tom. "O Gênio de Irará: Tom Zé." *Revista Caros Amigos.* N. 31, 1999: 28-35.

----. *Tropicalista Lenta Luta*. São Paulo: Publifolha, 2003.

Žižek, Slavoj (ed.). *Mapping Ideology.* London: Verso, 1994.

----. *The Sublime Object of Ideology.* London: Verso, 1989.

----. *The Ticklish Subject.* London: Verso, 1999.

Zuin, Antonio Alvaro Soares; Pucci, Bruno; de Oliveira, Newton Ramos. *Adorno.* Petrópolis: Vozes, 2000.

Audio-Visual Material:

Da Silva, José Américo Moreira (dir.). *Zé de Irará, o Tom da Bahia*, 2004.

"Ensaio: Tom Zé." *Programa Ensaio.* TV Cultura. Channel 2, São Paulo, July 10, 1991.

Gallo, Carla (dir.). *Tom Zé, ou Quem Irá Colocar Uma Dinamite na Cabeça do Século?* Celso Camargo, Priscilla Migliano, Carla Gallo (producers), 2002.

Levi, Renato (dir.). *Os Alquimistas do Som*. Documentary aired at TV Cultura. Chanel 2. São Paulo, May 4, 2004.

Matos, Décio, Jr. (dir.). *Fabricando Tom Zé*. Goiabada Productions. 2007.

"Roda Viva: Entrevista com Tom Zé." *Roda Viva.* TV Cultura. Channel 2. São Paulo, August 22, 2005.

Meirelles, Fernando. *Cidade de Deus.* DVD, 2002.

Zé, Tom (dir.). *Grande Liquidação*. LP. Columbia Records, 1968.
----. *Jogos de Armar.* DVD. Trama, 2004.
----. *Se o caso é chorar.* LP. Continental, 1972.
----. *Todos os Olhos.* LP. Continental, 1973.

Websites:

Tom Zé's official web site: http://www.tomze.com.br/.
Web site for Fabricando Tom Zé (bilingual): http://www.fabricandotomze.com.br/.

About the texts

"Ferreira Gullar: poetry and intensity" first appeared in Portuguese at *Luso-Brazilian Review*, vol. 51, number 1, 2014.

"Not Exactly Sex and Drugs: Reinaldo Moraes *Pornopopéia* between monadology and the partition of the sensible" was published in *Parallax*, vol. 20, issue 4, edited by Silvia López.

"Objectifying Failures in the 2010 São Paulo Biennale: the cases of Nuno Ramos and Gil Vicente" originally came out in Romanian at *Idea: arts+society*, vols. 36-37, 2010, translated by Alex Moldovan.

"Arthur Bispo do Rosário and the Ruse of Brazilian Art" was written for *Wasafiri*, vol. 30, number 2, 2015, an issue devoted to Brazil, edited by Fabio Akcelrud Durão and Suman Gupta.

"The Adventures of a Technique: dodecaphonism travels to Brazil" was included in *Traversing Transnationalism*, edited by Pier Paolo Frassinelli, Ronit Frenkel David Watson (Amsterdam: Rodopi Press, 2011).

"Appropriation in reverse; or, what happens when popular music goes dodecaphonic" appeared in *Latin American Music Review* v. 30, number 1 2009.

"Tom Zé's Unsong and the Fate of the Tropicália Movement" was a chapter of *The Popular Avant-Garde*, edited by Renée Silverman (Amsterdam, Rodopi Press, 2010).

"Fernando Meirelles' *City of God* 14 years later" has not been unpublished.

"Towards a Model of Inclusive Exclusion: Marginal Subjectivation in Rio de Janeiro" came out first in *A Contracorriente*, vol. 3, number 2, 2006. It was then reprinted in *The Afro-Brazilian Mind*, edited by Niyi Afolabi, Esmeralda Ribeiro, and Márcio Barbosa (Trenton: Africa World Press, 2007).

"T.W. Adorno in Brazil" appeared in *Atenea*, vol 24, number 2, 2004.

"Monologism of the multiple" was originally published in Spanish in *Tópicos del Seminario*, vol. 21, 2009, translated from the Portuguese by César González Ochoa; a French translation came out in *L'Amérique latine entre critique et théorie: un autre regard sur la littérature*, edited by Carine Durand and Sandra Raguenet, (Paris: Garnier Classique, 2015), and translated by the authors; the original can be found in *Teoria Literária e Suas Fronteiras*, edited by Alberto Pucheu, Flavia Trocoli and Sonia Branco (Rio de Janeiro: Azougue Editorial, 2014).

www.ingramcontent.com/pod-product-compliance
Lightning Source LLC
LaVergne TN
LVHW091118080826
845145LV00008B/1959

* 9 7 8 1 9 4 3 3 5 0 3 6 0 *